ISLAM

ISLAM

AN AMERICAN RELIGION

NADIA MARZOUKI

Translated by C. Jon Delogu

Columbia University Press
New York

Columbia University Press
Publishers Since 1893
New York   Chichester, West Sussex
cup.columbia.edu

Library of Congress Cataloging-in-Publication Data
Names: Marzouki, Nadia, author. | Delogu, Christopher Jon, translator.
Title: Islam, an American religion / Nadia Marzouki ; translated by C. Jon Delogu.
Other titles: Islam, une religion Américaine? English
Description: New York : Columbia University Press, [2017] |
Includes bibliographical references and index.
Identifiers: LCCN 2016044401 (print) | LCCN 2016047257 (ebook) |
ISBN 9780231176804 (cloth : alk. paper) | ISBN 9780231543927 (e-book)
Subjects: LCSH: Islam—Social aspects—United States. | Islam and
politics—United States. | Islamophobia—United States.
Classification: LCC BP67.U6 M3713 2017 (print) | LCC BP67.U6 (ebook) |
DDC 305.6/97—dc23
LC record available at https://lccn.loc.gov/2016044401

Columbia University Press books are printed on permanent
and durable acid-free paper.
Printed in the United States of America

COVER DESIGN: Jordan Wannemacher
COVER IMAGE: Illustration by Eric Deleporte

IN MEMORY OF AZIZA BEN KRAÏEM
AND BARBARA SNITKOVA

CONTENTS

CONCLUSION 195

FOREWORD

OLIVIER ROY

N adia Marzouki's book is much more than just a monograph about Islam in the United States. Through careful consideration of the relations between the West and its Islam, her study reflects on the vision that the West keeps of itself, especially when doubting its values and its own political culture. The debate about Islam is the symptom of a profound crisis, even if, of course, this debate takes up Islam either to reject it or integrate it. And these two "camps"—those who think that Islam is incompatible with the West (though which West?) and those who think that it can be integrated within it—are in agreement when it comes to defining Islam as the locus of the other, of difference, and of foreignness. "Living with one's differences," "multiculturalism," "reasonable accommodation," "tolerance"—all these terms deployed to conceptualize integration also cement in place the idea of an unsurpassable alterity.

The advantage of Nadia Marzouki's detour through the United States is to isolate the quasi-existential presence of Islam from the various parameters that cloud the debate more than they clarify it. If in both Europe and the United States the presence of a large Muslim population is recent, the place of that population is different. In Europe, Muslims are linked to three sensitive issues: immigration, social exclusion, and "the return of the sacred." In the United States, the debates on immigration and the socially excluded are hardly focused on the Muslim population but instead on Latinos (when it comes to immigration) and on African Americans (when it comes to social exclusion). Moreover, American Muslims, especially the foreign born, generally belong to the middle and upper classes, unlike their European coreligionists. Finally, America is familiar with the resurgence of religious practitioners, especially Christians, as illustrated by evangelicals and the Tea Party. In America, public demonstrations of religiosity are not on the face of it considered bizarre or expressions of fanaticism, as is often the case in Europe, including when it comes to Christianity. But the paradox is that, even after setting aside these three factors (immigration, social exclusion, religious visibility) that are associated with Islam in Europe, one nevertheless finds across a large portion of the American population the same rejection of Islam as a religion, a rejection that has boosted European populism of late.

In short, there is indeed an invariable rejection of Islam in the West that is independent of questions of immigration, social exclusion, and challenges to secularism and French *laïcité*. Islam is perceived as the absolute other whose very presence requires a rethinking of what constitutes the political bond, beyond the social contract and republican integration—that is, beyond the two founding elements that allowed one to conceive of the "*civis*" as composed of varying individuals and populations. Yet the vast amount of what's been written in the social sciences about the integration of Muslims in Western countries generally focuses on three questions: the theological question (Is Islam compatible with Western values?), the sociological question (How does one integrate a population that derives mostly from immigrant workers?), and the legal question (What standing should the religious practices of Muslims have, including the matters of veils, minarets, halal meat, etc.?). In other words, it considers the conditions of compatibility between Islam and Western societies by establishing entirely reasonable objectives. One can notice how, little by little, Muslims, with the exception of Salafists, define their faith in compatible terms (with values of self-realization instead of Sharia), enter the middle classes, and integrate within the institutional framework provided for religion (Mosque parishes, chaplaincies, etc.). But this scientific literature mostly leaves out the subjective question of "acceptability"—that is, the emotional reaction to the presence of Islam. Generally, these reactions, if recognized at all, are lumped into an unworthy category of subjectivity, as primitive reactions that ought to be surpassed by rational thought, or worse yet rejected out of hand under the heading "racism." And even if the number of studies of racism is increasing in the social sciences, inquiry into Islamophobia is either denied ("There is no Islamophobia, only racism" or "This is just an exercise in free speech") or disqualified (because it's racist, and therefore devoid of all pertinence). However, one hardly ever asks about what the rejection of the other means for self-affirmation. If Islam is perceived as unassimilable—in other words, as incompatible with the constitution of the political bond—then what does constitute the political bond?

In simple terms, Western political culture has two models of political bond: citizenship, which entails that the social bond is above all political and derives from the nation-state, and the social contract, which considers the state as a simple arbitrator over a contract decided on by free, equal, and rational individuals. The first paradigm is the ground of republican integration, so dear to the French, but is also active in countries of "positive law" (where law is the expression of the will of the "sovereign"); the second is the foundation of reasonable accommodation, the expression of a liberal conception of political life as practiced in countries of "common law" (where laws are above all contractual). But as we shall see, these two paradigms have hardly been successful at dissipating a malaise, as one notices both the failure of the liberal call for reasonable accommodation and the crisis of ineffectual calls to citizenship and political integration.

If we take three entirely distinct examples of what is supposed to regulate the religious within the public sphere—France's 1905 law affirming republicanism centered on the state, the Italian constitution as an expression of concordance with a privileged church, and Canada's principle of "reasonable accommodation"—one observes that all three have more trouble managing secularism than the religious. We can consider as examples a recent crisis in each country: the *eruv* in Montreal (an enclosure requested by an ultra-Orthodox Jewish community that consists of placing a white thread nine feet off the ground to encircle the neighborhood of the faithful, thus letting them circulate on the Sabbath); the Italian crucifix (which a nonreligious person requests be removed from the classroom of her son); and halal meat in the Quick fast-food restaurants in France (where a campaign is launched against the systematic provision of halal meat in certain restaurants and cafeterias). In the three cases, the argument in favor of the acceptance of the religious element in the public space is that it does not bother the nonbeliever for whom it has no meaning. The case of halal meat is clear: what serves as a religious symbol for the believer is merely a slaughtering technique for the nonbeliever (i.e., one that results in meat that contains less blood). This might pose a culinary problem, especially for someone who likes rare meat, but it is not a matter of moral conscience. As long as for economic reasons the halal or kosher meat is distributed in the private sphere, the 1905 law does not come into effect. Similarly, it would be impossible to prohibit the sale of communion wafers in supermarkets.

In all these cases, "secularism" is unable to chase out the religious (because courts refuse to exclude it), and "reasonable accommodation" does not work because the nonbeliever feels sensitive about the religious element—he demands (in vain, hence his anger) its exclusion from the public sphere even when it has nothing to do with proselytizing or any pressure whatsoever. The neighborhood that includes the Jewish community in Montreal refuses the *eruv*, the Italian schoolchild's parent refuses the crucifix, and a portion of French public opinion refuses the invisible halal. People want to exclude from public space either religion in general or the other religion while forgetting in the case of France that the 1905 law was not designed to exclude religion from public space but, on the contrary, to organize religion within that space. This is why the courts refuse to exclude the religious from the public sphere, and it is why frustrations mount against a law that seems to ignore emotions and feelings. The religious symbol, even if invisible, without practical consequences, and detached from all proselytizing (as with the Italian crucifix), is bothersome. Of course, it is especially bothersome when associated with a "foreign" culture, but not only: a nun in her wimple will attract stares in France, and a priest in a cassock or soutane is immediately taken for a fundamentalist. Legal proceedings multiply in areas where newcomers move in and request that church bells not ring at night (and roosters not crow). In short, the religious is meaningful even for the unbeliever, and this is why we can no longer speak of rational parties establishing reasonable legal rules for harmonious cohabitation.

The problem of religious liberty is therefore not just a matter of law, the courts, and a harmonization of different liberties (freedom of speech, freedom to choose, and freedom to not have a religion). It comes from deeper wellsprings that we are more and more coming to think about under the heading of identity. Of course, identity is the rallying cry of all populist movements. The reference to freedom of religion that is enshrined in all

Western constitutions runs up against a reaction based on identity. In a sense, then, populism runs counter to human rights. Therefore, it is one of the cornerstones of modern democracy that is at stake in the debate about Islam.

Consequently, one must look elsewhere to find what, in the eyes of Islam's opponents, constitutes the political bond—in something infrapolitical that allows for the establishment of a political community. This infrapolitics is elaborated in terms of culture or, more succinctly, as identity. As though identity, instead of being a product of the political bond, was in fact what made it possible.

However, since this identity is impossible to define, it is instead felt as affects, emotions, and anger. It is not a matter of rights, as a slogan in opposition to the construction of an Islamic center in Manhattan puts it, but of what ought and can be done: "Not a matter of rights, but of what is right," as Nadia Marzouki underlines.

As she says in her conclusion, the debate underscores well the question of the social bond and whether it supposes "sameness." And if yes, how does one define this sameness? The term "identity" appears everywhere today, but it is actually relatively recent within political science. It begins to be used often in the 1970s, and that use becomes exponential in the 1990s. People talk of a common "culture," of "Western values," and "European Christian identity"—something tells me that the old term "Judeo-Christian" was dropped in favor of just "Christianity"—while forgetting the extent to which the last centuries in the West have been more about civil wars than a harmony of values. No serious political scientist would speak of a culturally homogeneous France in the course of history—neither in religious matters (unless one is going to praise the revocation of the Edict of Nantes and the expulsion of Jews) nor in politics. Laïcs and "Cathos" (the nonreligious and Catholics) led distinct parallel lives in twentieth-century France. Finally, the European Christian identity that numerous laïcs regularly evoke has little in common with the values defended by the Catholic Church, which, on the contrary, believes that the dominant culture in Europe has lost touch with its Christian roots because for the Church, Christianity is a faith before being a culture. Likewise, the happy-hour gatherings of identity enthusiasts, who down sausages and wine as a way to thumb their noses at Muslims (and Jews), are far from the spirit of the Eucharist.

Wanting to define a Western identity is to deny the complexity of Western culture and leads to falling into a reductive incantation.

So then what should be done? Well, instead of looking for the truth hidden behind the debate, or the truth that the debate is hiding, it is worth asking if it is not the debate itself that creates a new world. In other words, we could ask if the emotions, the fears, and the angry feelings do not themselves bring together, paradoxically, a large number of those who are upset to debate not just about the other but with each other, and therefore to grant the other his or her dignity. In short, Westerners ought to take seriously their own conception of citizenship and liberty. Christian churches ought to reflect on the reference to Christianity. Is it a culture, and, if so, what does one do with the European Western culture that is opening itself to gay marriage? Is it a faith? But in that case, the Muslim believer is closer to it than the identity-obsessed atheist. Besides the small minority of extremists who go off enthusiastically toward civil wars, the fear of conflict is also a desire to overcome conflict. The other is called on to explain himself, but he also wants to express himself. He is called on to do so according to a code of polite manners that he attempts to comprehend. The debate creates its own formatting effects. There's an obligation to respond on the part of the Muslims who must therefore invent, outside of all theological dogmatism, the responses they will give both practically, in the observance of their beliefs, and in the formulation of their identity in order to define their new presence in the West. In this way, the incantatory quest for a new illusory identity can instead arrive at a new social compact.

ACKNOWLEDGMENTS

I wish to express my sincerest thanks to my mother and father, and to my sister, Myriam. I want to thank my French publisher at Le Seuil (Paris), Jean-Louis Schlegel, and my American publisher at Columbia University Press, Anne Routon, for extending to me their confidence and for their thorough advice and suggestions; to Christopher Jon Delogu, for his thoroughness and enthusiasm in translating this book. Thanks to Jase Short and John Green for their help during my research in Tennessee; to Denise Spellberg, for her pioneering, inspiring, and stimulating work, and for believing in this book; to Denis Lacorne, for his trust, encouragements, and most helpful feedback; to Zachary Shore, for his long friendship and stimulating comments during the revision process; and to Elizabeth Shakman Hurd, Winnifred Sullivan, and Anver Emon, for their precious input and support at various stages of this research. My work benefited from funding from the ERC-funded ReligioWest project at the European University Institute (Florence), and from important feedback from the research team there. The Centre Raymond Aron in Paris (CNRS-EHESS), where I have worked since 2013, has proved to be a very amicable and collegial place that afforded me unique research conditions to finalize this project.

I am particularly grateful to Olivier Roy for all these years of encouragement, teaching, and inspiration.

ISLAM

INTRODUCTION TO
THE AMERICAN EDITION

A Euro-American Debate over Islam

"In France, it's illegal for a Muslim woman to wear a head scarf at a public school. In the United States, it's illegal for a clothing store to refuse to hire a Muslim woman because she wore a head scarf to her job interview."[1] This is how a journalist at the *New York Times* recently summarized the differences between the French and American debates over Islam. In June 2015, the U.S. Supreme Court recognized the discriminatory character of the decision by the clothing merchant Abercrombie & Fitch to not hire Samantha Elauf because she was wearing a head scarf. This ruling stood in sharp contrast to another one made in France a month earlier. In May 2015, a middle-school principal in the Ardennes twice sent home a student because he judged her skirt to be "too long" and claimed it constituted an "ostentatious symbol" (*ostentatoire*) of religious affiliation.[2] The contrast between these nearly simultaneous decisions is striking. However, is it correct to go from this juxtaposition to taking each case as exemplary of two presumably opposed "models" for the public management of Islam? My uneasiness with this sort of opposition was one of the main reasons that led me to write this book. Such attempts at classification seek not only to isolate distinct political forms but also to place them in a hierarchy. Thus one finds oppositions between "open" and "closed" secularisms, or else "authoritarian" and "liberal"; and Muslim communities are labeled "well integrated" or "excluded," and the like. These approaches are seductive not only because they feed into what Freud called "the narcissism of small differences" but also because they make increasingly complex societies more readable. However, by insisting only on the irreducibility of social structures, juridical forms, or political traditions, one overlooks considering the capacity for hybridization inherent to and enabled by the circulation of ideas, fears, and individuals.

A major feature of the evolution of public controversies over Islam in the United States and Europe since 2000 is the trend toward a standardization of anti-Muslim arguments and of the objects around which Western fears and fantasies crystalize. The differences when it comes to legal rules and habits about the separation of the religious and the political, the sociological particularities of Muslim populations, and colonial histories are well known. And yet one can notice the anti-Muslim narrative becoming more formulaic and narrow on both sides of the Atlantic since 2000. Themes such as Islamization in disadvantaged suburbs; the use of mosques as training camps for jihadists; the oppression of Muslim women by their brothers, husbands, or fathers; stealth jihad; and *taqiyya* are the standard talking points in the discourse of anti-Muslim groups in both the United States and Europe—a discourse that has contaminated the mainstream public debate everywhere.

THE AMERICAN AND FRENCH REACTIONS TO THE *CHARLIE HEBDO* ATTACK

The reactions provoked by the attacks against the headquarters of the newspaper *Charlie Hebdo* and the kosher supermarket Hyper Casher on January 7–9, 2015, are a telling illustration of this process of synchronization and increasing interconnection between the debates over Islam and Muslims in Europe and the United States. Certainly, at first glance, the reactions were expressed in a different register in France and the United States. In France, the *Charlie Hebdo* attack was mostly presented as a cultural aggression against *laïcité* (France's particular separation of church and state spheres that dates from 1905) and freedom of expression. French Muslims were publicly called on to collectively condemn the violent actions of the Kouachi brothers, Chérif and Saïd. With the exception of a few discordant voices—notably the researchers Olivier Roy, Didier Fassin, Farhad Khosrokhavar, Jean Baubérot, and François Burgat—the collective rhetoric was marked by a sense of duty and calls for unity. In America, responses were more moderate, perhaps on account of the geographical distance from the events and the cautionary effect of numerous cases of inept media bungling since 2001. With the exception of a few news anchors who evoked the supposed existence in Europe of lawless "no-go zones" occupied exclusively by Muslims, the news analysis tended to be more nuanced and carefully critical than in France.[3] Whereas the French debate was saturated with dogmatic interpretations of *laïcité* and declarations of the "right" to blasphemy, in the United States the discussion was about responsibility, accountability, contextualization, and a moral obligation toward an economically disadvantaged category of the population. While condemning the attacks and repeating their attachment to the principal of free speech, several American commentators expressed doubts about the alleged national unity on the day (January 11) that multiple massive public demonstrations took place simultaneously in Paris and many large French cities. "We have been here before," declared Adam Shatz in a blog of the *London Review of Books* on January 9, two days before the Sunday demonstrations.[4] According to Shatz, the slogan "Je suis Charlie" ("I am Charlie," though it can also be read as "I *follow* Charlie"), which was spontaneously adopted and relayed mechanically by a large portion of the French public, intellectuals, and political class, reveals a nostalgia for the period immediately after the September 11 attacks when it was still possible to entertain illusions about a clear distinction between the good guys and the bad guys.[5] The *Doonesbury* cartoonist Garry Trudeau condemned the brutal execution of his French colleagues but also raised a question about the social usefulness of satire when it is systematically targeting a disadvantaged social group. "Satire should punch up, not down," he affirmed, while pointing out the difference between the right to offend and the obligation to offend.[6] Anthony Faiola, reporting from France for the *Washington Post* on January 13, wrote of the uncomfortable feelings among French Muslims who were constantly being asked to apologize for a murder that they did not commit.[7] Dalia Mogahed, a director of research at the Institute for Social Policy and Understanding and a consultant to the White House Office of Faith-Based and Neighborhood Partnerships, posted a declaration on her Facebook page beginning "JeSuisDalia" to denounce the propensity of many to condemn all French Muslims for an act committed by two individuals. "I am Dalia. I represent a community of exactly one. I answer for the crimes of exactly one person. I apologize for the actions of exactly one woman."[8] On the *Daily Show* for January 13, 2015, host Jon Stewart mocked the noticeable presence at the January 11 mass march of several heads of state famous for their lack of respect for free speech. In April 2015, six members of the PEN writer's association opposed awarding a medal for "Courage and Freedom of Expression" to *Charlie Hebdo*.[9] The novelist Peter Carey justified this position, denouncing "the cultural arrogance of the French nation, which does not recognize its moral obligation to a large and disempowered segment of their population."[10] An open letter to the PEN directors, signed first by the six protesting authors and then by two hundred more writers, points out the difference between what is permitted by law and what is morally appropriate: "[T]here is a critical difference between staunchly supporting expression that violates the acceptable, and enthusiastically rewarding such expression."[11]

THE OVERLAPPING DEBATES ON ISLAM IN THE UNITED STATES AND IN EUROPE

These divergent assessments of the reactions to the attacks on January 7–9, 2015, do not permit one to conclude that there exist two opposed models for understanding and managing Islam. As noted, there has been a standardization and increasing interconnection of the types of questions and forms of debate that are happening, even if they may give rise to differing responses. Specialists of religion in France have criticized for years the paradoxical process of a sanctification of the Republic and a sacralization of *laïcité*, but they start from premises that are different from those underscored by American analysts. For Olivier Roy, the French stigmatization of Muslims is a direct effect of the transformation of *laïcité* into religion-phobia more than the manifestation of postcolonial treatment: "I think today we are more in a state of hyper-*laïcité* than in an extension of the colonial set-up. This hyper-*laïcité* affects all religions, but more so Islam. It is more a refusal to take into consideration religion in the public space—it is a religion-phobia."[12] American specialists often reproach their French colleagues for underestimating the continuity of state treatment of Islam even after the official end of colonialization as well as the process of racialization that is at work in the rejection of Muslims. The French reply to these criticisms by pointing out the American tendency to overestimate racial and postcolonial factors—a bias they see as linked to the history of America's formation as a nation. It would be wise to avoid essentializing either position. A new generation of French researchers is making its mark through attentive examinations of the racial dimension behind the othering of Muslims.[13] In America, social scientists such as Mayanthi Fernando and John Bowen have gone beyond the racialist aspects and shed light on the properly religion-phobic dimension of discrimination against Muslims in France.[14] At any rate, it is clear that these quarrels between different academic chapels on either side of the Atlantic demonstrate the increasing overlap between discussions on Islam in Europe and the United States.

The back-and-forth discussion provoked by Michael Walzer's January 2015 article published in the magazine *Dissent*, in which he accuses American intellectuals on the left of having improperly closed their eyes to the defects of Islam and Islamism, also illustrates this process of unification when it comes to the manner of debating Islam on both sides of the Atlantic.[15] The denunciation of an alleged collusion between leftist intellectuals and Islamists has been routine practice in the French public debate since the late 1990s.[16] It is therefore interesting to see the same debate reappear in the United States fifteen years later. To strengthen his criticism of the term "Islamophobia," Walzer refers to the French author Pascal Bruckner.[17] Instead of confirming the hypothesis of distinct models, this cross-cultural weaving of references and arguments in the debates on Islam in the United States and Europe gives rise to convergent lines of questioning. Disagreements over Islam that formerly were treated behind closed doors, as it were, within distinct national territories are increasingly cited and recited across different contexts, and these activities have real social and political consequences.

In short, the *Charlie Hebdo* affair is not just a French story treated *intra muros*. In its wake, questions were asked in the United States about the way Americans had discussed Islam since 2001 and about the limits that should or should not be imposed on the liberty to caricature a religion in the American context. The affair also gave the Islamophobic activist Pamela Geller the idea of organizing a caricature-the-Prophet contest in the town of Garland, Texas (near Dallas), that took place on May 4, 2015. The organization of this event provoked the anger of two extremists associated with the Islamic State of Iraq and Syria (ISIS), who ended up shooting at several people in the vicinity and were then shot dead. These acts of violence, in turn, served as the pretext for the organization of an anti-Muslim rally on May 30, 2015, mounted by right-wing motorcycle enthusiasts who defended free speech in front of a mosque in Phoenix, Arizona. One sees clearly how in only a few months, an attack and polemic that erupt in Paris trigger other attacks and polemics in several American cities. Emmanuel Todd's contrarian book *Qui est Charlie?* (*Who Is Charlie?*) turns up in a review in the pages of the *New Yorker*.[18] The extreme-right politician Marine Le Pen is granted space on the opinion pages of the *New York Times* after the attacks of January 2015.[19] The same welcome is extended to the controversial novelist Michel Houellebecq ten months later after the attacks in November.[20] Going in the other direction, one may observe the *Daily Show*'s sketches about French prejudices against Islam, and France also expresses its indignation at the Islamophobic murder that took place in faraway Chapel Hill, North Carolina.

My book starts off from the observation that, despite the well-known differences in political traditions, constitutional setups, and sociodemographic characteristics between Europe and the United States, the polemics and policies concerning Islam are increasingly interdependent. In this regard, one could repeat the comment made by Nilüfer Göle, who notes that a public European space is being created in a negative, paradoxical way as a result of the standardization of polemical debates over Islam.[21] In a way, the presence of Muslims in Europe and America contributes to giving coherence to an otherwise elusive Western public space. Positioning Islam as otherness allows one to create and give substance to a common public space, defined in a reactive manner by values and traditions presumed to be opposed to those of Islam.

Could it be, then, that the Western disputes over Islam are not, as is commonly believed, the direct result of certain legal traditions and particular sociological characteristics? My hypothesis is that the public controversies over Islam are not simply the latest manifestations of the contradictions and internal breakdowns of each "tradition" or "model" (in the United States, the contradiction between open secularism and persistent racism; in France, the contradiction between an ideology of equality and an intransigent and exclusive *laïcité*). The disputes over Islam in the Unites States and Europe reveal a more profound and transversal conflict within the majority of secular democracies—one that concerns the definition of the very meaning of the political community. The contemporary controversies over Islam expose fundamental misunderstandings about the social contract and democracy. What the disputes over mosques, wearing the veil, Sharia, and halal all put on display is the opposition between two distinct registers for the justification of the conditions for belonging to the political community. One of them, in conformity with the liberal philosophical tradition, insists on the normative dimension of constitutional rights that guarantee the equality of citizens. The other register, by insisting on a populist interpretation of the U.S. Constitution, evokes another source of normativity, founded this time on the appropriateness of certain emotions and behaviors. Therefore, this book does not seek to conduct or present the results of a comprehensive or exhaustive sociological field study of American Muslims; its goal is to understand the sources of discord, the misunderstandings, and the rancor that surround the political definition of living together democratically when these conflicts crop up in controversies over Islam in the United States.

A FRENCH-TUNISIAN PERSPECTIVE

My analysis has of course been partly inspired by my knowledge of the French debates over Islam, but what is presented here is not just a "French" perspective on Islam in America. In France, there is a longstanding affection for analyzing American social, historical, and political life—from Alexis de Tocqueville to Thomas Piketty, from François Cusset to Justin Vaïsse.[22] However, throughout the preparation of this book, I made it a point to bring in for questioning the tendency of both countries to caricature each other. This study is the result of many years spent in the United States—during my doctoral studies, which allowed me to do exchanges at Berkeley and Princeton; as a postdoc at Yale; and then during shorter stints since 2010 to do research in New York, Washington, D.C., and Tennessee. Each of these stays gave me the chance to further my research project as I conducted interviews and observed debates unfold day to day, but they also led me to discover new ways of thinking about the relation between religion and politics. It was very nourishing for me to have the chance to spend the 2004/2005 school year on the UC Berkeley campus, the same year that the media hurricane about banning the veil in public schools was in full force back in France. It was during that year that I discovered the work, still largely unknown in France, of thinkers such as Talal Asad and Saba Mahmood. Their critiques of liberalism and secularism altered and sharpened my perception of Western polemics over Islam and the stakes involved.[23] But during my years in the United States, I was also often surprised at the uncomprehending looks and even disappointment that I received from some of my interlocutors when I expressed my reluctance to view France as simply an Islamophobic and racist power whose policies toward Muslims had not changed one bit since colonial times.

My discomfort with the mania on both sides of the Atlantic to resort to drawing caricatures of those on the other side probably comes from the fact that my perception and interpretation of the world developed through my attachment to a small country with a Muslim-majority population and unknown to most Americans before 2011—Tunisia. This book is influenced, inevitably, by personal experiences in the place where I spent the first sixteen years of my life and to which I have remained close ever since. It is this insider/outsider status vis-à-vis my *two* countries of origin, France and Tunisia, that most likely explains my allergic reaction to essentialist categorizations. It may also be the source of my interest in the effects of mirroring, hybridity, and circulation—in other words, for the portion of freedom and creativity that individuals possess beyond and despite the weight of structures, traditions, and systems. In fact, these circulatory systems have existed for a very long time and have played a more important role than certain strict comparatists are generally willing to admit. It was a pleasant discovery during my research years, for example, to learn that one of the first instances of the diplomatic recognition of Islam by the United States occurred in 1805 under President Thomas Jefferson, who received at the White House Sidi Sulayman Mellimelli, the envoy of the bey of Tunis. Instead of serving dinner at 3:30 P.M., then the customary time, Jefferson asked that the meal be served "precisely at sunset" in order to respect the prescribed time for the interruption of fasting during Ramadan.[24] In August 2012, during an Iftar ceremony organized at the White House, President Barack Obama mentioned this historic event: "Thomas Jefferson once held a sunset dinner here with an envoy from Tunisia, perhaps the first Iftar at the White House, more than 200 years ago."[25]

HYBRID ORIGINS AND IDENTITIES

This book may be situated in the tradition of "French" observers of American political life, but it is even more influenced by those analyses that examine the processes of weaving and hybridization of identities and forms of argumentation beyond the borders imposed by what are commonly referred to as "area studies." This type of analysis has been developing in France since the 1990s, for example, in the work of Jocelyne Dakhlia, whose research aims to break up the essentialist categories of an alleged "Mediterranean world" or a "Muslim world." *Les musulmans dans l'histoire de l'Europe*, co-edited by Jocelyne Dakhlia and Bernard Vincent, brings together new contributions that encourage rethinking the history of the relation between Europe and the Muslim world in ways beyond the prism of fracture and conflict.[26] The goal is to reveal the "Islamic past of Europe" and the ancient history of "Muslim presences in Europe." In the United States, a similar approach can be found in the research of the historians Denise Spellberg and Kambiz GhaneaBassiri.[27] Their work corrects the mistaken belief that the encounter between Islam and America is something recent, and instead analyzes this encounter not as a shock between two constituted bodies but as an open set of hybrid and ambivalent phenomena. The goal of this line of research is not to pacify the history of relations between Islam and the West, nor to deny the erratic character, often invisible and numerically limited as well, of the Islamic presence in Europe and America before the nineteenth century. These studies seek to reposition Islam by situating it within the interiority and intimacy of Western societies, which in turn are no longer viewed as unified and homogeneous integrating bodies. This epistemological postulate of a constitutively networked and co-extensive relation between Islam and Europe, or Islam and America, has been a major source of inspiration for this book. This study is not a historical investigation in the traditional sense but rather an offshoot of this type of problematization of the relations between identity, religion, and politics.

By defining Islam as an American religion, my analysis does not exactly follow the work of those interested in the process of the Americanization of Islam. Rather, it is inspired by recent publications that show one cannot think properly about certain fundamental ideals of liberal democracy and secular America independently of their relation, if only in theory, with Islam. Between the 1980s and the early years of this century, important studies were conducted about the waves of migration and the processes of integration of Muslims in America.[28] While making an essential contribution to the understanding of the diverse ways of practicing Islam in America, these studies are constructed on lines of questioning about "trajectories" and "stages" of integration, and the "compatibility" of Islam and America—as though the heterogeneity of these two objects were self-evident. Starting in the late 2000s, another current of thought emerged that begins from the inverse presupposition. The latter posits that the encounter between Islam and America is not the outcome of a slow teleology of integration. On the contrary, this thesis views the encounter as a point of departure that underlines the ambivalence, from the start, of American liberal-secular democracy and exposes what this democracy simultaneously engenders in both the most progressive direction (the principle of religious freedom) and the most inegalitarian direction (slavery and racism). Starting in the eighteenth century, Islam intervenes (albeit in a purely hypothetical form) in the debates concerning religious freedom. In the nineteenth century, the figure of the Muslim slave also plays an important role in the conflicts that oppose slaveholders and abolitionists. Spellberg has shown how, in the constitutional debates of the state of North Carolina, several Federalists opposed the introduction of a religious test for candidates to public office. She cites as evidence the words of William Lancaster, a delegate to the North Carolina Convention, who on July 30, 1788, makes the following declaration: "But let us remember that we form a government for millions not yet in existence. . . . In the course of four or five hundred years, I do not know how it will work. This is most certain, that Papists may occupy that chair, and Mahometans may take it. I see nothing against it."[29] Dial forward to September 2015, when 29 percent of Americans (and 43 percent of Republicans) remain persuaded that President Obama is a Muslim and that Islam is a foreign body within America, and it's clear that Spellberg's book marks a major turning point when it comes to thinking about the relations between Islam and America. After Spellberg, the focus would no longer be on investigating the process that allows an alleged foreign body to be progressively absorbed or accepted by the American nation, or about reflecting on the efforts at harmonization between two heterogeneous entities. Following the new direction opened up by Spellberg's research, as I do in my book, means not asking how Muslims become good Americans but asking how Americans come to take responsibility (or not) for this original, founding hypothesis that makes a place for Catholics, Jews, and Muslims in the social contract.

WHEN THE FRINGE BECOMES MAINSTREAM

Since the publication of this book in France in May 2013, American debates about Islam and Muslims have not let up. Whether via news outlets, blogs, and editorials or in other forums for discussing foreign and domestic policy, questions about the rights of Muslims and the acceptability of Islam are increasingly a part of everyday debates in the United States. The local battles over Sharia that I discuss in this book have continued since 2013.[30] State legislatures, notably in Texas, have continued to debate bills banning all reference to foreign law.[31] Laws of this type have passed in North Carolina (August 2013) and Alabama (November 2014). In these two states, Muslims represent less than 1 percent of the population, and no troublesome legal conflict linked to Islamic law had occurred in either of them that would justify the need for such legislation.[32] Thus legislation prohibiting foreign laws remains a solution to a nonexistent problem, just as the legal specialists of the American Civil Liberties Union (ACLU) demonstrated in 2011.[33] The true purpose of these laws also remains the same—to reinforce the populist vision about the otherness and dangerousness of Islam. Muslim American organizations such as the

Council on American-Islamic Relations (CAIR) and associations for the defense of civil rights continue on their side to resist these projects and to inform the public about what Islamic law is and about the harmful stigmatizing effects of the anti-Sharia bills. The pursuit of exclusion paradoxically creates a form of inclusion. The sociologist Mucahit Bilici observes that the anti-Sharia projects "negatively recognize Islam and include it in American law by trying to exclude it."[34]

Local controversies triggered by the opposition of residents in certain neighborhoods to a mosque construction project are still a regular occurrence. The motives invoked to oppose are always questions of zoning and the risk that increased traffic on Fridays would disrupt the tranquility of the neighborhood. In some cases, the arrival of Christian Arabs fleeing civil war and persecution has contributed to the transplantation of interreligious Middle Eastern conflicts to small-town America and resulted in improvised alliances of convenience between Arab Christians and anti-Muslim Americans. In September 2015, Chaldean Christians from Iraq, who make up 5 percent of the 130,000 inhabitants of Sterling Heights, Michigan, launched a virulent campaign against a local mosque construction project. To justify their opposition to what they referred to as the "mega-mosque," these Iraqis recycled the well-worn arguments about the risk that it would serve as a training camp for terrorists and that it would lead to the collapse of real-estate prices in the neighborhood.[35] Despite the counterarguments of Muslims, the city's planning commission rejected the mosque proposal. Mayor Michael Taylor claimed that the decision was based on "objective land use criteria and not emotional feelings tied to religious beliefs."[36]

Disputes over mosques also reveal internal differences within Muslim communities that turn on conflicts between generations, differing theological visions, and conflicting attitudes toward a democratic organization of the mosque. In May 2015, a significant conflict erupted, again in Michigan, when the imam Hassan al-Qazwini announced that he was leaving the Dearborn Islamic Center of America in protest over the opaque and authoritarian management of its board of directors. This imam, who had led prayers at this Shiite mosque for eighteen years, departed along with the members of the Young Muslim Association who had complained about the mosque's insufficient inclusion of young people and women.[37] The simplistic media coverage of the mosque controversies tends to obscure the profound differences that exist within Muslim communities. The divergent views are the understandable expression of the wide diversity of origins, beliefs, practices, and daily lives of American Muslims. Yet these disagreements are often resolved in a discreet, semiclandestine manner. Muslims, sensing they are constantly being watched and under suspicion as accomplices to terrorism, compensate by projecting the image of a harmonious and peaceful community. The pressure exerted by the Manichaean thrust of the media debate inhibits the public expression and development of the diversity inherent to Muslim American communities.[38] This pressure requires that they position themselves first along the bipolar axis Muslim versus anti-Muslims, and in so doing they reinforce, despite themselves, the polarization of a debate from which they would most likely prefer to extricate themselves.

ISIS: NEW FORMS OF AN OLD DEBATE

Since 2013, debates have been marked by the arrival on the media and political stage of the phenomenon known as the Islamic State, or ISIS. The mediatization of the brutality orchestrated by ISIS has considerably slowed the meager gains in the public conversation over Islam, which until then was making some progress at conveying the complexity and variety of Muslim societies. The most passion-driven reactions to the attacks of 2001 had begun to yield, albeit with difficulty, to somewhat richer and more nuanced discussions, thanks notably to the expert public testimony produced by some think tanks and by some media outlets. The reality of a long and costly war in Iraq had moderated enthusiasm for the traditional hawkish discourse of a good U.S.-led coalition opposing an axis of evil. The "Arab Spring" uprisings, especially in Tunisia and Egypt, allowed Americans to discover an uncharacteristic image of the Muslim world—the sight of young people demonstrating, independently of any religious references, against dictatorship and corruption. Since 2013, the meticulous care that ISIS brings to the staging and dissemination of their horror shows has been a major blow to the efforts of all those in the West and in Muslim-majority societies who have been trying to initiate a more factual and nuanced discussion. Talking points organized around a "clash of civilizations," the alleged intrinsic violence of Islam, and its incompatibility with Western values have returned to center stage and have once again been energetically exploited by populist politicians and Islamophobic activists.

If the crimes committed by ISIS appear to present unheard-of levels of savagery and media savvy, the intellectual and political analysis of these events has done little beyond recycle well-worn lines of reasoning. An article by Graeme Wood, for example, "What ISIS Really Wants," rehashed the old two-sided debate between an explanation based on ideology (Islam explains everything) and an explanation based on social and geopolitical structures (Islam explains nothing).[39] As Lisa Stampnitzky has remarkably demonstrated, this either/or approach to the problem contributes to the same type of depoliticization of analysis as that produced by the studies of terrorism that circulated widely starting around 2000.[40] This is what leads anthropologist Darryl Li to affirm that "discussions of jihad today are like a secularized form of demonology. They stem from a place of horror that shuts down serious thinking about politics . . . to reinforce this sense of radical cataclysmic difference."[41] Li regrets that by systematically linking the matter of jihadist violence to that of Islam, the analysis collapses into a closed discussion around the single question of authenticity. One may note that most discussions about ISIS turn on the question of determining if its terror strategy is fundamentally Islamic or, on the contrary, a disfiguration and departure from what would be "true" Islam.[42] However, by obsessing over whether the enemy is truly or falsely Islamic, the properly political dimension of the ISIS phenomenon ends up being neglected. The habit of stating the problem of terrorism and jihad exclusively in terms of more or less Islamic radicalization impedes thinking about the question of radicalness itself. By approaching the phenomenon as a matter of radicalization, understood as a denaturing of authentic Islam or a deviance from an acceptable civic posture, one bars oneself from thinking about the dimensions of *political* and *autonomous* choice that are proper to the jihadist engagement. In contrast, Li calls for "taking radicalism seriously as a political orientation, whether its idiom is Islamic, communist or anarchist."[43] For the most part, however, discussions of ISIS have unfortunately reinforced the tendency that's been around since roughly 2005, and which I discuss in this book—the normative routinization of the most provocative and irrational arguments about Islam.

THE UNHINGED VERBIAGE AGAINST ISLAM
IN THE 2016 PRESIDENTIAL CAMPAIGN

The 2016 U.S. presidential campaign, which was already in full swing in 2015 and frequently marked by the provocative outbursts of a loudmouth Republican candidate, businessman Donald J. Trump, offers a good illustration of this normalization process. In November 2015, Trump stated his support for the idea of an increased surveillance of Muslims.[44] A month later, he proposed prohibiting all Muslims from entering the country.[45] During a town-hall meeting in the fall of 2015, he noticeably failed to correct the remarks of a participant who affirmed that President Obama is a Muslim, saying: "We have a problem in this country, it's called Muslims. Our current president is one."[46] The claim by another Republican candidate, Ben Carson, that a Muslim could never be elected president also caused a stir. At a press conference on September 21, 2015, Muneer Awad, the director of CAIR, reminded his audience that article 6 of the U.S. Constitution explicitly states that "no religious test shall ever be required as a qualification to any office or public trust under the United States."[47]

Some Republican candidates did denounce these moves to stigmatize Muslims. Senator Ted Cruz (R-Tex.), former Florida governor Jeb Bush, and Senator Lindsey Graham (R-S.C.) criticized Trump's pronouncements and underlined their un-American character. This difference in attitude toward Muslims is consistent with the account given in this book about the divergent opinions within the Republican Party—ranging from personalities such as former representative Newt Gingrich who are obsessed with the Islamization of America to others such as Senator John McCain (R-Ariz.) who warn about the danger of a new McCarthyism. This presidential campaign confirms that since 2012, Islam has been a decisive issue in the ongoing battle within the Republican Party between those who, like Republican National Committee chair Reince Priebus, call for the party's strategy and discourse to move back to the center toward the preoccupations of young people, women, and minorities and those who support the party's rightward shift.[48] But despite the opposition voiced by some important figures within the Republican Party, the repeated provocative statements by the most extreme candidates have a harmful effect. As I show in chapter 3, on the anti-Sharia movements, the effect consists in successfully nudging the default setting of public debate on Islam further and further to the right. One notes that certain political figures who in the past had distinguished themselves by their refusal to yield to anti-Muslim paranoia did not speak out clearly against the pronouncements of candidates such as Trump. One example is New Jersey governor and Republican candidate Chris Christie, who, in 2010, had firmly denounced those opposed to the construction project of the Islamic center near New York City's Ground Zero. He also expressed his disagreement with the anti-Sharia movement, calling them "crazies," and publicly supported Judge Sohail Mohammed, the first Muslim American to be named a superior court judge. In 2015, Christie's statements against welcoming all Syrian refugees and his hesitation about denouncing Trump's outbursts were deeply disappointing to Muslims in New Jersey. "He has abandoned us and has moved on," declared Mohammed Hameeduddin, the Muslim American mayor of the city of Teaneck. "He's going more toward the position of the national Republican primary voter."[49]

The divergence noted in this book between Republicans and Democrats continued to be in evidence during the campaigning in 2015. All the Democratic candidates quickly denounced the Islamophobic statements of their Republican adversaries. During a campaign stop at the University of Minnesota on December 16, 2015, former secretary of state Hillary Clinton strongly criticized Trump's proposal to bar all Muslims from entering the country. The same day Senator Bernie Sanders (D-Vt.) and Representative Keith Ellison (D-Minn.) met with leaders at a mosque in Washington, D.C., to reaffirm the full citizenship and belonging of American Muslims. In his State of the Union address on January 13, 2016, President Obama also repeated that "it's just wrong" to stigmatize citizens based on their Muslim faith.[50] On February 3, 2016, President Obama, during his first official visit to a mosque, also quoted Thomas Jefferson and mentioned that Jefferson owned a Quran.[51]

However, despite the obvious gulf that separates the two parties, the unhinged and widely circulating extreme discourse against Muslims limits the practical effectiveness of civil counterstatements by Democrats and Muslims. Moreover, since all the time and space allotted to them is devoted to these urgent counter measures, there comes to be only a single standard reply: *No, Muslims are not terrorists, and they have the same rights as other American citizens.* There is no time remaining to broach themes such as the diversity of American Muslims, their relations with other religions, or the multiple forms of their engagement in the civic and political life where they live. My study, which focuses on the period 2008 to 2013, comes to a conclusion similar to that of Christopher Bail, whose study of the period 2001 to 2008 appeared in 2015.[52] Having conducted a quantitative analysis of the influence strategies of 120 organizations engaged in the debate over Islam, Bail shows the fringe organizations have an exceptional capacity to influence the terms of the debate and captivate the attention of journalists. If the American conversation on Islam is sliding ever rightward, it is not because the discourse of extremist anti-Muslim organizations is reflecting or in harmony with supposed Islamophobic predispositions of the American public. Rather, it is because the resources of these organizations, when it comes to media access and sheer money, give them unprecedented power to manufacture and naturalize hate speech and hateful feelings.

FROM WORDS TO DEEDS

The increasingly unhinged character of public discourse creates a climate that favors the passage from words to deeds. The number of assaults against Muslims and attacks against mosques increased considerably during the fall of 2015 after the attacks in Paris. Gunshots were fired outside a mosque in Connecticut, and threats were made against an Islamic center in St. Petersburg, Florida, among other incidents. On Facebook, there have been calls to murder Muslims in Dearborn, Michigan, where one-third of the 96,000 residents are Arab Americans. Soiled pages of the Quran have been thrown at a mosque in Pflugerville, Texas. Pigs' heads are regularly placed at the entrance to mosques, such as in Philadelphia, and there have been attempts at arson—for example, at the mosque in Coachella, California.[53]

The murder of three students at the University of North Carolina at Chapel Hill in February 2015 is without a doubt the Islamophobic act that most upset the American people and international opinion. What the Chapel Hill tragedy illustrates is not simply an arbitrary and reprehensible execution of three young Muslims by an Islamophobic individual. The arguably more salient feature is that it stages three exemplary

American citizens opposed by an individual who perceives himself and is perceived by others as basically lost and a loser. All the testimonies and commentaries compiled after this triple murder entirely agreed that Deah Barakat; his young wife, Yusor Abu-Salha; and Yusor's sister, Razan Abu-Salha, were model students, actively engaged in the associative life of their community, part of a large circle of friends, advancing toward successful professional careers, and proud of their American identity. In May 2014, Yusor Abu-Salha had given an interview posted on the site of the organization StoryCorps, an oral-history project, in which she expressed her strong attachment to her country:

> Growing up in America has been such a blessing. . . . Although in some ways I do stand out, such as the hijab I wear on my head, the head covering, there are still so many ways that I feel so embedded in the fabric that is, you know, our culture. And that's the beautiful thing here, is that it doesn't matter where you come from. There's so many different people from so many different places, of different backgrounds and religions—but here we're all one, one culture.[54]

Her murderer, Craig Hicks, on the contrary, represents the archetype of the small-time white guy, down and out, unemployed, in and out of marriage several times, and a self-described libertarian partisan of gun-ownership rights who would spend his evenings alone, spewing hate about other religions on social media. Contrary to what was affirmed by some commentators, one cannot deny the Islamophobic dimension of Hicks's act and view it as simply excessive anger resulting from a disagreement over a parking space. And yet Hicks's act is also more than the violent expression of theological-political discord. It is an affective attitude—examined in these pages—whose features are rage, resentment, and a consciousness of finding oneself falling behind or being downgraded. This attitude can lead to a reactionary acting out via a sacralization of territory—it might be land in one's neighborhood where a mosque risks going up or something as small as a parking spot. This study seeks to demonstrate that Islamophobic words and deeds in America express, above all, the rage and resentment of part of the population that considers itself bumped downward and reacts to this experience of lost status and wounded honor by seeing certain territory and the U.S. Constitution as holy.

THE AFFIRMATION OF THE LANGUAGE
OF RECOGNITION

All the same, it's important not to get stuck on this somber overview because alongside and despite the unleashing of words and deeds of hate, the recognition of Muslims on political, legal, and cultural levels is growing stronger. This is the effect of the matching efforts of the tenacious engagement of Muslim Americans and the support—if not always widespread, at least more audible—of a portion of media personalities and politicians, civil rights organizations, and Jewish, Catholic, and Protestant leaders. The banalization of hate speech has, in turn, revived a discourse of equality and pluralism. The virulence of certain hateful acts and utterances has had the positive effect of forcing a certain number of journalists, politicians, and association presidents to come out of their silent shells and articulate a clear position. It is perhaps this that most distinguishes the specifically American character of the debate on Islam from its European counterparts. In Europe, and notably in France, the discourse in favor of equality and against discrimination toward Muslims, restrained as it mostly is to certain academic circles, has become almost inaudible to the larger public. Populist rhetoric, *laïcité* preaching, and identity politics have gained hegemonic status and together have turned Islam and Muslims into the principal enemy of the nations of Europe.[55] Unlike in the United States, these discourses in Europe cut across partisan and ideological lines. The ramped-up focus on *laïcité* in France can be found coming from leaders on the left and the right. And it's the Socialist Party, borrowing a tactic usually associated with the playbook of the Far Right, that proposed the highly controversial measure of punishing those convicted of terrorism by stripping them of their nationality—a measure interpreted as largely symbolic but that would have the effect of establishing an illegitimate distinction between citizens of older "French" stock and citizens of Arab origin.[56] Thus, despite the striking standardization of their lines of reasoning, the American public debate over Islam is different from the French debate on one important point: in the United States, the virulence and absurdity of Islamophobic utterances by certain political figures limits but does not completely inhibit the development of a battle of ideas. The firmness and clarity with which two leading American newspapers, the *New York Times* and the *Washington Post*, have condemned Islamophobia in news pieces and editorials on an almost daily basis since 2015 has no equivalent in the mainstream European print media.[57] In France, every article or utterance denouncing Islamophobia is almost systematically paired with someone's countervailing statements affirming that blasphemy and offending Islam are civil rights and that Muslims lack a sense of humor and critical distance. In the United States, however, in reaction to the unleashing of verbal violence that has become more and more widespread, one can witness the clear affirmation of a discourse that takes up the work of historians to show that the Founding Fathers had already envisioned the full compatibility of Islam with American citizenship. At the same time that in France sociologists are being scolded by Prime Minister Manuel Valls, who accuses them of wanting to "excuse" terrorism as they try to explain its causes, in the U.S. historians' arguments are increasingly being used in the media battle against Islamophobia.[58]

In reply to the literalist and fundamentalist interpretations of history and the Constitution that populists close to the Tea Party regularly deploy, journalists, academics, and other specialists advance another reading of the history of the country's founding principles and of religious freedom. In September 2015, after the Republican candidate Ben Carson stated he did not believe a Muslim was fit to become U.S. president, Denise Spellberg responded with an article titled "Ben Carson Would Fail U.S. History."[59] Similarly, it was history and the Constitution's basic principles that were turned to when underlining the absurdity of the arrest of fourteen-year-old Ahmed Mohamed on September 14, 2015—the day he walked to school with a clock that he had built by himself but that one of his professors mistook for a bomb. In her reply to this incident, Spellberg recalls that such profiling of Muslims is contrary to the principle of religious freedom as defined by Thomas Jefferson, who coincidentally had also once designed a clock:

> Using the Polygraph to write five years before his death, Jefferson, our first "infidel" president, championed the rights of Muslim citizens, writing that he intended his Statute of Virginia for Religious Freedom "to comprehend within the mantle of its protection, the Jew and the Gentile, the Christian and Mahometan, the Hindoo, and infidel of every denomination," wherein he wrote these immortal words: "our civil rights have no dependence on our religious opinions."[60]

Along the same lines, several nonspecialized media outlets have run stories analyzing the ancient presence of Muslims in New York.[61] In the *New York Times*, for example, David Dunlap retraced the ancient history of a Muslim quarter known as "little Syria," and he reminds readers that, for New Yorkers, Muslims have long been their "neighbors" and not foreigners.[62]

THE FORMATTING OF PUBLIC STRATEGIES OF SELF-PRESENTATION

This book demonstrates how, paradoxically, through arguments that borrow from the themes and forms of European disputes, Islam as built in the United States becomes an American religion in a double sense—first through the strategies of recognition adopted by Muslims and second through the formatting of Islam as a faith. The mode of public presentation of self as practiced by Muslims is formatted with strategies of affirmation and recognition that have been used by other religious and cultural minorities. This mode is defined entirely by the legal-political norms and expectations of the American public. It is as citizens that Muslims intervene in the numerous controversies described in this book. It is in the name of respect for citizen equality and for the First Amendment, not with verses from the Quran, that they claim their rights. The content of their arguments and the style of their strategy, both inspired by the example of civil rights organizations and other associations that defend religious minorities, show that it's out of the materials of *American* politics, law, and the culture generally that Muslims are building the norms of their discourse and their public actions. In political and legal battles, their audience and interlocutor is the American public, not some hypothetical globalized *ummah*. In other words, the myths of a double allegiance, of a fifth column, of foreign infiltration, of clever disguises, or of a project to subvert the Constitution are discredited day after day by the actual practices and demands of the majority of Muslims. The idea of Islam's fundamental foreignness to America is equally rejected by civil rights organizations, legal defense councils, think tanks, political leaders, researchers, local associations, and ordinary individuals who have mobilized since 2001 to defend Muslim rights. As a result, Muslims have won big symbolic victories in the courts. Some months before the Supreme Court's decision concerning the treatment of Samantha Elauf by Abercrombie & Fitch, an appeals court recognized in January 2015 the validity of a complaint by a group of imams, activists, and student protestors who denounced the illegality of a surveillance program targeting Muslims developed by the New York Police Department.[63]

But the courts and other forums for public debate are not the only battlefields where Muslim Americans have made significant gains. They are also winning recognition for themselves in artistic spheres, sports, and the fashion world. Since roughly 2000, Muslim comedians have gone after stereotypes by following in the footsteps of Jewish and Mormon minorities who have sought to reverse the sting of social stigma through humor. Some of these artists have become true cultural entrepreneurs and have successfully exported their brand into mainstream culture. Troupes such as Allah Made Me Funny, Axis of Evil, and the comedy documentary *The Muslims Are Coming* (2013) ridicule the constant equation of Islam with terrorism. Mucahit Bilici has pointed out that airports—the ultimate "no joke zone"—have become the privileged setting where these Muslim humorists like to play out their sketches. The goal of this humor is to underscore the common humanity shared by Muslims and other citizens beyond political and religious differences. "Ethnic comedy is unfamiliarity packaged in a box of familiarity, a glimpse of charisma before it is routinized," notes Bilici.[64] The same goal is pursued in the web series "Halal in the Family," broadcast in September 2015 on the site Funny or Die. This miniseries, created by producer Miles Kahn and Aasif Mandvi, an actor and comic reporter on the *Daily Show*, presents scenes of a Muslim family living in a typically American suburban house. The four episodes in the series treat with humor the daily situations that Muslim Americans have to go through, such as dealing with the permanent mistrust and suspicion of the neighbors, the teasing of the kids at school, and diplomatic relations with other minorities.[65] The representation in visual media of Islam and Muslims has slowly improved with the appearance of positive or harmless Muslim characters in series such as *Quantico*, *The Brink*, and *Community*. Orientalist stereotypes are still very common, as can be seen in the series *Homeland*, but this aesthetic reductionism is also called out more often and more quickly than before.[66] During shooting for the series, artists who had been recruited to write graffiti in Arabic on walls of the set cleverly exposed the Islamophobic undercurrent of the series by writing slogans such as "Homeland is a joke."[67]

Muslims have also made their mark in the world of fashion, comics, and sports. The African American former basketball star and convert to Islam Kareem Abdul-Jabbar (born Lew Alcindor) has regularly spoken out against Islamophobia. G. Willow Wilson invented a young adolescent unveiled female character for Marvel comics who faces the same problems confronted by any American teenager. The humor usually derives from mocking common prejudices and insisting on the common humanity of all Muslims, yet other artistic forms are exploring with more nuance the complexity of the modes of identification among American Muslims. The play *Disgraced* by Ayad Akhtar, which ran in New York between 2012 and 2015, explores the internal contradictions of Amir Kapour (played first by Aasif Mandvi and later by Hari Dhillon), a successful architect who lives in a very beautiful New York apartment with his wife Emily, a non-Muslim and artist. The play opens with a dinner scene between Amir and his wife and another couple, an American Jew, Isaac, and his wife, Jory, an African American. The well-appointed, modernist apartment and the menu (fennel salad and roast pork) illustrate the perfect integration of these two multicultural couples and their relaxed attitudes toward religious dogmas. And yet the play evolves in such a way that the internal contradictions of all the characters, especially Amir, are put into dramatic relief. Through the story of these two couples, Ayad Akhtar seeks to evoke a more universal condition than the one of Muslim Americans. In an interview he gave to the *New York Times* in October 2014, he explained that he saw the "Muslim-American experience . . . as a repository of more eternal American themes of rupture and renewal."[68]

ISLAM AS CIVIL RELIGION

It can also be said that Islam is an American religion in a second sense. Islam is developing as a religion in a way that is in conformity with the normative definition of what a religion is in the American tradition— defined by a double ideal of post-Protestant secularism and civil religion.[69]

Islam is successfully attaining recognition in the American imaginary and public space but at the price of a normalization of the field of interventions and the types of life it makes possible. To be American, Islam must become simply a faith, a form of spirituality that is soluble within civil religion. In the American post-Protestant context, the condition of inclusion for many religions within the civil religion is the moderate neutralization of a religion into faith or spirituality. The acceptability of Islam and Muslims in the eyes of the American public operates—just as was the case for other minorities such as the Jews and the Mormons in the past—via a standardization of Islam as faith. This process of self-conformity to a norm was very visible during the Sharia controversies. To fight against the state legislatures that proposed laws banning all reference to Islamic law, Muslim associations and leaders concentrated their efforts on articulating one clear message: *Sharia is not a legal code but a code of ethics that serves to guide the spiritual formation of the individual.* This strategy made sense in the context of general suspicion about the loyalty of Muslims who were being accused of allegiance to a parallel legal code in competition with the U.S. Constitution. This message notwithstanding, it remains that Islamic law, even if there is a great deal of internal diversity, possesses a strong normative and legal dimension, and therefore it cannot be easily reduced to a simple ethical or spiritual guide. To affirm that Sharia is a spiritual ethics is to engage in a process of self-conformity to the collective norms of what is defined as acceptable religiosity within a secular context. Thus when explaining his path to conversion, Kareem Abdul-Jabbar explains why it was that he did not join the Nation of Islam: "Although I was greatly influenced by Malcolm X, a leader in the Nation of Islam, I chose not to join because I wanted to focus more on the spiritual rather than political aspects."[70]

This distinction of the object "religion" into two subcategories—one, inoffensive, that is about interiority, faith, and spirituality; the other, potentially dangerous, that broaches the public expression of political and legal demands—did not get started with debates on Islam. Numerous researchers, from Talal Asad to Courtney Bender, have shown that American secularism and pluralism are not neutral concepts with respect to each religion.[71] Rosemary Hicks underlines that these concepts "carry the imprint of Protestant traditions and thus privilege specific (sometimes secularized) Protestant practices and understandings of religion instead of creating an even space in which various groups interact."[72] In the same perspective, my book shows that in the numerous controversies over mosques, Sharia, and terrorism, the strategy of Muslim Americans to gain acceptance has been to insist on the spiritual, internal dimension of Islam, thus contributing to a reaffirmation of the normative distinction between an acceptable and a dangerous religiosity. Whether through humor in stand-up comedy and sitcoms, or through interreligious dialogue initiatives, Muslim Americans wish to get across two arguments: "We are citizens with the same rights as you," and "We are human beings just like you because we have a faith that is equivalent to yours"—and this second message is even more important than the first. Invoking the recognition of a humanity common to all individuals and the equivalence of all faiths leads to the depoliticization of the speech of Muslim Americans and a notable reduction in the power for criticism and dissensus that this speech could potentially represent. To be acceptable, Islam must be rebuilt as a "modern" civil religion—in other words, as above all a type of faith or spirituality. The visions of the world suggested by diverse possible interpretations of Islamic theology or law are, in principle, discarded as elements troubling to the American civil religion or even considered as dangerous or anti-American. The study by Bilici shows how the public discourse of the leading Muslim organizations is founded on a strategy of resignification of Islam in two phases. First, Muslims "reposition their faith from Muslim to Abrahamic and from Abrahamic to American civil religion."[73] By participating in ecumenical initiatives or by mocking stereotypes, Muslims seek to free Islam from the position of alterity into which a large portion of the public places it: "Islam becomes a 'religion' in neighborly contact with other 'religions,' primarily Christianity and Judaism. Nearness establishes the equivalence of Islam, Christianity and Judaism as 'religions.'"[74] But this strategy of inclusion and integration contributes to a dilution of Islam into the myth of the American civil religion: "The language of 'religion' gives way to that of 'faith,' which makes Muslimness a part of the unity of American civil religion."[75]

This study of American controversies over Islam since 2008 thus reveals a double process of formatting: first, that of anti-Muslim arguments on both sides of the Atlantic, and second, that of Islam as a faith. Through this analysis, my book asks about the ever-increasing fragility of the liberal argument on which rests the defense of Muslim rights. The participants in anti-mosque or anti-Sharia demonstrations affirm not so much their opposition to a liberal discourse based on equality of citizens' rights and religious freedom but rather the nonpertinence of this discourse. They do not deny that Muslims have rights. They simply declare their upset feelings at the fact that Muslims have the nerve to want to exercise their rights when, to them, it's not appropriate to do so: "It's not about rights; it's about what is right," the demonstrators will say. Anti-Muslim words and deeds, therefore, reveal much more than a coherent anti-liberal or anti-egalitarian ideology. They are signs of an affective disposition characterized by the visceral feeling of having been offended, betrayed, dispossessed—and by a need to have this wound recognized. This type of public claim that entails the disqualification of the liberal discourse of rights, here judged inadequate for grasping and responding to the specificity of certain collective feelings, is not only to be found at anti-Muslim demonstrations. It is the same type of affect that mobilized Yale University students in the fall of 2015. Shortly before Halloween, a professor circulated an e-mail in which she called into question the administration's instructions to students asking them not to wear costumes that might offend minorities. The professor, Erika Christakis, took the side of free speech and defended the capacity of students to decide for themselves about the appropriateness of wearing this or that costume. Her letter, in turn, unleashed widespread protest in which students denounced its inappropriate and offensive character that they saw as disrespectful and insensitive to the reality of racial discrimination on campuses.[76] Even if this campus affair and the controversies over Islam are very different, one finds in both the same argument—"it's not about rights but about what is right"—and the same call to defend a certain territory, whether a plot of land in the case of the mosque controversies or a "safe space" in the case of the Yale students and their campus life. The recurrence of this type of claim, which can be mobilized for reactionary or progressive agendas, leads to wondering about the growing precariousness of the liberal norm in struggles for equality.

Already fragile, these norms must not become disqualified, since it is thanks to them that Muslim Americans have succeeded in winning numerous legal battles in the courts. By closely examining controversies over Islam, this book intends to expose the politically structuring character of this opposition between a liberal-legal norm and an affective norm. The theoretical analysis of this opposition extends beyond this book's goals. What this study does underscore, however, is the potential, both inclusive and depoliticizing, of each normative register of action. To invoke affective feelings is to propose a ritualist vision of the community, one founded on a mimicry of feelings and ways of life. Certainly, placing the struggle on the legal plain of claims for rights leads to the real integration of Muslims; however, this inclusion entails that Islam must conform to the norms of what counts as acceptable religiousness within a given legal and political tradition. In these two understandings of the political community, what is excluded, or at least strongly retrained, is the possibility for disagreement, for difference, and therefore of the political.

INTRODUCTION

The 2004 French law that prohibits wearing conspicuous religious symbols in public schools provoked much perplexity and even indignation in the United States. The law appeared to go entirely against the American definition of religious freedom as a fundamental individual right and the principle of its free exercise as guaranteed by the First Amendment of the Constitution. The questions and moralizing multiplied: What right had the French state to intervene in the regulation of religious practices? Why did the French have the mischievous obsession of always instituting new laws to settle the least little problem? Did young Muslim women really need to be protected by the republic? But France is hardly the only target of America's wrath. Several countries are regularly denounced for their intolerance toward this or that religious minority: Why do the Germans refuse to recognize Scientology as a religion? Why do Italians oppose the construction of mosques? Why are the Belgians afraid of a few burkas? One institution in particular has for many years played an essential role in the construction of this narrative that places an exceptional America—champion of religious freedom—in opposition to an aging Europe that is increasingly insular, intolerant, and racist. The United States Commission for International Religious Freedom is an independent, bipartisan group created by the federal government in 1998 to make recommendations to the U.S. State Department about the condition of religious liberties around the world. Based in Washington, D.C., it names in its annual report the good and bad countries, the latter being referred to as "countries of particular concern." France was placed on the bad list in 2004, and all of Europe in 2010. As for the "Muslim world," it is of course where the commission sees religious liberties to be most at risk and where the United States should make it a priority to intervene.

But even though the United States is fond of presenting itself as a model and world arbiter for the protection of religious freedom, the past few years have seen an increase in the number of cases that concern the rights of American Muslims. Moreover, the arguments put forward in these controversies are strangely similar to those we've been hearing in Europe since 2000. Everywhere there are debates about the size of new mosques that neighborhood Muslims want to build, and speculation about what is going to be preached inside them. In California, a number of families organize to prohibit circumcision in the name of respecting children's rights. Certain Americans, in a curious display of Jacobinism, have even turned to Washington and demanded the passage of a federal law prohibiting all reference to Sharia law in U.S. courts. In various places people are starting to dispute a Muslim woman's right to wear a veil in the workplace or at school. There are protests against the efforts of Muslim parents to obtain an officially recognized school holiday for an Islamic festival day, Eid al-Fitr. The authorities of an airport negotiate with a Muslim taxi union that refuses passengers transporting bottles of alcohol. Customers erupt in protest against a health-food supermarket chain that wants to sell halal products to make more money during the month of Ramadan. All these debates sound strangely familiar. So what has come over the Americans? How is it that they've turned to having discussions about Islam in nearly the same terms as Europeans?

This book asks two questions. First, why in the past years has Islam become for a large portion of the American population not just a security problem or foreign policy issue but a true problem of domestic politics? And second, to what extent do these polemics express something beyond a problem with Islam, but really a more profound questioning of a certain conception of liberal, secular democracy?

One could be tempted to explain the appearance of these arguments as simply an offshoot of the memory of September 11, 2001. But even if the trauma provoked by those attacks counts for something, it could not alone explain the sizable malaise surrounding Islam. September 11, 2001, certainly marks a turning point. "On Sept. 10, 2001, nobody in America seemed to know anything about Islam. On Sept. 12, 2001, everybody seemed to know everything about Islam," quipped Leon Wieseltier in a *New York Times Book Review*.[1] But it is certainly since the election of Barack Obama, the first African American president—who is considered a Muslim by 11 percent of the population according to a 2012 Gallup poll and whose nationality is doubted by a large contingent of right-wing conspiracy theorists—that controversies related to Islam have multiplied.[2] In a social context marked by a serious economic crisis, ferocious opposition by the Republican Party to President Obama's plan to reform the health care system, the success of the Tea Party, and a noticeable tendency toward extremism of the American Right, Islam has become, like in Europe, a focus of questions and a source of discord. Unlike during the two terms in office of George W. Bush (2000–2008), the talk is no longer simply about how to halt the progress of radical Islam in the Middle East so as to safeguard the interests and security of the country. Now it's about asking about the place of Islam in America and about the intentions of Muslims. What goes on in mosques? Is Sharia a religious or legal code? Is Islam a religion? Do Muslims deserve to be Americans?

The development of a fear of subversion or of an imminent Islamic invasion of America is apparently all the more enigmatic since Muslims barely represent 0.6 percent of the American population. Also, since they have very diverse ethnic and national origins, they are far from constituting a homogeneous, unified community that could pose any significant threat or hold political weight. On average, their socioeconomic standing is quite similar and slightly above the national average, and they tend to be conservative on moral and social issues—in other words, far from the myth of a marginalized, excluded population inclined toward seditious behavior. Moreover, in contrast to the European context, the figure of the Muslim in America is not clearly equated with "immigrant." In the United States, that figure is first of all the "Latino," who is Catholic—except when he converts to Islam, and that is occurring more and more often. Therefore, the American case is also interesting because even though Islam is not a metaphor for immigration, it provokes fears and arguments similar to those one hears in Europe.

The 2012 presidential campaign revealed the persistent mistrust and specific fear of Islam. Although when first announced Mitt Romney's candidacy raised many questions about the plausibility of a Mormon president, in the end the religion of the Republican candidate caused less of a stir than some had thought it would. The campaign even contributed to a relatively speedy normalization of views about the Mormon religion in the American media. Even though many Christians on the right still refuse the idea that Mormonism is a part of Christianity, a majority of the population considers it a mainstream religion whose American-ness is not in question. But this is not the case for Islam, which is still widely perceived as irreducibly foreign and dangerous even if the Muslims living in the United States are, and proclaim themselves to be, resolutely American.

How is one to analyze the persistence and even amplification of this fear of Islam in a country that prides itself on its long history of acceptance and progressive assimilation of all religious minorities? To what extent are these public anti-Muslim incidents serving as substitutes for the expression of more fundamental anxieties and unhappiness about the very significance of liberal democracy? These questions are worth asking because what's striking about the polemical debates that have occurred in the United States since 2008 on the subject of mosques, Sharia, and the sale of halal products is the systematic association between anti-Islam arguments and arguments hostile toward liberal secular democracy. Pointing out the danger of a certain mosque or of the hidden agenda of a certain Muslim association is always closely tied to antiliberal, populist reasoning. How is it, antiliberals decry, that these elite judges and these liberal civil rights organizations remain so blind to the "danger"? Why are liberals so stubborn about wanting to guarantee the same rights to all citizens, they continue, when it is so important to submit Muslims to an exceptional regime? Judges, political leaders, and liberal activists have made every effort to denounce such remarks as contrary to law, the Constitution, and the principle of separation of church and state, yet it has quickly become clear that countering these statements with the language of law and the Constitution offers no satisfying full-proof comeback. Attempts to defend Muslim rights in the name of respect for liberal secular principles have failed to convince a significant portion of the population. The question that the controversies raise is therefore not just about the reasons for the persistent fear of Islam. Of more fundamental importance is the question of liberalism's capacity (as a philosophical, political, and legal theory) to resolve current tensions and problems linked to the acceptance of Islam.

What do arguments over Islam teach us about the widespread hatefulness toward liberal democracy and secularism? To what extent does the liberal tendency to put forward law as the principal instrument for resolving the current conflicts fittingly and effectively respond to the demands and unhappiness expressed in these controversies?

Since 2000, the theme of the encounter between "Islam" and "the West" has been the focus of a large number of studies in both academia and the popular media. One notes, however, that this debate has generally remained very normative—organized mostly around deciding if, yes or no, Islam is "compatible" with democracy, *laïcité*, women's rights (and, more recently, the rights of children and animals), and if Muslims are capable of integrating into Western societies. One witnesses here the relentless opposition and confrontation between those who affirm that there is nothing about Muslims that would prevent their integration and those who maintain that Islam is fundamentally contrary to all liberal principles. Each of these two possibilities is put forward with more or less documentation and less or more polemically. The argument in favor of the unexceptional and unproblematic status of Islam can be developed along liberal, republican, or postcolonial lines of argument.[3] The essentialist and culturalist thesis can be found in the writings of notable continuators of the work of the Middle Eastern specialist Bernard Lewis as well as, in more nuanced form, in the numerous analyses performed by authors who claim a firm attachment to the European Enlightenment tradition or to that of Islamic rationalism.[4]

Independently of the way in which each participant positions himself in this debate, the very terms of the discussion are problematic insofar as they presuppose an overly large homogeneity both when it comes to Islam and when it comes to what constitutes liberal democracy. The longer the debate is pursued, the more one notices it being uncritically accepted that the only pertinent question is what are the conditions of possibility for the encounter between an ensemble of practices, norms, and discourses vaguely associated with Islam and an ensemble of rules and behaviors that are associated with liberal democracy and secularism. There is, however, a third line of analysis that aims to go beyond the binary opposition of the essentialist thesis and the anticulturalist approach by showing the multiplicity and similarity of fractures and transformations that have taken place both in Muslim communities and societies and in Western societies.[5] By adopting this perspective, this book seeks to contribute to a reformulation of the problem by asking not about "Islam and democracy" but instead about liberal secularism's confrontation with itself. The antagonism in need of understanding is not the conflict between Islam and America but a dispute that America is having with itself. The question of interest here is not to know "what failed" in Islam or in the Muslim world. I am more interested in taking the occasion of these specific debates about Islam to inquire into the unhappiness and misunderstandings that are surfacing with respect to liberal secularism as a political theory and legal regime.

Despite the fundamental differences that exist between Europe and the United States when it comes to the history of religious freedom and the sociology of Muslims, one can observe a paradoxical convergence of Euro-American argumentation on Islam. It is this paradox that my book underlines by questioning the presupposition of a radical opposition between American and European models for the protection of religious freedom. According to this presupposition, it is generally agreed that since September 11, 2001, the United States has, to say the least, tense relations with the Muslim world. Yet it is continually stated that American Muslims are considerably wealthier and better educated than their lumpenproletariat Muslim counterparts in Europe, and generally live in peace in the United States without provoking arguments and affairs on the scale one observes in Europe. Also over the same period, an entire media machine in America got started with the aim of explaining why Europeans detest Muslims so much, and of course France remains the favorite target of American commentators. It's hard to keep track of the number of scholarly or general studies that demonstrate—often by means of disturbing historical shortcuts and despite obvious ignorance of the history of French laïcité and of the operation of the country's political institutions—that Muslims in France are essentially all discriminated against, excluded, and under suspicion. These writings offer exhaustive lists of the judged and the judges, such as "the Jacobin State," "the Republican model," "authoritarian secularism," "postcolonialism," and "intransigent feminism." Even if in certain of these publications one can find pertinent and detailed critiques of French policies toward Islam, these concepts have become the bass notes of a dominant refrain, the common labels that American researchers and public intellectuals use to perpetuate, often with a patronizing tone, an idea of American exceptionalism and a corresponding European malediction in the treatment of Islam. But if Americans like to caricature Europeans, the latter are no less capable of slinging it right back. A large majority of European peoples, with perhaps France in the lead, continue to describe the United States as a homogeneous society composed of white, racist, Islamophobic evangelical fundamentalists ready to bomb any troublesome Muslim country, large or small.

The aim of this book is therefore to understand how these two models, supposedly so diametrically opposed, arrive at the same crux—the incompatibility of Islam with "Western values." Could it be that beyond the large differences between the Muslims of Europe and those in the United States, and between the types of arrangements between the religious and the political on each side of the Atlantic, these so-called models are not so different after all? In other words, is it possible to claim that these "models" are becoming increasingly similar not just because of a shared malaise about Islam but also because of an expanding reexamination of the very political principles that they are founded on? How is it that the European and American debates on Islam offer a distorted image, a parodic representation of the ideal of rational collective deliberation over theories of liberal politics, an ideal that continues to play a decisive normative role in the way Western democracies see themselves and represent themselves? Surely nothing is further from this ideal than the way debates are conducted, in Europe and the United States, about mosques, minarets, burkas, public prayer, Sharia, or the condition of Muslim women. Instead of the liberal ideal of an exchange of reasoned arguments, we find streams of absurd reasoning founded on burlesque analogies and speculation. Resentment and bad faith take the place of the famous "agreeing to disagree," while the tone of exchanges fluctuates between violence and buffoonery. Rumors and revelations posted on any website are accepted as proof. The testimony of counterfeit intellectuals with dubious qualifications is taken as seriously as the statements of legal or academic experts and theologians. The controversies over Islam amount to a cacophony of the deaf and represent exactly the inverse of the ideal situation of rational communication and collective deliberation as stipulated by normative liberal theory. And yet, as absurd, burlesque, and shrill as they are, these polemics also produce positive effects. The parties reach ways of mutually adjusting, learn to get to know each other, and develop new rules for living together. The controversies divide but most of all they go in circles. However, after going in circles long enough, the conflicting sides learn more about each other, even if the upshot may be to detest each other all the more.

Chapter 1 recalls the principal historical and sociological characteristics of Muslims in America, and shows that from a legal point of view, what they seek is no different from what other religious minorities request.

Chapter 2 analyzes the different controversies surrounding the construction of mosques and examines the opposition between, on the one hand, the legal logic and, on the other, the repertoire of emotions and moralizing that is central to the arguments of a large portion of the public.

Chapter 3 considers the anti-Sharia movement, which seeks to banish from the courts all reference to Islamic law and asks about the particular conception of democracy that underlies this exceptional and unconstitutional treatment of Muslims.

Chapter 4 examines the way the Tea Party seized on the Islamic question starting in 2010 and how its tactics operate within a long-standing rhetorical tradition of populism and a form of paranoid rationality that expresses an illiberal conception of democracy.

Chapter 5 looks at how the treatment of Islam as a matter of foreign policy reveals less clear distinctions than those observed in domestic quarrels between moral registers, law, and security. The policy of exporting the principle of international religious freedom is founded mostly on a culturalist approach that opposes an intolerant Muslim world to a persecuted Christian world.

1

MUSLIM AMERICANS

A Religious Minority Like Any Other?

A DYNAMIC AND PLURALIST RELIGIOUS LANDSCAPE OF INTEGRATED MUSLIMS

A study conducted in 2008 by the Pew Forum on Religion and Public Life depicts a diverse and dynamic religious landscape.[1] It leads one to question perceptions that are still too prevalent in Europe, of an evangelical, white, bigoted, aging America.[2] The United States in the Obama era is characterized by a high level of religious pluralism and a strong tendency for individuals to go from one religion to another or to change denominations. More than 25 percent of Americans over eighteen years old say they left the religion in which they were brought up for another. The cliché that says America is pious and hostile to secularism is also stripped away: nearly 25 percent of Americans age eighteen to twenty-nine say they are have no religious affiliation. Although 51 percent of Americans are members of a Protestant denomination, there is high fragmentation within this group. Today there are over one hundred denominations (26.3 percent of the population belongs to an evangelical church and 18.1 percent to "mainline" Protestant churches). Overall, 23.9 percent of Americans are Catholic, 1.7 percent are Mormon, 1.7 percent are Jewish, 0.6 percent are Orthodox Christians, and 0.6 percent are Muslims.

The research findings reveal important differences between age groups. Although more than 62 percent of Americans seventy years old and up are

Protestant, only 43 percent of eighteen- to twenty-nine-year-old Americans are. Similarly, 25 percent of Americans age eighteen to twenty-nine declare no religious affiliation, whereas only 8 percent in the seventy and up age group do so. These statistics suggest that America is definitely undergoing a certain amount of secularization (especially among younger generations) and a diversification of the religious spectrum, with a notable decline over the long term of the numerical weight of Protestantism as compared with other religions. The study puts forward the hypothesis that "if these generational patterns persist, recent declines in the number of Protestants and growth in the size of the unaffiliated population may continue."[3]

Among the striking characteristics of the American Muslim population are its relative youth, from the standpoint of both their age upon arrival in the United States and their average age: 63 percent of American Muslims are first-generation immigrants, and 45 percent of them arrived after 1990.[4] However, even though they tend to be recent arrivals in the United States, a large percentage are American citizens: 37 percent of them were born in America, and 70 percent of Muslim immigrants born abroad are today American citizens.[5] Nearly all Muslims who arrived before 1980 are now American citizens. This population is relatively younger than other religious communities: 29 percent of Muslims are between the ages of eighteen and twenty-nine (as against only 14 percent of mainline Protestants); 48 percent are between thirty and forty-nine years old. Only 5 percent are older than sixty-five (compared with 28 percent of mainline Protestants and 29 percent of Jews). Consistent with the overall youth of this community, 53 percent of Muslims have no children; 19 percent have two children. These figures give the lie to the idea of burgeoning families, a favorite myth among conspiracy theorists who spread fear of invasion.

Concentrated mostly in the Northeast (29 percent) and the South (32 percent), the Muslim population is composed of people who self-identify as white (37 percent, versus 91 percent of mainline Protestants), as black (24 percent), as Asian (20 percent), and as Hispanic (4 percent).

The socioeconomic standing and education levels of Muslims are comparable to national averages, with 16 percent having annual incomes of more than $100,000 (versus a national percentage at this income level of 18 percent, and compared with 16 percent of Mormons, 46 percent of Jews, and 43 percent of Hindus) and 35 percent reporting annual income of less than $30,000 (versus a national percentage at this level of 31 percent, with 47 percent of those belonging to historically black churches with this income). Fourteen percent of Muslims have an undergraduate university diploma, and 10 percent have either a master's degree or a doctoral degree (compared with the national percentage of 11 percent, though the number is 35 percent for Jews and 48 percent for Hindus).

The study describes the religiousness of Muslims as strong but not dogmatic, and more open than that of Mormons, Jehovah's Witnesses, or evangelicals. Eighty-two percent of Muslims affirm having an absolute belief in God (compared with 41 percent of Jews and 39 percent of Buddhists), and 17 percent participate in a religious service more than once a week, which is less than Mormons (31 percent), Jehovah's Witnesses (71 percent), and evangelicals (30 percent). Seventy-one percent say they pray every day, which is also less than Mormons (82 percent), Jehovah's Witnesses (89 percent), and evangelicals (78 percent). When it comes to sacred texts, 50 percent of Muslims say they believe the word of God is totally true (compared with 62 percent of members of historically black churches and 59 percent of evangelicals, whereas only 22 percent of mainline Protestants think so, and 10 percent of Jews). Only 33 percent of Muslims say there is only one acceptable interpretation of a sacred text (as against 77 percent of Jehovah's Witnesses and 54 percent of Mormons). Finally, 81 percent of Muslims categorically reject suicide attacks, while 1 percent say they are justified to defend Islam against its enemies.

When it comes to politics and ideology, a plurality of Muslims are Democrats (37 percent; only 7 percent are Republicans) but are often conservative on social and moral issues. Nineteen percent describe themselves as conservative, 24 percent as liberal, and 38 percent as moderate. A majority of Muslims support the Obama administration's reforms, notably of the health care system, and say they favor a strong government (21 percent are in favor of small government versus 70 percent who favor strong government). Along these lines, 59 percent believe that government should take a more active role in defending moral behavior. Muslims are divided on the question of abortion: 35 percent consider it wrong in most cases, and 35 percent say it is permissible. However, 61 percent say that society should discourage homosexuality.

Another study conducted by the Gallup Institute in 2011 indicates that the political participation of American Muslims is lower than that of other large religious groups.[6] Only 65 percent of them are registered to vote, compared with 91 percent of Protestants and Jews, although this may be partially due to the relative youth of the Muslim population since the average age is thirty-six. The study reveals that Muslims tend to deplore the numerous acts of discrimination they are subjected to but on the whole tend to be optimistic about the future, and 82 percent say they are very happy with their lives. This optimism is not shared by the rest of the population: "It is striking to see that Muslim Americans are considerably more satisfied with the way things are in the country (56%) than the general public."[7] This situation derives in part from the fact that Muslim Americans are generally happier about the political situation of the country since Obama's election as president. They also seem to have suffered somewhat less, on average, from the economic crisis of 2008; 46 percent of American Muslims say they are in very good financial shape, compared with only 38 percent of the general population.

The study especially underscores the ordinariness of Muslim Americans and their high level of conformity in different areas of everyday life. Muslims answer in the same numbers as the general public when it comes to how much time they spend watching television, playing video games, or tending to the recycling of their garbage. Thirty-three percent say they have collaborated with neighbors to settle some community problem, compared with 38 percent of the general public who say they have. In other words, even if one can dispute the pertinence of certain questions or the criteria used in these studies, they paint a picture that is very different from what is suggested by a number of polemicists.[8] American Muslims do not constitute a unified community of dangerous extremists turned in on themselves. They are a relatively young population who tend to be economically comfortable, Democratic-leaning though morally conservative, but not fundamentalist. The Muslim community is strikingly normal, in fact, and appears in many ways to be highly "American."

A recent study by the Brookings Institution offers important information on the general state of relations between religions, ethnic communities, and age groups.[9] The findings also overturn the distorting cliché that would see a sharp opposition between a homogeneous American society and a marginalized Muslim population. The study underscores the widely different attitudes among different generations. White non-Muslim Americans of the so-called millennial generation (those born between 1980 and 2000) have much more regular contact with African Americans, Hispanics, and Muslims than do those sixty-five years old and higher. A high percentage of whites of all ages say they have experienced discrimination just like minority groups, and six out of ten Republicans say that discrimination against whites is now as big a problem as discrimination against minorities. One can ask if there are adequate reasons and evidence for this claim, but the fact that so many white Republicans in the population make it suggests that the paradigm of an offensive, imperial white America at war against Islam (the paradigm frequently deployed in anti-Islamophobic arguments) is itself inadequate. According to the Brookings Institution study, 68 percent of millennials of all religious affiliations have a favorable opinion of Muslims (compared with only 47 percent of Republicans and 46 percent of people over age sixty-five). Similarly, 60 percent of the general population, all religions and political affiliations combined, regret that too many Americans consider all Muslims to be terrorists.

Muslims are hardly the only group that incites fear or skepticism. Forty-nine percent of Democrats and 56 percent of those aged eighteen to twenty-nine have a favorable opinion of atheists, but only 38 percent of Republicans and 35 percent of those over sixty-five also have a favorable opinion of atheists. Many people are either ignorant or doubtful about Mormonism. Twenty-seven percent of the population say they know nothing about Mormonism, and 41 percent do not think Mormonism is a Christian religion. Fifty-seven percent of evangelical Christians reject the notion that Mormonism falls within Christianity. Mormons are generally considered more negatively among younger adults, perhaps because of the Mormon Church's opposition to gay marriage. The level of hostility toward Mormons is about the same among conservatives and liberals; 21 percent of conservatives and 22 percent of liberals say they have a negative view of Mormons: "Just as in the past there were Left and Right versions of anti-Catholicism; today there are two ideological currents against Mormons."[10]

The study reveals the very clear difference between Democratic and Republican feelings toward Muslims. On the question of a Muslim teaching at an elementary school in their neighborhood, 66 percent of Democrats and only 44 percent of Republicans see nothing wrong with this. More than half of Democrats (57 percent) compared with 37 percent of Republicans say they would favor the construction of a mosque in their neighborhood, and 58 percent of Democrats and 45 percent of Republicans accept the idea that Muslims should be able to kneel and pray in airports.

By insisting on the integration and normalness of Muslim Americans, these studies reassure a nervous public. By doing so, they also reaffirm the glorious story of a tolerant, multicultural, multiethnic America still capable of surmounting its differences and being a source of hope and a force in favor of integration and moderation. By seeking to show the exemplary integration of Muslim Americans, the studies reformulate indirectly the theme of America's exceptional destiny. The 2007 study by the Pew Institute already insisted on the difference between Muslims in America and those elsewhere in the world, notably in Europe: "Generally speaking, the 2007 study showed that Muslims living in the United States are middle class and moderates, largely assimilated, satisfied with their lives, and moderate on international questions, especially compared to Muslim minorities in several European countries that were studied by the Pew Global Attitudes Project."[11] The 2011 study confirms this gap between American Muslims and other Muslims around the world.

It is thus within this religious landscape characterized by high levels of pluralism, a great fluidity of membership, and a tendency toward a certain standardization of practices and even doctrines that I analyze the present-day controversies over Islam. These are political disputes that oppose Democrats and Republicans but that also divide the Republican Party. These debates also reveal radically divergent ways of conceiving of and living out daily political life. They suggest a clear face-off between a liberal sensibility and reactionary, populist feelings. But there is absolutely no way one can reduce them to, as one often hears it repeated in Europe, a war between a united, white, evangelical majority and a Muslim minority. Evangelical Protestantism is certainly an important part of the American religious landscape, but its power is not hegemonic. What's more, it does not hold a clear set of positions regarding Islam.[12] Insofar as proselytism and political engagement are essential aspects of this type of Protestantism, Islam could certainly appear as a threatening competitor religion; but in fact it occupies a relatively moderate place in its social and cultural agenda. Even among fundamentalist evangelicals—and Sébastien Fath underlines that not all evangelicals are fundamentalists—Islam is not a central preoccupation.[13] Of course, from a theological point of view, many fundamentalists consider Islam to be a false religion, and the members of these churches are more inclined to have an unfavorable opinion of Islam. Some fundamentalist pastors have joined activist movements opposed to the construction of mosques or to Sharia. But a fight against Islam is far from being the main battle of these groups. First, not all fundamentalists engage actively in politics. Second, among militant causes, stopping abortion, gay rights, and the Obama administration's health-care reform and promoting prayer in schools and the teaching of creationism are all much more important to them than mosques, head scarves, and Sharia. Evangelical fundamentalists may not be big admirers of Islam, but secular humanism remains their number-one enemy.[14] Therefore, I shall not be analyzing the controversies over Islam based on a simplistic paradigm of "culture wars." Stereotypes, ignorance, and fear of Islam do exist across a large portion of the population. But the scale of recent debates and activism cannot be explained by an Islamophobic predisposition that would be culturally determined among a majority of Judeo-Christians. It is the political will of a minority of activists and organizations that is at the origin of the leading controversies, and these conflicts are precisely political more than they are religious or cultural.

ISLAM: A HISTORICALLY AMBIGUOUS AMERICAN RELIGION

Even if it did not always have the visibility that it acquired starting in 2001, Islam was at the heart of the principal battles that forged the American republic and its democracy. Muslims have not been mere extras or passive victims within a Protestant, white, racist culture. They have actively contributed to the transformation or the destabilization of that culture. To a great extent, the history of Islam in America is the history of America itself. However, an exhaustive retelling of this history is not the object of this study. It suffices to say that starting in the seventeenth century, Islam was perceived as an unusual religion. Its very status as a religion was regularly doubted, but it was also credited with a particular capacity for mediation, resistance, transformation, and even redemption within the nation. Numerous historical studies have insisted on the idea of the Americanization and progressive normalization of Muslims. But in fact these Muslims are represented less as individuals of an exotic culture who little by little "integrated" but instead as liminal, transitive figures, thanks to whom America has undertaken a reconciliation with itself on several occasions.

Despite the near total lack of sources that would relate the life of Muslim slaves in their native Africa, historians have been able to produce a relatively precise image of the way these first Muslims were perceived. The survival of Muslim slaves imported from Africa was made possible by a double process of what historian Kambiz GhaneaBassiri calls "denegrifiction" and "reislamization."[15] Starting in the seventeenth century, a form of hierarchy was established that considered the Muslim slaves as less "Negro" than the other slaves. Racist observations by white masters about a given skin color, hair texture, or education level contributed to the development of the semicivilized figure of the "Moor." Similarly, Islam, although considered inferior to Christianity, seemed more respectable than pagan beliefs and other forms of spirituality. A number of Muslim slaves participated in this construction, as is illustrated by the itinerary of Ibrahim Abdulrahman, the "Prince of slaves." Born in Timbo in West Africa in 1762, this soldier's son went to study in Mali in 1774. Upon his return in 1788, he was captured and sold to slave dealers and later turned up in Natchez, Mississippi. Thanks to the quality of his work and his education, he rose rapidly to become overseer on the cotton plantation of Thomas Foster, where he started a family and cultivated his own plot of land. Cyrus Griffin, the editor in chief of the local newspaper, the *Southern Galaxy*, offers this description: "That Prince . . . is a Moor, there can be but little doubt. . . . The Prince states explicitly, and with an air of pride, that not a drop of negro blood runs in his veins. He places the negro in a scale being infinitely below the Moor."[16]

Before Abdulrahman was liberated by order of President John Quincy Adams in 1828, a number of those in favor of his emancipation attempted to demonstrate that he was practically Christian. Afterward, during his travels through the North, as he tried to raise money with the help of the American Colonization Society to buy the freedom of his children, he was presented as a Christian convert and said to have been baptized in a Baptist church. Abdulrahman left some doubt about the truth of his conversion, all the while understanding the advantages that a Christian identity could give him, as one sees in his reply to the Reverend Thomas Gallaudet, who had sent him a copy of the Old Testament in Arabic as well as an Arabic translation of Hugo Grotius's *On the Truth of the Christian Religion*: "After I take this book home, I hope I shall get many to become Christians. I will show them the path of the Christian religion."[17]

As shown by GhaneaBassiri, in pre–Civil War America, the Islamic religion of the African slaves played an important role in debates about the
condition of slaves. While numerous defenders of slavery insisted that it
was something positive that had contributed to improve the Africans' condition, others point to the Muslim slaves as proof of a kind of civilization
among Africans. The abolitionist Theodore Dwight pointed to the examples of slaves such as Abdulrahman, Umar Ibn Said, and Job Ben Solomon
to show that blacks could be educated and civilized. The abolitionists' interest in Islam was purely strategic. They did not have any true admiration for
Islam comparable to what one can witness, for example, in France around
the same time among the Islamophile followers of Auguste Comte.[18] The
praise of Islam was a rhetorical tool that allowed them to score points in
polemical arguments about humanity and black culture. Like all of his
contemporaries, Dwight thought that Mohammad was a false prophet,
and the abolitionist bishop Benjamin Bosworth Smith claimed that the
Quran was simply plagiarized from the Old Testament. Other critics of
slavery insisted that it should be possible to use Muslim slaves in the efforts
to evangelize Africa: "These [Arabic-speaking people] would appear to be
superior in culture and civilization to surrounding people. . . . The way is
open for evangelizing them through the Arabic language, by means of men
who should be trained for the purpose in an Arabic department of the
Liberia College."[19] The Muslim African slaves were thus perceived as transitive, ambiguous, borderline figures who constitute simultaneously both
a separation from and a link between different entities: "As liminal figures,
African Muslims provided an avenue by which some Anglo-Americans
advanced a very different understanding of an English or American community in which the existing boundaries between races and religions were
temporarily blurred, mainly, for commercial and missionary purposes."[20]

In post–Civil War America with slavery now abolished, Islam continues to play a role that is both central and paradoxical in debates about
America's civilization, identity, and progress. In a context influenced by
the evolutionary thinking of Charles Darwin and Herbert Spencer, ideas of
Protestantism's superiority compared with other religions and of America's
exceptional status take hold. The pastor Josiah Strong affirms in his successful publication *Our Country: Its Possible Future and Its Present Crisis*
(1885) that America's triumph was founded on two principles that date
from the Reformation and the Age of Reason—Christian spirituality and

civil liberty. For him, other religions were not only inferior but dangerous for the progress of humanity. Catholicism was considered an authoritarian religion consistent with a lesser-evolved stage of humanity. By the end of the nineteenth century, the practice of comparing religions became commonplace in both academia and among the general public. Another successful publication, this one by the Unitarian minister and professor of theology at the Harvard Divinity School, James Freeman Clarke, is a good example of this enthusiasm for comparing religions. In *Ten Great Religions: An Essay in Comparative Theology* (1871), Clarke asserts that Protestantism is the single truly whole and universal religion, the other religions being what he calls partial religions because they are intimately linked to an ethnic community. For him, Islam cannot be characterized as a universal religion, because even if it has expanded beyond the borders of a particular ethnic community, "Mohammedanism has never sought to make *converts* but only *subjects*, it has not asked for belief, but merely for submission."[21]

The Parliament of the World's Religions, organized in 1893 in Chicago as part of the World's Columbian Exposition, furthers the mainstreaming of these ideas of a hierarchy of religions and their common but unequal relationship to humanity. In his inaugural discourse, Charles Carroll Bonney, a leading organizer of the exposition and president of the World's Congress Auxiliary and a layman in the Swedenborgian church, made the following declaration: "While the members of this Congress meet, as men, on a common ground of perfect equality, the ecclesiastical rank of each, in his own church, is, at the same time, gladly recognized and respected, as the just acknowledgment of his services and attainments. But no attempt is here made to treat all religions as of equal merit. Any such idea is expressly disclaimed."[22] His defense of Christianity is not a call to establish a Christian theocracy but rather a vision of a secularized world characterized by faith in America's exceptional status.[23]

Starting in the twentieth century, Islam plays an essential role in black American nationalist movements while still retaining the same ambiguous, semireligious status. The first prophets and founders of Afro-American Islam made it an essential tool in the struggle for equality. But this strategy led to the development of the idea that Afro-American Islam was necessarily part of a language of resistance more than a "true" religion. In a study titled *Christianity, Islam and the Negro Race* (1887), Edward Wilmot Blyden presents Islam as essential to the progress of Africa and

Afro-Americans but says little about Islam as a religion. Although a severe critic of Christianity, Blyden never converted to Islam but was convinced that the emancipation of blacks could only come via Islam: "Nowhere can one find any community of Negro Christians who are autonomous and independent. Haiti and Liberia, the so-called Negro republics, are struggling simply to survive. . . . However, there are numerous communities and Negro Mohammedan states in Africa that are autonomous, productive, independent and dominant."[24]

Along the same lines, the principal mission of the Moorish Science Temple of America, created in 1925 by Noble Drew Ali, and the Nation of Islam (NOI), created in 1934 by Wallace Fard, was to offer African Americans an organization, a place, a style of life, and a vocabulary that would permit them to make sense of their past and alter their status as second-class citizens.[25] As shown by Kambiz GhaneaBassiri, the rewriting of black American history and the imagination of a more promising future would pass through Islam: "While black Muslims in the antebellum period played a passive role, for the most part, in the processes of their 'de-negrofication,' in the interwar period, the prophetic founder of the Moorish Science Temple . . . actively appropriated Islam in a 'de-negrofying' process that was designed to ascribe his followers a positive national identity."[26]

The prevailing view in the historiography of Afro-American Islam is that of a slow evolution from heterodoxy toward orthodoxy. Afro-American Islam at the beginning of the nineteenth century was said to be heterodox and syncretic, taking inspiration from both Judaism and Christianity, from African customs, and from Hinduism. Born from a mixture of intellectual sources and a variety of religious models, it supposedly remained heterodox with respect to the Sunni orthodoxy until Warith Deen Muhammad—the son of Elijah Muhammad, who had directed the NOI starting in 1934—took over the direction of the NOI in 1975 following the death of his father. After renaming the temples of the NOI "mosques," replacing the title of "minister" with that of "imam," and eliminating the NOI security forces known as the "Fruit of Islam," the son changed the name from Nation of Islam to the American Society of Muslims. Thus it is said that the arrival of Warith Deen Muhammad as director of the NOI marks the beginning of the normalization of Afro-American Islam and of a rapprochement between Afro-American Muslim communities and Muslim communities of Middle Eastern origin.

Researchers have lately put into question the implications of such a narrative. For example, doesn't the insistence on aspects of heterodoxy and fantasy within the sources of Afro-American Islam contribute to discredit black Islam? Certain authors thus reject the thesis according to which a deformed, heterodox Islam was introduced by self-proclaimed prophets to credulous blacks in search of a messiah within the ghettos of midwestern America.[27] They talk instead about the first contact between African Americans and Islam taking place within an international context of exchange with orthodox Muslims. They insist especially on the important role played by the encounter between black soldiers and European and North African troops during the First World War and how this led to the discovery of orthodox Sunni Islam. Thus it is said to be a network of intellectuals and not dishonest door-to-door salesmen who introduced Islam into black neighborhoods.

Outside this historiographical debate, the prevailing image throughout the United States of black Islam is that of a religion of resistance whose role is primarily social and political. African American communities excluded by the white, Protestant majority are said to have found in Islam a language and an ideal institutional vehicle to protest against racism, poverty, and lack of recognition. This is why Afro-American Islam is associated with and sometimes reduced to an Islam of prisoners and prisons. It was in prisons that Afro-Americans gradually converted to Islam starting in the 1920s and then massively starting in the 1950s—just as they would also sympathize with Che Guevara or Marxism. The centrality of the figure of Malcolm X in the historiography of Afro-American Islam not only expresses a widely shared admiration for his role in the civil rights movement. It also reinforces the rarely questioned assumption that the Islam of black Muslims has more to do with politics than with faith.[28] Perceived as a religion of the disadvantaged or disenfranchised, Afro-American Islam comes sometimes to seem like a second-class religion, and the sincerity and authenticity of the faith of Afro-American Muslims seems often to be doubted.[29]

The same paradoxical process of rendering Islam invisible as a religion can be observed among the immigrant Muslim populations originating from Southeast Asia and the Middle East that began to settle in the United States starting around 1900. In order to integrate into society, they insisted first on their national and ethnic origins rather than on their religious affiliation. It is not until the end of the 1980s that a discourse develops to deliberately affirm and promote an American Islam that would transcend differences of national and ethnic origin. Initially, many immigrants underwent or freely engaged in a process of de-Islamification analogous to what was experienced by Muslim African slaves. To avoid discrimination, many of those who arrived at the beginning of the twentieth century even took Christian names and remained very discreet about their faith.[30] Immigrants from India and Syria fought to be recognized as belonging to the racial category "white" so as to gain easier access to American citizenship that foreigners of color were denied. Through the 1960s, immigrant Muslims mostly accepted the dominant paradigms that defined American identity as white and Protestant. Rather than putting them in question, they tried to blend in and remain quiet about their religious and ethnic characteristics:

> Immigrants from regions with significant Muslim populations did not question the axiological assumption that participation in American modernity and progress was related to America's national character as a white, Christian nation. . . . In other words, they did not challenge the racism and bigotry involved in the conflation of whiteness, Protestantism, and progress; rather, they argued for their inclusion within this matrix. They not only argued that they were "white," but they also believed it.[31]

In the many studies published starting in the 1980s about the religion of these immigrants, a paradoxical form of religion is evoked. The practices of Muslims of Arab or Asian origin are analyzed mostly from the standpoint of questions about relations between ethnic and cultural communities. Filled with good intentions, this multiculturalist approach aims to show that Muslims are capable of integrating into American society. But by presenting Islam as exclusively an ethnic and cultural attribute of certain minorities, it comes to ignore once again the fact that Islam is a religion. Those who take more interest in the precise doctrinal content of Islam develop the idea of the "reciprocal enrichment" of both Islam and America. Muslims would supposedly help or even save an American society in crisis that has lost its way and forgotten its own values. From this point of view, Muslim values not only are compatible with American values but actually represent the quintessential version, while American society is on the verge of falling into decadence. Others put the accent on the fortuitous opportunity that democratic American society represents for Islam because in this context true Muslim values will be able to fully express themselves. Researchers sympathetic to the school of John Esposito and the Center for Muslim-Christian Understanding at Georgetown University insist therefore on the correspondence and dialogue between Muslim and Christian values. Although provocative and counterintuitive, this approach remains faithful to the teleological narrative of Muslim integration and the American idea of progress.

Whether as an instrument of evangelization, resistance, or integration; as the language of mistreated minorities; or as a potential source for a regeneration of American values, Islam throughout American history has appeared as a paradoxical form of religion. Although derided as inferior, heterodox, or dangerous, it has also been recognized—and feared—for its power to influence within political, social, and cultural spheres. Perceived as both an ultrareligion (a religion of absolute transcendence that incarnates a type of radical alterity) and an antireligion (a fake religion of false prophets and political militants), Islam scares and divides people, but it also creates bonds and contributes in a decisive way to a redefinition of racial, ethnic, and cultural boundaries.

ISLAM: FROM GEORGE W. BUSH TO BARACK OBAMA

The election of Barack Obama as president marks a major turning point in the national debate over Islam. Between 2001 and 2008, within the context of the wars in Afghanistan and Iraq, the public debate was mostly centered on the fight against radical Islam. The theme of "Islam as a religion of peace" that was important in the discourse of the Bush administration was no longer convincing after Barack Obama's arrival in the White House in 2009. Despite the many real cases of discrimination against Muslims who have come in for criticism since the attacks of September 11, 2001, the public had been adhering mostly to the idea of the good American Muslim, distinct from Middle Eastern extremists and especially from the stigmatized proletariat Muslims of European suburbs (*banlieues*). Starting in 2008, the criticism of Islam becomes more virulent, more systematic, and often includes open hostility toward President Obama. The number of media stories concerning Islam in the United States increased during this period even though the official discourse on Islam of the Obama administration was not radically different from that of President Bush.

In the years following the attacks on the World Trade Center, those in government, think-tank experts, and the foreign policy establishment all share roughly the same idea that it's necessary to promote "moderate Islam" in Muslim countries in order to neutralize the advance of "radical Islam." The experience of the Cold War serves as a point of reference: the strategic aid given to anti-Communists within Europe's civil society, especially in Eastern Europe, is cited as the example to follow.[32] With radical Islam posited as the equivalent of Communism, moderate Islam must play the role of the non-Communist Left. Numerous experts offer up criteria to differentiate moderates from extremists. The authors of a report published in 2004 by the Rand Corporation establish a correlation between the theological conceptions of Muslims and their attitude vis-à-vis American politics.[33] To distinguish "true" moderate Muslims from duplicitous ones, it is important, says the Rand report, to take into account both the political preferences that Muslim leaders express in public and their conceptions of the Quran. The only "true" moderates are those who have a nonliteral view of this sacred text. Thus the Rand experts are entirely closed to the idea of distinguishing between an "intransigent" believer's attitude toward sacred texts and a "fundamentalist" attitude toward the society and the world. For them, intransigence implies or is a necessary concomitant of fundamentalism.[34]

With the arrival of President Obama in the White House in January 2009, the containment strategy with regard to radical Islam gradually yielded to a new tactic—engagement with the Muslim world.[35] This idea rests on a particular conception of the Muslim world as one with a distinct political culture largely influenced by religion. Insofar as the political behavior of Muslims can be explained as reflecting or following from religious values, the American strategy should aim to restore Islam's "true" values. The theory of engagement takes up a culturalist and idealist presupposition but translates it positively: because certain religious and cultural values may alter behaviors, the proper thing is to try to shape those values so as to foster social and political attitudes that are deemed desirable. In his June 4, 2009, speech in Cairo, President Obama expressed his wish to break with his predecessor's paradigm of containing radical Islam:

"This cycle of suspicion and discord must end. I've come here to Cairo to seek a new beginning between the United States and Muslims around the world, one based on mutual interest and mutual respect."[36]

Obama insisted that Americans and Muslims belong to a common humanity defined by the same hopes and the same fears. The unilateralism and the imperial ambition to transform the Muslim world in a few months that were characteristics of the Bush administration's "Greater Middle East Initiative" were rejected as unrealistic. Islam was now considered as a resource to be used to improve relations between the United States and the Muslim world, and was no longer considered simply as a threat. In the June 4, 2009, speech, Obama defined Islam as the comprehensive category that ought to be actively kept in mind for fashioning solutions to a variety of conflicts in the Middle East and Central Asia. The president underscored with several quotations from the Quran that the "true" Islam promotes tolerance and freedom, and he criticized a minority of extremists for having betrayed the true values of Islam. Finally, he underlined the similarity of values and interests between the Muslim world and the United States: "America and Islam are not exclusive and need not be in competition. Instead, they overlap, and share common principles—principles of justice and progress; tolerance and the dignity of all human beings."

The rhetoric of the Obama administration is positive, friendly, and pragmatic in contrast to the public discourse of his predecessor, which appeared more offensive and idealistic. However, the goals are the same: defend the nation's domestic security and its exceptional role in the world. Obama's declaration represents more a courteous translation of the realist's paradigm—the containment of radical Islam—than a true political and theoretical alternative.

There is no doubt a wish to break with an earlier period by establishing calmer relations with Muslims thanks to several indirect initiatives to build an official, moderate American Islam. But one can observe today, as under President Bush, a certain blurring of borders between domestic policy and foreign policy, between civil liberties and national security, and between governance and theology. A discourse that favors combating the radicalization of American Muslims has developed—a discourse that takes inspiration from theories used within foreign policy projects in Iraq, Afghanistan, Yemen, and Saudi Arabia as well as in Europe.[37]

General Douglas Stone began a program of "religious enlightenment" in Iraqi prisons that includes organizing meetings between moderate imams and radicalized prisoners in order to point the way to another conception of their religion. To further these efforts, American officials created a sort of comparative glossary that presents radical and moderate verses from the Quran "in order to refute detainees when they use certain passages to support a radical interpretation of Islam."[38] In 2010, the independent, nonpartisan, federally funded United States Institute of Peace published a report, *Countering Radicalization in America: Lessons from Europe*, that claims the United States "must be prepared to intervene in ideological and theological matters."[39] The program Prevent, implemented in the United Kingdom in 2007 to counter "domestic" radicalization, was an important source of inspiration for the United States. The British program aims both to correct deviant behavior thanks to a variety of educational and socializing initiatives and to disseminate among "at-risk" populations the necessary arguments and analyses in favor of moderate Islam. The American attempts to imitate the model of Britain's Prevent project are initiated at precisely the moment when modifications to the program are being considered in response to widespread criticism and doubts about its actual effectiveness. Muslims are not a passive target in such projects to establish a moderate Islam. Certain religious leaders, such as the imam Mohamed Magid, the executive director of the All Dulles Area Muslim Society, have become quasi-official representatives of American Islam.[40] The recent history of leading Muslim organizations also confirms these attempts to construct an American Islam. Since the end of the 1980s, these organizations, unlike those started in the 1960s, are not satisfied with simply providing a Muslim-friendly space and theological teaching to its members.[41] Their purpose is no longer simply to provide immigrant Muslims with services related to daily religious practice but to defend their civil rights and encourage them to participate in local and national political debates. This is the explicit mission of two current organizations that are the most engaged in controversies relating to Islam: the Muslim Public Affairs Council (MPAC) and the Council on American-Islamic Relations (CAIR).[42]

Even if these initiatives are motivated by good intentions and aim to improve relations between governing bodies and Muslims, they represent a rather curious form of governance where theology is blended with national security concerns.[43] Expert in national security law Samuel Rascoff argues that "counter-radicalization, puts the government in the position, vis-à-vis Islam, of serving as a kind of official theologian, taking positions on the meaning of inevitably contested religious concepts and weighing in on one side of debates that rage within a particular faith tradition."[44]

THE LEGAL DEFINITIONS OF RELIGION AND RELIGIOUS FREEDOM

If Islam has appeared throughout American history as a paradoxical sort of religion, how do Americans define a "true" religion? Independent of the prejudices and feelings of the nation's different religious communities, what are the criteria that legally distinguish a true religion from a nonreligion? Lawmakers, judges, and other civic leaders have tried to answer this question since the nineteenth century in order to deal with the claims of numerous religious minorities. Mormons, Catholics, Seventh-Day Adventists, Jehovah's Witnesses, Amerindians, and Jews have regularly called into question, through the courts, a certain normative definition inspired by Protestantism of the true religion in order to have their rights recognized. The questions that revolve around Islam are not fundamentally different from those asked about all these other religions. Since the nineteenth century, American courts have had to resolve conflicts about religious freedom and determine the meaning of the two clauses of the Constitution's First Amendment—the establishment clause and the clause of free exercise—as well as the relationship between these clauses: "Congress shall make no law respecting an establishment of religion, or prohibiting the free exercise thereof."[45] Because the Constitution does not define what a religion is, it has been necessary to develop over time criteria that allow a line to be drawn about what constitutes acceptable religious behavior, while refraining to give a positive definition of religion. To properly understand today's debates about Islam, one must keep this long tradition of legal discussions about the First Amendment in mind.

In 1878, the Supreme Court specified for the first time the meaning of the "free exercise" clause in the case of *Reynolds v. United States*. George Reynolds, a member of the Church of Jesus Christ of Latter-day Saints— that is, the Mormons—was convicted of bigamy in violation of the Morrill

Anti-Bigamy Act (1862), which declared the practice of having multiple spouses illegal. Reynolds attempted to argue in his defense that the law violates the free exercise clause of the Constitution and that "plural marriage" was for him a religious obligation. The Supreme Court justices rejected his argument and ruled that Reynolds's religious liberty was not infringed by the Morrill Act. In effect, the Court's decision established a distinction between religious beliefs and the actions that follow from them. If the free exercise clause protects beliefs, it does not authorize all actions committed in their name. Since the Constitution provides no definition of religion, the justices are left to inquire into what the Founding Fathers may have meant by the term. They refer notably to the Virginia Statue for Religious Freedom and in particular to a letter from 1802 written by Thomas Jefferson to the leaders of the Danbury Baptists. In this letter, Jefferson makes a clear distinction between actions and religious opinions:

> Believing with you that religion is a matter which lies solely between Man & his God, that he owes account to none other for his faith or his worship, that the legitimate powers of government reach actions only, & not opinions, I contemplate with sovereign reverence that act of the whole American people which declared that their legislature should "make no law respecting an establishment of religion, or prohibiting the free exercise thereof," thus building a wall of separation between Church & State.[46]

The *Reynolds* decision strengthens the idea that what the free exercise clause must protect is freedom of belief and of conscience and not the total sum of religious practices. Chief Justice Morrison Waite asserts that "[the Danbury letter] may be accepted almost as an authoritative declaration of the scope and effect of the amendment thus secured. Congress was deprived of all legislative power over mere opinion, but was left free to reach actions which were in violation of social duties or subversive of good order."[47]

Winnifred Sullivan, an authority on religion in American courts, notes that the Reynolds affair is also significant because it is one of the first cases where the Supreme Court justices make use of an expert's testimony to help them define what a religion is. Justice Waite cites the views of the jurist and political philosopher Francis Lieber, who associated polygamy with a savage mode of life proper to "Asian" and "African" peoples:

"Polygamy has always been odious among the northern and Western nations of Europe, and, until the establishment of the Mormon Church, was almost exclusively a feature of the life of Asiatic and of African people." The judge refers to Lieber's testimony to argue that polygamy is contrary to public order: "Professor Lieber says, polygamy leads to the patriarchal principle, and which, when applied to large communities, fetters the people in stationary despotism."[48]

The restrictive approach adopted in the *Reynolds* case has since been put into question on several occasions. In *Sherbert v. Verner* (1963), the Supreme Court chose a more flexible interpretation of the free exercise clause. Adele Sherbert, an employee in a textile mill in South Carolina and a member of the Seventh-day Adventists, was fired after she refused to work on a Saturday, a day on which, according to her religion, it was forbidden to work. She sued her employer, who was refusing to grant her unemployment compensation. This time, Justice William Brennan rendered a decision in Sherbert's favor, affirming that to deprive the employee of unemployment benefits because she had respected a religious precept was in violation of the free exercise clause: "[T]o condition the availability of benefits upon this appellant's willingness to violate a cardinal principle of her religious faith effectively penalizes the free exercise of her constitutional liberties."[49] The Supreme Court makes use of this case to define the criteria of a superior interest of the state (a "compelling state interest"), which asserts that, before adopting a measure that limits the free exercise of an individual, the government must be able to prove that the protection of a compelling state interest (such as the safety of a given population) is at issue.

Nevertheless, in 1990, with the case of *Employment Division v. Smith*, there is a return to the more restrictive approach that prevailed in the *Reynolds* case. This case opposes two members of the Native American Church (NAC) to the human resources department of the employment board of the state of Oregon. Alfred Smith and Galen Beck, who were employed as psychologists at a drug-rehabilitation center, were fired for having consumed peyote at work. The state of Oregon refused to grant them unemployment benefits on the grounds that they had been fired for misconduct. An appeals court reversed the first decision by accepting the argument of the two members of the NAC for whom the consumption of peyote was said to be a religious obligation, and therefore the denial of benefits was a violation of their religious freedom. The Supreme Court rejected this argument and asserted that the free exercise clause could not be invoked to justify infractions of generally applied neutral laws such as the prohibition of certain drugs by the state of Oregon. The law in question applied to everyone and did not specifically target members of the NAC. Judge Antonin Scalia referred to the reasoning applied by the Supreme Court in the *Reynolds* case and underlined that even though the First Amendment prevents the government from regulating beliefs by law, it is under no obligation to protect any and all practices. Accepting the reasoning of the two employees would have had dangerous consequences, says the Court:

> The rule respondents favor would open the prospect of constitutionally required religious exemptions from civic obligations of almost every conceivable kind—ranging from compulsory military service . . . , to the payment of taxes . . . , to health and safety regulation such as manslaughter and child neglect laws . . . , compulsory vaccination laws . . . , drug laws . . . , and traffic laws . . . , to social welfare legislation such as minimum wage laws . . . , child labor laws . . . , animal cruelty laws . . . , environmental protection laws . . . , and laws providing for equality of opportunity for the races. . . . The First Amendment's protection of religious liberty does not require this.[50]

The goal here is not to retrace the complete trail of jurisprudence on the First Amendment but to underline with this brief review of some of the most important cases the long-standing and complex history of the debates about religious freedom that date from long before the question of Islam occurs. The general question of what exactly is to be protected by the First Amendment—beliefs or practices—has been argued over since the nineteenth century.

Another matter that has been debated for a long time in American courts is what criteria are to be used to define practices and symbols as religious or cultural. In *Lynch v. Donnelly* (1984), the Supreme Court had to rule on whether the presentation of a Nativity scene in a public space represented a form of indirect establishment of a religion or if it was simply an acceptable cultural practice. A group of residents in Pawtucket, Rhode Island, lodged a complaint against the city, claiming that exhibiting the usual scene of Christ's birth in the business district of the city constituted an official establishment of the Christian religion. A district court and a court of appeals ruled in favor of the plaintiffs, but the Supreme Court overturned the decision. In a 5 to 4 vote, the Court ruled that the presence of the Nativity did not aim to promote a particular religious message but had "legitimate secular purposes."[51] Justice Warren Burger, author of the opinion of the Court, underscored that the symbol of the Nativity had been part of Western culture for a long time. It was simply a part of the celebration of a public holiday, not of a religion. It was said to have a symbolic value comparable to references to God in American courts or to the words "In God We Trust" printed on American currency: "Those government acknowledgments of religion serve, in the only ways reasonably possible in our culture, the legitimate secular purposes of solemnizing public occasions, expressing confidence in the future, and encouraging the recognition of what is worthy of appreciation in society. For that reason, and because of their history and ubiquity, those practices are not understood as conveying government approval of particular religious beliefs."[52] It is worth noting that the most ardent opposition to this decision came from a Catholic judge, William Brennan, who refused to see the Nativity reduced to a religious symbol: "The crèche retains a specifically Christian religious meaning. . . . The nativity scene is clearly distinct in its purpose and effect from the rest of the Hodgson Park display for the simple reason that it is the only one rooted in a biblical account of Christ's birth."[53] The Catholic judge, by his attachment to a religious interpretation of the Nativity's symbolism, proves to be the one most in favor of a strict separation of religious space and public space.

To help determine which characteristics are pertinent for defining a religion, there has often been recourse to the opinions of experts, including theologians, sociologists, and historians of religion. But this use of expert testimony raises numerous questions. This can be seen from the experience of Winnifred Fallers Sullivan, a religion scholar who has been asked to testify many times in court. Of particular note was her participation in the case of *Warner v. Boca Raton*, which concerned a family whose relatives were buried in the municipal cemetery of Boca Raton, Florida. Despite a city ordinance that authorized cemetery decorations up to a certain size, certain families had placed objects of a larger size on graves. When the city council suddenly decided to have these decorations removed, the families filed a suit on the grounds that the removal was a violation of their right to free exercise. The question debated by the court was whether the decorations placed on the graves corresponded to a true religious practice that merited protection. Five experts, three for the plaintiffs and two for the city of Boca Raton, where invited to state their views. In the opinion of the two experts for the defense, the funerary decorations did not constitute an essential part of the religious practice of the plaintiffs but was merely a folkloric custom. Sullivan asked whether it is even possible to arrive at a legally neutral definition of religious freedom and about the usefulness of turning to this type of expert testimony. What is the value of these testimonies? In what way do they allow one to arrive at a fairer decision? How can one think that consulting religion specialists can help arrive at a consensus when one knows how divided the academic field of religious studies is? "If each American is entirely free to make her own decision about her religious standpoint and activity, in what sense can religious expertise be legally 'scientific,' or even 'assist' the trier of fact [judge or jury]?"[54]

Given the complexity of the question (How shall religion be defined, and who shall do the defining?), Sullivan was led to the hypothesis that religious liberty is quite simply impossible. She was not claiming that freedom of conscience and practice should not be protected but that it is impossible to satisfactorily solve the dilemma that, for the judge, consists in trying to protect religious freedom without relying on some standard of what's religious. Any judgment will inevitably be based on some theological or philosophical conceptions or on cultural presuppositions of a judge or experts. A neutral legal definition is impossible—it is always influenced by dominant conceptions within a given society about what constitutes a "true" religion. Religious minorities will thus have more trouble convincing others to consider different conceptions of the category "religion" as normal and acceptable. This imbalance is not necessarily the result of conscious intentions of some cultural majority to dominate minorities. It is more the result of the inherent ambiguity of the First Amendment. If today Muslims are particularly targeted, similar questions have been asked about all religions. In the Boca Raton case, it was Jewish and Catholic families that brought the suit. The judge and experts for the defense asserted that the cemetery decorations were simply a nonessential form of folklore. Most American religious communities have, to varying degrees, been forced to resist this attempt to construct a hierarchy between what a judge considers to be of essence to a religion and what he or she dismisses as simply a popular custom. Thus when constrained to judge between a religion's essence and its incidental features, the judge is obliged, despite everything, to tread into the territory of theology. Therefore, when Sullivan speaks of the impossibility of religious freedom, she means the impossibility of a perfectly neutral, fair, secular treatment of individuals. For her, the challenge of interpreting the First Amendment is made all the more difficult by the fact that American culture is both separationist and evangelical.

Even though American society is often described as more religious than European societies, it is also more attached to the principle of the separation of church and state and is much less tolerant of state interference in religious affairs. Trials against the government financing of school textbooks used in religious schools and of teacher salaries in these private schools or against the public display of religious symbols are regular occurrences. At the same time, American culture is profoundly evangelical, thanks to the dominant belief that considers the true place of religion to be in one's individual, sincere, and authentic faith, and not in an orthodoxy imposed by clergymen. This is the view expressed by Judge Kenneth Ryskamp in the Boca Raton case. When he asserts that all religious beliefs are true, he implies that the truth of the religion is seated in the belief. What counts is what one believes, not the height of the crosses that one places on the graves. While recognizing the validity of each person's point of view, the judge nevertheless concludes that the practices that the plaintiffs want to see protected derive from a type of superstition that does not deserve to be protected. This evangelical approach, while seemingly egalitarian and desirous of emancipating individuals from the tutelage of clerics and their dogmas, ends up producing its own form of orthodoxy that views certain religions as truer than others.

For all these reasons, Sullivan questions the usefulness of the specifically legal concept of *religious* freedom. She proposes that it simply be thought of within the category of individual freedoms: "What is arguably impossible is justly enforcing laws granting persons rights that are defined with respect to their religious beliefs or practices. Forsaking religious freedom as a legally enforced right might enable greater equality among persons and greater clarity and self-determination for religious individuals and communities. Such a change would end discrimination against those who do not self-identify as religious or whose religion is disfavored."[55] This brief look at legal debates about religious freedom proves that today's controversies about Islam cannot simply be understood as expressions of hostility toward Muslims since September 11. They are, rather, part of a long and complex history of questions and debates over the First Amendment.

BEYOND A CRITIQUE OF ISLAMOPHOBIA

To explain the increase in the number of controversies, leaders of Muslim organizations along with their liberal allies turn mostly to the paradigm of Islamophobia. After first appearing in the 1980s, this paradigm became even more popular after 2001. CAIR and MPAC, for example, publish every year a series of notices and reports denouncing the many aspects of this phenomenon. In its 2009/2010 report, CAIR condemns Islamophobic declarations and actions while at the same time recognizing that all religious minorities have been the object of exclusionary reactions.[56] The study's title, *Same Hate, New Target*, captures the main idea—that "virtually every minority in our nation has faced and in most cases continues to face discrimination."[57] CAIR defines Islamophobia as "close-minded prejudice or hatred of Islam and Muslims. An Islamophobe is an individual who holds a close-minded view of Islam and promotes prejudice against or hatred of Muslims."[58] The report does specify, however, that not all criticism of Islam can be characterized as Islamophobic: "It is not appropriate to label all, or even the majority of those, who question Islam and Muslims as Islamophobic."[59]

In May 2011, an exhaustive report was published for the first time by a non-Muslim organization, the center-left think tank Center for American Progress. The report, *Fear, Inc.*, defines Islamophobia as "an exaggerated fear, hatred, and hostility toward Islam and Muslims that is perpetuated by negative stereotypes resulting in bias, discrimination, and the marginalization and exclusion of Muslims from America's social, political, and civic life."[60] This phenomenon is said to be the work of a small number of organizations, foundations, intellectuals, and media outlets linked together by common financial interests and possessing considerable power to harm. This network constitutes what the report's two main authors call the "Islamophobia Megaphone." It is made up of three types of actors: rich foundations that fund different projects, such as the Richard Mellon Scaife Foundation, the Russell Berrie Foundation, and the William Rosenwald Family Fund; "misinformation experts"; and the "Islamophobia echo chamber." Among the experts cited are Frank Gaffney and his think tank, the Center for Security Policy; Robert Spencer and his website, Jihad Watch; and Steven Emerson and his Investigative Project on Terrorism. The echo chamber of Islamophobic misinformation is constituted by certain media outlets, the Christian Right, some politicians and grassroots organizations such as the American Congress for Truth (ACT! for America), the Tea Party, and the group Stop Islamization of America.

In a report published in June 2012, the Southern Poverty Law Center (SPLC), an organization dedicated to defending civil rights and combating racist white supremacist groups, also denounced the proliferation of Islamophobic declarations and deeds. This phenomenon is thought to be not simply the product of activism by rich right-wing foundations but a symptom of a changed attitude of the American Right: "The last decade has seen major changes in the American radical Right. What was once a world largely dominated by a few relatively well-organized groups has become a scene populated by large numbers of smaller, weaker groups, with only a handful led by the kind of charismatic chieftains that characterized the 1990s."[61] According to the SPLC, this evolution is in part attributable to the context of economic crisis and the growing malaise among a portion of the white population that is fearful about the erosion of its majority status. The U.S. Census Bureau predicts that by 2050, the category "non-Hispanic white" will constitute less than half of the country's population. The proliferation of anti-Muslim behavior coincides with a radicalization of right-wing, antigay religious groups as well as an unprecedented multiplication of "patriot" groups whose first target is the federal government. The SPLC claims that in 2008, only 149 such groups existed, but the number has reached 1,274 today. Among the new leaders of this radical Right—less charismatic than those of the 1990s but more numerous and extreme in their views—one finds leading figures of anti-Muslim movements such as Frank Gaffney, Brigitte Gabriel, and David Yerushalmi. Another "megaphone" person listed is Joseph Farah, the executive editor of WorldNetDaily, a news website of the radical Right.

Farah, a specialist on conspiracy theories and a leader in the "nativist" movement, has been determined to show since 2008 that Barack Obama is not American and that Muslims are preparing to take over America. John Weaver, a pastor in Georgia's Freedom Baptist Ministries and a member of the racist neo-Confederate movement, was a long-time member of the Council of Conservative Citizens, an extremist group known for inciting racial hatred throughout the southern United States. Weaver has described African Americans as an inferior race and openly declares his opposition to interracial marriage. There is also Alex Jones, the radio host of the *Alex Jones Show*, who explains to his listeners five times a week that rich corporations aided by the United States are plotting to dominate the world; that the federal government was behind the 1995 Oklahoma City bombing of the Alfred P. Murrah federal building and the September 11 attacks on New York City and Washington, D.C.; and that the Federal Emergency Management Agency, the government organization charged with responding to natural disasters and terrorist attacks, is in the process of building concentration camps.

Even though use of the term "Islamophobia" has spread in recent years among liberals and Muslims, it is heavily criticized by their adversaries. The British American journalist Christopher Hitchens rejected the term, calling it a "stupid neologism . . . which aims to promote criticism of Islam to the gallery of special offenses associated with racism."[62] Similarly, David Prager, a conservative columnist and radio host, has often protested against this term, whose sole aim, he believes, is to intimidate Americans and prevent them from articulating the slightest criticism of Islam. The defenders and opponents of the term regularly face off in the American media. Prager, Hitchens, and Ibrahim Hooper, the spokesman for CAIR, held a debate on November 13, 2010, on CNN that took up the following question: What is the proper name to describe the actions of a student of Ukrainian origin who several times threw the Quran in the toilets of his university? For Hitchens and Prager, this was simply a case of the exercise of free speech; for Hooper, the student's action was an expression of hatred aimed to intimidate Muslim students and destroy their self-esteem.

Whatever one thinks of the term "Islamophobia," the number of public controversies over Islam has clearly grown since 2008. It was especially in 2010—coincidently, the year of the electoral success of various Tea Party groups and individuals—that local movements in opposition to the construction of mosques were the strongest. In 2010, the Department of Justice published a report assessing the ten years that had passed since the implementation of the Religious Land Use and Institutionalized Persons Act, a law protecting the freedom to build religious edifices as well as the rights of prisoners.[63] The report notes that since 2000, 7 percent of the investigations into the application of this law concern violations of the rights of Muslims. The latter, however, represent only 0.6 percent of the population (3 percent of the cases concerned the rights of Buddhists, who represent 0.5 percent of the population; and Jewish rights violations concerned 6 percent, and they are 1.7 percent of the population). Following the controversy surrounding the construction of an Islamic community center in Manhattan, a number of disputes of the same kind broke out in a kind of domino effect across several states including Tennessee, Florida, and North Carolina, where Muslims make up less than 1 percent of the population. Starting in the summer of 2010, a group of lawyers, right-wing think-tank experts, and foundations launched a legal battle to gain passage of a law that would prohibit reference to Islamic law in American courts. In March 2011, Representative Peter T. King (R-N.Y.), already active in the Manhattan controversy, organized in Congress a day of public hearings specifically about the radicalization of Muslim communities and the alleged lack of cooperation by Muslims to oppose it. In the spring of 2012, the revelation by two journalists that a very anti-Islam film was being used as part of a training program by the New York Police Department also provoked a storm of controversy. In all these cases, one finds nearly the same individuals and organizations turning up. It strongly suggests that there is indeed a coherent network of actors and institutions that have similar material interests, the same vision of the world, and considerable power of nuisance.

But the history of American Islam is not only about this fight between networks of Islamophobes and Muslims. One reason is that many youth activists, grassroots organizations, interfaith coalitions, professors, public intellectuals, experts, think tanks, and media liberals are firmly opposed to such campaigns. Besides the groups Center for American Progress and SPLC, media celebrities such as Jon Stewart, Keith Olbermann, Stephen Colbert, and Rachel Maddow have regularly used their shows to ridicule the arguments of Gaffney and Gabriel and their followers. Media Matters for America, a watchdog group founded by the journalist David Brock, and the blog *Loonwatch* also regularly expose the factual mistakes that underlie the alarmist analyses of the opposing camp. Finally, important political figures also oppose Islamophobic attacks. They include the Muslim representative Keith Ellison but also Republicans such as Senator John McCain and the former mayor of New York Michael Bloomberg.

Moreover, if Islamophobia is effective in stirring up militant action, it does not adequately explain why the anti-Muslim actions and declarations are on the rise, or the effects that these actions have on the individuals concerned. Analyses based on Islamophobia explain the present conflicts in essentially two points: the imperial project of the United States and a feeling of fear. In one study from 2011, Islamophobia is defined as an American ideology that developed after the Cold War by means of which the United States seeks to keep its domestic populations tame while projecting its force abroad. The Islamophobic ideology would thus reflect the imbalance of international forces and America's hegemony over the Muslim world. In this view, a multitude of individuals from neoconservatives to hawkish Democrats to Christian evangelicals and even certain cooperative Muslims constitute "a systematic structure" that is almost impossible to break.[64] Another study from 2012 also defines Islamophobia as the ideology of an imperial project. But here the genealogy of the phenomenon dates from long before the Cold War: from the time of the Crusades to the Obama administration, the same Islamophobic "spirit" is said to have traversed the West and permitted Western powers to defend their interests both abroad and at home.[65]

For others, Islamophobia is not a symptom of a politics of power but of a general sentiment of the West's decline, of a sort of inward turn and fear of the other. Thus, for example, the philosopher Martha Nussbaum explains the controversies in Europe over burkas and minarets as well as the Manhattan mosque affair as resulting from the spread of fear of the other and an unsettled identity.[66] Nussbaum repeats a well-established presupposition in Western research on Islam, particularly in American university discourse, while also affirming that America remains more tolerant than Europe, which is considered to be attached to a Romantic ideal of the nation that combines religious tradition and culture.

These analyses that explain relations between America and Islam via claims about imperialism or fear nevertheless contain several problems. First, they start out with such a broad level of generality that they have difficulty explaining the specific quality and the complexity of relations between Muslims and non-Muslims. They therefore produce an essentialist and static image of the ongoing confrontations and make Muslims look like a passive community of victims devoid of any capacity to act and resist. Second, these explanations attribute an excessive coherence to the networks of anti-Muslim individuals and groups and in a way end up reproducing the conspiratorial approach that they intend to combat. The radical, populist Right may favor conspiracy theories, but one finds the liberal Left also indulging in conspiracy approaches even if their facts are better documented and their arguments more subtle. In a special issue devoted to Islamophobia by the leftist magazine the *Nation*, one learns of the key role played by Nina Rosenwald, the founder of the Gatestone Institute think tank, in the financing of several Islamophobic projects (including those of David Horowitz and the aforementioned Frank Gaffney and Brigitte Gabriel). One also learns of Rosenwald's links to the Israel lobby: after having served as a leader of the pro-Israel lobby American Israel Public Affairs Committee, she remains active in several other pro-Israeli organizations. Rosenwald has ties to Norman Podhoretz, the neoconservative activist and former editor of *Commentary*, and she is also affiliated with the Hudson Institute, a conservative think tank highly critical of Islam. The information contained in the *Nation* and in the report of the Center for American Progress is accurate, but what should one make of this enumeration of facts? There surely exists in the United States a small network of people and institutions with large amounts of money, common interests, and a shared hostility toward Islam and Muslims. They may be influential, but they are certainly not all-powerful. If, as we shall see in chapter 3, figures like Gaffney, Horowitz, Yerushalmi, and Gabriel are gifted with a harmful talent as megaphone mouths, they nevertheless remain more or less marginal, including within the conservative movement and the Republican Party. Large opposing forces exist in the media, in expert circles, in daily local political efforts, and especially in the law. Even if the Islamophobic network has a certain political and media influence and manages through outcries and well-financed campaigns to push the conservative and Republican agenda to the right, American law remains the surest guarantee of the rights of minorities, and notably Muslims. The shouting from Islamophobes has gotten loud, but their media impact stands in inverse relation to their legal victories, which have been rare.

Finally, it must be said that theories of empire or fear (from Nussbaum and others) express a form of consensual indignation that may irritate, amuse, or insult the members of Islamophobic groups but have very little chance of changing minds. Curiously, the indignation derives from a posture identical to that of many Islamophobic experts and activists. The ones who cry out, denounce, and demystify posit themselves as morally superior and intellectually more insightful than their adversaries. The whole thing ends up going in circles, with each being outraged at the weakness or blindness of the other. Not only is this type of discourse unhelpful for understanding how Islam is constructed and understood in the United States, but the likelihood that it could eventually improve relations between Muslims and non-Muslims seems low. To overcome the politics of fear and the intolerance that are developing in the West, Nussbaum asserts that it is urgent to return to an ethical philosophy based on Socrates. Specifically, she recommends three remedies: reaffirm political principles of equal respect for all citizens; revive a rigorous critical faculty capable of exposing incoherencies and egotisms; and develop a capacity for generous imagination that allows one to see the world as it is seen by someone of another religion.[67] One can at least wonder how effective such a pedagogical program would be at convincing a majority.

The action of anti-Muslim groups has a double effect. If they are truly successful at intimidating, discriminating against, and excluding Muslims from certain facets of political and social life, they have also inadvertently contributed to popularizing a positive image of Muslims. The interpretation of contemporary debates that uses only the magnifying glass offered by the Islamophobic model obscures an important dimension of the public representation of Muslims—what Olivier Roy has called "Islamonarcissism" also known as New Muslim Cool. This attitude, which consists of turning the stigma into a badge of honor that makes one proud to be Muslim, has become common among ethnic and cultural minorities in the United States. The suggestion is that the simple fact of being Muslim is the sign of some form of natural radicalness, a positive difference, or even an innate capacity to be more just, intelligent, and closer to the truth or to humanity. To be Muslim in post–September 11 America is not simply to be a victim of discrimination or the object of ridicule and caricature. Today it is a way to project oneself as radical, critically aware, young, other—in short, a new way of being "cool." These two tendencies,

Islamophobia and Islamo-narcissism, are the effect of the questioning and transformations that were caused by the September 11 attacks. But they also descend from an older discursive tradition—the obligation for minorities to prove their loyalty and their capacity to integrate. As part of one's odyssey within this exceptional democracy, contestation is an essential way of proving one's loyalty—on condition, of course, that it threatens neither national security nor public order, and contributes, on the contrary, to the nation's prosperity and progress. A number of Muslim intellectuals, artists, and activists are working to show themselves playing a decisive role in awakening or saving an America that has forgotten its core values and become prey to excess individualism, avarice, and hubris. The documentary film *New Muslim Cool* was a big hit among Muslims and liberals.[68] The film tells the story of the life of a rap artist of Puerto Rican origin, Hamza Pérez, a former drug dealer and former Catholic who now fights to improve conditions in his community through the medium of Muslim rap and hip-hop and works as a volunteer chaplain in a prison. Of course, this redemption story about a former "bad guy" corresponds to the standard script of many blockbuster American movies. Along the same lines is the reality show launched in November 2011 by Discovery/TLC, *All-American Muslims*, which pursues a similar normalization of the figure of the American Muslim. The show follows the daily lives of five Muslim families in Dearborn, Michigan, and films Muslims portrayed in roles that are typically American, such as the Little League baseball coach, the patriotic policeman, or the father who declares his family to be what's most important to him.[69] In its own way, the show contributes to constructing a different image of Muslim Americans. After Italian Americans (Jersey Shore) and Asians (K-Town), Latinos and Muslims have their own reality shows that offer the same mixture of caricatures, stereotypes, pathos, and narcissism.

2

THE MOSQUE CONTROVERSIES

Moral Offense and Religious Liberty

One-third of America's mosques were constructed in the past fifteen years. Between 2000 and 2010, their number went from 1,209 to 1,925. The diversity of American mosques reflects the heterogeneity of Muslim communities, composed of individuals with widely different ethnic and national origins. The mosques not only have different rituals and conceptions of doctrine but also are of different physical sizes and styles, ranging from garages and apartment rooms to edifices with a minaret. Some also double as community centers with schools, a restaurant, a fitness center, or even a cemetery. Funding sources also vary, from local dues paying to generous Saudi donations. While certain mosques concentrate their efforts on local community needs, others, such as the Al-Farooq mosque in Atlanta, Georgia, opt for a more missionary approach. Some rigorously follow rituals as well as a Salafist type of teaching; others, such as the Al-Farah mosque in New York City directed by Imam Abdul Rauf, are noted for a more ecumenical approach open to the influences of mystical and Sufi currents, while others even allow women to lead certain prayers. A survey of about one hundred mosques distinguishes five categories of faithful: modernist, literalist, mystic, African American, and mixed.[1] These different types certainly do not have fixed identities. Tensions and divergences may exist within a single mosque. Some are growing rapidly while others may be close to shutting down. The audiences in each mosque are constantly changing according to the tastes and life paths of the faithful who live in a country known for its high rate of professional and geographical mobility as well as strong competition on the religious "market."

PROTECTION OF RELIGIOUS FREEDOM

American Muslims benefit from the same legal protections that all other religious communities receive. The right to construct a place of worship and the freedom of assembly for religious purposes are guaranteed by the First Amendment, the Civil Rights Act of 1964, and the Religious Land Use and Institutionalized Persons Act (RLUIPA) of 2000. The Civil Rights Act prohibits all discrimination based on race, color, gender, nationality, or religion. Article 7 of this law requires employers to respect the religious practices of their employees, such as honoring the Sabbath and wearing religious clothing. Similar protections are promulgated in the RLUIPA, which was unanimously approved by Congress on September 22, 2000.[2] Supported by a large coalition of Republican and Democratic legislators, the RLUIPA strengthens the religious freedoms of the incarcerated. It also aims to solve problems posed by urban zoning codes that relate to the construction of houses of worship. At the moment of the law's passage, its two main sponsors, Senators Edward Kennedy (D-Mass.) and Orrin Hatch (R-Utah), explained that "zoning codes frequently exclude churches in places where they permit theaters, meetings halls, and other places where large groups of people assemble for secular purposes."[3] The 2000 law stipulates that "no government can impose or have applied a rule concerning the use of land that imposes a substantial constraint on the religious observance of a person, including a religious assembly or institution, unless the government can prove that the imposition of the constraint on this person, assembly, or institution a) serves to defend a compelling state interest; and b) is the least restrictive means for defending this compelling state interest."[4]

Thanks to the RLUIPA, many religious communities have been able to better defend their right to construct parochial schools, places of worship, and faith-based social services. RLUIPA-related cases that have gone to court concern all religions, but an inventory reveals a large number of cases about Islam. A September 2012 study notes thirty-five unresolved conflicts about the construction of mosques that were tracked carefully by the Department of Justice.[5] Granted, the number is small compared with the total number of projects, most of which carry out the construction of mosques without any problems or resistance. Nevertheless, these relatively few cases are striking for the virulent emotions they've provoked and for the repercussions they've had beyond their local municipal contexts at a national level. The fury of the debates often bears no relation to the size of the Muslim community at issue. City councilors and, more often, neighborhood associations mobilize against projects to build or expand a certain mosque, which may often be referred to as "an Islamic cultural center." Even though opponents of these mosques describe themselves as firm believers in the constitutional principle of religious freedom, they eagerly deploy any number of reasons to prove that the principle cannot apply to Muslims. Often seemingly neutral reservations are put forward: the risk of increased traffic and parking problems, noise, waste management, or other environmental concerns. A businessman opposed to the construction of a sixty-foot minaret on the roof of a mosque in Santa Clara, California, said he had nothing against minarets per se but was worried that such an architectural feature would lower neighborhood property values.

However, these apparently benign arguments quickly give way to more pointed speculation about the place of Islam in America. Mosques are represented as the Trojan horses of radical Islamic groups in American suburbs. Opposing arguments mounted by these neighborhood associations are based on a series of inferences that foster the belief that a simple mosque is somehow going to subvert the Constitution of the United States. In ways similar to the incidents in Europe that have multiplied since the end of the 1980s, the mosque controversies in the United States are an indication of how much the visibility of Islam disturbs and upsets an increasing number of people.

THE CASE OF THE MANHATTAN ISLAMIC CENTER

The Ground Zero controversy erupted in the spring of 2010 over the construction of an Islamic cultural center at 51 Park Place in Lower Manhattan.[6] Abandoned after having been partly damaged by falling debris on

September 11, 2001, the building at this address had for some years been used as a prayer site by the members of the nearby mosque Al-Farah. Built in 1923 and rented over a period of years first to the clothing store Syms and then to the Burlington Coat Factory, the building was sold during the financial crisis in July 2009 for only $4.85 million to the property-investment company Soho Properties. The president of this company is the businessman Sharif El-Gamal, and among the shareholders is the imam Feisal Abdul Rauf, who said he intended to found an organization on this site dedicated to intercultural and interfaith dialogue called the Cordoba Initiative.

FROM A PROJECT OF INTERCULTURAL DIALOGUE TO A SYMBOL OF CONQUEST

The first official reactions to the project were very positive and insisted on the legality of the project and its contribution to improving intercultural relations. "If it's legal, the owners of the building have the right to do what they want with it," declared a spokesman for Michael Bloomberg, New York's mayor at the time, in December 2009. The New York police commissioner, Raymond Kelly, stated he has always had good relations with Imam Rauf and rejected the alarmist predictions that had circulated. Lynn Rasic, spokesperson for the National September 11 Memorial Association, whose board of directors included Daisy Khan, the wife of Feisal Abdul Rauf, applauded "the idea of a cultural center that strengthens relations between Muslims and people of all faiths and horizons." Rabbi Arthur Schneier, the spiritual leader of the Park East Synagogue on the Upper East Side since 1962, also expressed his enthusiasm for the project.

However, starting in April 2010, in a political context marked by intensifying Republican opposition to President Obama's reform projects and with the midterm elections on the horizon in November 2010, the Cordoba Initiative became the special target of polemicists closely associated with the Tea Party. Pamela Geller, the author of the blog *Atlas Shrugs*, and Robert Spencer, the editor of the anti-Islam website Jihad Watch, became two of the leading forces that mobilized against the project at 51 Park Place.[7] Since 2000, Geller's blog has denounced the violence and lack of freedom that she believes are inherent to Islam. An admirer of the Dutch parliamentarian Geert Wilders and of the English Defense League, Geller criticizes liberal Jewish intellectuals such as Noam Chomsky and George Soros for their "self-destructive" attitude and calls on them to join her in encouraging Israel to retake control of Gaza.[8] Robert Spencer, who holds a master's degree in Catholic history from the University of North Carolina at Chapel Hill but is self-taught when it comes to theology and the history of Islam, created the website Jihad Watch in 2003. The site's stated mission is to denounce "the concerted effort of Islamists around the world to destabilize non-Muslim societies." An active member of the Melkite Greek Catholic Church, Spencer has written several books on Islam and has published articles in *FrontPage*, a magazine edited by the neoconservative David Horowitz.[9] Spencer receives the support of polemicists and leading neoconservative political figures such as the historian Daniel Pipes, former CIA director James Woolsey, and Frank Gaffney, the founder of the Project for a New American Century. Coauthors of a book severely critical of the Obama administration, and cofounders of the group Stop Islamization of America, Geller and Spencer warned about the symbolic victory that would result from allowing the construction of a mosque so close to the place where the two World Trade Center towers collapsed.[10] Spencer writes, "The Twin Towers, after all, were the symbol of America's economic power. Placing a mosque by the site of their destruction (at the hands of Islamic jihadists) symbolizes the taming of that power."[11]

On May 25, 2010, despite the intensification of these attacks, the community board of Lower Manhattan voted 29 to 1 (with 10 abstentions) in favor of the Cordoba Initiative.[12] Even though it had only consultative significance, this vote is further proof of the rift that was opening up between the way legal and technical experts were evaluating the project and the way it was being interpreted by a large part of the population. Far from ending the dispute, the community board's decision exacerbated the hostile feelings of the project's opponents. The vote galvanized the opposition of Tea Party activists. Geller and Spencer called on the members of its group to demonstrate on June 6 at the corner of Liberty and Church Streets (near Ground Zero) in protest against the decision. On their signs were such telling slogans as "You can build a mosque at Ground Zero the day we can build a synagogue in Mecca," "Everything I need to know about Islam I learned on September 11," "It's the Jihad, stupid," and "Mayor Bloomberg, your shameful silence disgraces the ashes of 3,000 New Yorkers." Opposition to the Islamic cultural center then became a pretext for promoting a variety of causes, such as the rights of Coptic Egyptians, the rights of Muslims to abandon Islam or to convert, the national security of Israel, and the survival of Christianity in Western society. During the demonstration, the Dutch parliamentarian Geert Wilders made a speech in which he tried to warn the American people about the danger that would come with the Islamization of the country, a scenario that according to him is already weakening Europe. Joseph Nasrallah, an activist of Coptic Egyptian origin, spoke in the name of "all American Copts" to denounce Islam's strategy of dissimulation (*taqiyya*). Sam Khoshbaten, an Iranian American, speaking "in the name of the Iranian community," expressed his condolences to all the victims of the terrorist attacks and sharply criticized the Iranian president at the time, Mahmoud Ahmadinejad. After the June 6 demonstration, former Muslims who had converted to Christianity, groups of Muslims who now self-identify as atheist or unreligious, and members of the group Why We Left Islam were all invited on television shows to express their indignation over Imam Rauf's project. On August 20, 2010, during an interview on Fox News, Mosab Hassan Yousef, who had converted to Christianity in 1999 and claims that he is the son of a member of Hamas and a former spy for the Israeli Shin Bet, described Imam Rauf as "crazy" and "dangerous," and pronounced a warning about the risk of division (*fitna*) of the American people.[13]

Barely a month after the June 6 demonstration, the decision of the Landmarks Preservation Commission again displayed the large gap between the legal and technical experts and the public's perceptions.[14] At the end of a raucous day of speechifying at Hunter College during which speakers vehemently expressed their opposition to the transformation of the building at 51 Park Place, the nine commissioners decided in a unanimous vote not to classify the building as a "landmark." They argued that it did not exhibit enough architectural and aesthetic features to deserve that honor. In so doing, they removed the last legal means that would have allowed the project's opponents to block the conversion of the building into an Islamic center.

THE TEA PARTY DOUBLES DOWN

Starting in June 2010, the Cordoba Initiative became a central issue among Republicans and Democrats competing in the midterm elections in November. While Andrew Cuomo, the attorney general of New York and the Democratic candidate for governor, affirmed his support of the principle to respect religious freedom, Rick Lazio, a former member of the House of Representatives from Long Island and a Republican candidate for governor that year, cast doubt on the integrity of Imam Rauf.[15] Proclaiming himself a spokesman for the victims of September 11, Lazio sent a letter on July 7 to Cuomo demanding that he investigate the funding sources for the Islamic cultural center. Lazio sought in this way not only to discredit his Democratic opponent, Cuomo, but also to outpace his Republican rival, Carl Paladino.[16] A former Democrat who was then supported by the Tea Party movement, Paladino ran in opposition to abortion and homosexuals but was often tripped up by his extramarital affairs.[17] His campaign was centered on reforming the state's school system, cutting taxes, and criticizing the project to reform America's health-care system.[18] Starting in July 2010, the denunciation of the Cordoba project became a major theme of his campaign. What occurs then is a sort of bidding war between the two rival Republican candidates. In a radio interview given on July 22, Paladino warns Imam Rauf, saying, "As governor, I will seize the power of expropriation by eminent domain to block the construction of this mosque and make instead a war memorial out of the site rather than allow a memorial to honor those who attacked the country."[19]

On August 3, 2010, on Governor's Island, facing the Statue of Liberty, Michael Bloomberg made a public stand in favor of the Islamic cultural center. Responding indirectly to the threats made by Paladino, the New York mayor stated,

The simple fact is this building is private property, and the owners have a right to use the building as a house of worship. The government has no right whatsoever to deny that right—and if it were tried, the courts would almost certainly strike it down as a violation of the U.S. Constitution. Whatever you may think of the proposed mosque and community center, lost in the heat of the debate has been a basic question—should government attempt to deny private citizens the right to build a house of worship on private property based on their particular religion? That may happen in other countries, but we should never allow it to happen here.[20]

On August 13, 2010, on the occasion of the ceremony of *iftar* (the end of fasting) organized each year by the White House, President Obama also spoke out in favor of the Cordoba project and stated that Muslims are full American citizens like any other.

However, the position for or against the initiative of Imam Rauf does not necessarily define itself along ideological lines of Left versus Right, Democrat versus Republican. Certain individuals on the right of the ideological spectrum speak out in defense of Imam Rauf on the grounds of defending individual liberties. Representative Ron Paul (R-Tex.), the originator of many of the themes of the Tea Party and a self-described libertarian, rejects the attitude of those opposed to the mosque, considering such opposition to be an illegitimate encroachment on individual freedom.[21] On August 23, 2010, Paul posted a statement on his blog in which he condemned the positions of the Right and the Left as equally demagogic: "Conservatives are once again, unfortunately, failing to defend private property rights, a policy we claim to cherish. In addition, conservatives missed a chance to challenge the hypocrisy of the left which now claims they defend property rights of Muslims, yet rarely if ever, the property rights of American private businesses."[22] In similar fashion, the Republican Grover Norquist, the president of Americans for Tax Reform, a lobby opposed to tax increases, defends the Cordoba center in the name of the right to private property.[23]

RIGHT VERSUS RIGHTS

The Ground Zero controversy is defined by the confrontation of two distinct lines of reasoning, one based on rights and expert testimony on behalf of the public, and the other based on political, media-driven debates. Between December 2009 and September 2010, several decisions were made that, in theory, could have put an end to the controversy: the May 25 vote of the community board, the July 13 decision of the Landmarks Preservation Commission, statements by the FBI and the New York Police Department, and the insistence by both Mayor Bloomberg and President Obama that the Cordoba project was consistent with two fundamental American rights—freedom of religion and the right to private property. However, rather than ending the controversy, each of these moments actually touched off more opposition in certain quarters, and each also saw new actors entering the fray. How could the controversy take on such proportions when there was no legal or material justification for opposing the construction of this Islamic cultural center?

"This is not a debate about religious freedom," said a spokesperson for Paladino to the Landmarks Preservation Commission on July 13, 2010. "If it was about religious freedom," he continued, "we would not be discussing the matter. The problem is simple: it's the siting of this structure." For many of those opposed to the Islamic center, the Cordoba project was perhaps legal, but it was nevertheless an affront to the victims of September 11—an outrage, a provocation, a monstrosity. "It shows such lack of respect to place a mosque so close to what we consider as a sacred space," deplored one participant in the July 13 hearings. "I'm ashamed that you could even be considering such a project after all that we have endured, and not just us New Yorkers but the entire country. We have suffered terribly. How can you authorize this when it is so painful for us?"[24]

The Manhattan controversy offers an inverted image of the polemic that started in Europe after the publication of caricatures of Mohammad in a Danish newspaper. In 2006, as in 2010, the discourse of rights (freedom of speech in 2006, freedom of religion in 2010) was set up in opposition to a normative discourse about religious and moral sensibilities. In each controversy, the roles of Muslims and their detractors are reversed, but the structure of the debate is the same. In fact, those opposed to the Cordoba Initiative readily point out the similarities between the two debates. During the June 6 demonstration organized by Stop Islamization of America, there were signs that reproduced the caricature of the Prophet wearing a turban shaped like a bomb. One sign with the words "And they think a caricature is insulting!" clearly offers the opponents of the Cordoba project a quick comeback not only to Imam Rauf and his allies but to all Muslims who in 2006 were offended by the publication of those caricatures. On July 13, one participant underlined the importance that Muslims accord to religious symbols so as to complain all the more about their lack of sensitivity toward American suffering:

> I have Muslim friends, but I am against this project. We ask Imam Abdul Rauf to have the decency to admit that it's a sensitive matter and truly an offense for us. We must be respectful toward Muslims, I have no problem

with that, but where is the respect that they owe us? There are plenty of places where they can build this mosque. In the Muslim world symbols are taken very seriously. For example, the Prophet Mohammad, when it came to those caricatures, what did they do? They went into the streets, they organized riots and killed fifty people. There's proof of the importance of symbols for you.[25]

The reasoning developed in the debate about the caricatures that underscores European intolerance toward Muslims is here produced in mirror image. To those who warn the American people about the rise of intolerance and racism, opponents of the Cordoba project reply that it's the Muslims who, with their insensitivity to American suffering, are showing intolerance. At the July 13 hearings, one speaker explained it this way: "What I don't understand is why the Muslim community does not show a little tolerance toward us. Why don't the Muslims say, 'OK, we'll build this mosque somewhere else'? All I see are attempts to divide us, and when you divide, you conquer. . . . I want to see a little tolerance toward us—we lost three thousand people."[26] In the debate about the caricatures, the wounded sensibilities of Muslims stood in opposition to the freedom of speech defended by the journalists and secular political figures. The New York debate presents the inverted situation where the Muslims and others defending the Cordoba project based their argument on the neutral secular principle of religious freedom.

NATIONALISM AND A REDEFINITION OF THE SACRED THROUGH SUFFERING

The argument based on moral offensiveness shows both a form of outward-looking deprovincialization of the American debate about Islam by erecting a mirror-image copy of the themes developed in the European controversies and a nationalist reassertion of the sacred status and sovereignty of the American "homeland." While some opponents of the mosque rely on the classic paradigm of a "clash of civilizations" and go on about conflicts between Judeo-Christian values and Islam, the majority of those who invoke the moral offensiveness argument explain their feelings as coming from the sacred character of Ground Zero more than by any specifically Judeo-Christian association. The sacredness comes from the enormity of the attack and not from any one religious source. If the two are evidently linked, it is nevertheless the suffering of the victims' families that is sanctified more than their religious identity. The destruction of the World Trade Center had the effect of redefining the value of objects found at the site of Ground Zero. Simple pieces of debris were transformed into sacred symbols. But this transvaluation process is complex, as one can see from the number of scandals involving objects found at the site and the controversies that have erupted about what criteria to apply to establish their new value and ownership.[27] For example, an FBI agent helped himself to a vase from the store Tiffany & Co. and displayed it in the agency's office in Minneapolis. To justify his action, he said he believed that the vase had certainly lost all its commercial value and that no one could accuse him of stealing.[28] However, a man who pretended to be a Red Cross volunteer so as to more easily steal some cheap clothes from a Century 21 store located near the towers was convicted of theft, despite his efforts to claim that the clothes no longer had any value. Independent of such dubious cases, declaring an object or a plot of land sacred was essentially linked to the memory of the attack. Defining the site of Ground Zero as sacred was, above all, a reaffirmation of the sovereignty of the American nation. After all, the terrorist attacks were not understood as being directed against the Port Authority or Larry Silverstein, the developer of the World Trade Center, but against the American government: "If the regime of private property causes the sovereign to recede into the background behind a world of law, the 9/11 attacks, violating the sovereign's control over space and violence, reconjured it."[29]

The dispute that erupted a few months later, not about a Muslim place of worship this time but about a cross, also suggests that what's at stake is the sacralization of a territory and of national sovereignty more than any affirmation of an anti-Muslim, Christian identity. In July 2011, the group American Atheists lodged a complaint against Mayor Bloomberg, the Port Authority of New York and New Jersey, and the World Trade Center Foundation. The group's complaint voiced its opposition to the public display at the National September 11 Memorial & Museum, which was scheduled to open on September 11, 2011, of two pieces of steel retrieved from the debris at Ground Zero and made into a cross. The opponents said that displaying this "Ground Zero cross" violates the First Amendment: as a Christian symbol, they argued, the cross has no place in a museum owned and paid for by the government, even if the museum is managed by a private foundation. In a public statement released on July 25, 2011, David Silverman, the president of American Atheists, points out that "no other religions or philosophies will be so honored. There will only be a Christian symbol in the middle of OUR memorial. As a gesture of public accommodation, the memorial ought to either allow us (as well as other religious philosophies) to include our own symbol in the museum, and one of equal size, or it should withdraw its plan to display the cross. Equality is an all or nothing contract."[30] The suit filed by American Atheists provoked anger among several Republican legislators and conservative lawyers, as well as skepticism among some secular liberals, because for most Americans this cross is not a Christian symbol but a symbol of national solidarity. Representative Michael G. Grimm (R-N.Y.) announced the draft of a bill that would make the cross a national monument: "This cross was a symbol of hope and freedom at a time when New Yorkers were battling against feelings of loss and destruction. . . . By defining the cross at the September 11 Memorial as a national monument, we will insure that this symbol of liberty continues to honor those whom we have lost and those who kept faith."[31] The action taken by American Atheists was criticized not only by conservative Christians but also by many journalists, intellectuals, religious leaders, and political figures, including liberal Democrats. They all denounced the trial as grotesque, excessive, and inappropriate, and insisted on the exceptional character of the Ground Zero site.

The exchange that took place on July 13, 2010, between the Landmarks Preservation Commission and the public testimonies at those hearings clearly reflects the divergent ways of attributing value to places and objects. The commission opened the day of hearings with a presentation explaining why, in its view, the building at 51 Park Place could not receive the status of historical monument. "The property does not meet enough of the conditions to be so classified. Its attributes are not unique nor are they celebratory. The building does not meet the criteria."[32] This conclusion was consistent with observations made by different commission members since 1989, the year when discussions to give the building a special status began. A large portion of the audience, however, refused to accept this decision and saw the building as the sole "survivor" of the

September 11 attacks and therefore unique. Speaking of the building as though it were a heroic person, several testimonies clearly intended to show that "this building deserves the status of 'landmark' for historical reasons." While conceding that the aesthetic qualities of the building are debatable, one person nevertheless asked the experts to modify the criteria used to determine whether the building deserves landmark status: "The building is not attractive, so I understand why you would not want to classify it as a monument; but insofar as it was involved in the events of September 11, there can be no question about its historical significance. We should not forget what happened on September 11. We are in the process of losing our history and it's up to you to save it." By transforming the Ground Zero neighborhood into a memorial site, the idea was also to keep alive awareness about the danger that Islam represents so that such attacks occur "never again."

The opponents of the Cordoba construction project define the legitimate source of Muslim rights in a specific way. While they recognize that the Constitution guarantees to all the right to religious freedom, they request that Muslims not exercise their right in this instance. However, the emotion and suffering, as irrational as they may seem, become the legitimate source of another type of right—the right to not be offended. Many testimonials compared the suffering caused by the memory of September 11 to the suffering of survivors of the Holocaust. Recalling that "Holocaust survivors are entitled to express irrational feelings," the national director of the Anti-Defamation League, Abraham Foxman, says regarding the families of victims of September 11 that "their distress entitles them to express viewpoints that others would categorize as irrational or bigoted." The Anti-Defamation League also made a public statement in which it concedes that Muslims have the right to construct a mosque at 51 Park Place but declares such a project inappropriate:

> Those in favor of the Islamic center may have every right to build on this site, and they may have even chosen this site to disseminate a positive message about Islam. The bigotry shown by those who have attacked them is unjust and to be condemned. But ultimately this is not a question of rights, but a question of what is right. In our view, to construct an Islamic center in the shadow of the World Trade Center will unnecessarily create more victims and cause more pain—and that is not right.[33]

In a similar vein, the archbishop of New York, Cardinal Timothy Dolan, speaking at a homeless shelter on August 17, 2010, mentioned the decision made by Pope Jean-Paul II in 1993 to prohibit the construction of a convent at Auschwitz out of respect for the memory of the victims of the Holocaust. In citing the controversy over the Carmelite convent, and without attempting to explicitly refute the right of Imam Rauf to construct a mosque at Ground Zero, the archbishop nevertheless appeals to his feelings and sense of decency to encourage respect for the pain of the victims of the September 11 attacks. Cardinal Dolan's reference to the pope's attitude in 1993 is part of an argument that is more patriotic and nationalistic than religious in character. The archbishop speaks not in the name of Catholics and Christians but in the name of Americans and as a guardian of the memory of the September 11 attacks. Similarly, the controversy about the Carmelite convent and the removal of the large cross that had been erected there was more about the identity of the Polish nation than anything to do with abstract conflicts between Judaism and Catholicism. In the post-Communist context of the 1990s, when the affirmation of the Catholic religion was intrinsically linked to expressions of nationalism, those who favored maintaining crosses near the Auschwitz site were fighting for the recognition of "Polish rights" to the site, and in doing so they were rejecting the Polish identity of Poland's Jews.[34] Even though the context and stakes in the Manhattan affair were very different, one notices there an analogous attitude among the opponents of the Cordoba project. The latter transformed the Ground Zero neighborhood into a sacred site that only non-Muslim Americans have a right to own. By recalling the Muslim origins of the terrorists and by associating the Cordoba project with the memory of the attacks, they put in question the Americanness of the Muslims who are behind the Cordoba Initiative as well as the patriotism of the non-Muslim supporters of the project.

The rejection on July 7, 2010, by New York State Supreme Court Judge Paul Feinman of the suit filed by Timothy Brown, a retired fireman, against the Landmarks Preservation Commission, Soho Properties, and the mayor of New York, put an end to the controversy—judicially speaking, at any rate. The court decided in effect that the suit brought by Brown, a client represented by the American Center for Law and Justice, a group of evangelical, conservative lawyers, did not offer sufficient grounds to indict the commission. The former fireman who was among the first responders at the site on September 11 did not prove convincingly enough how the destruction of the building situated at 51 Park Place would cause him "injury in fact." Brown had tried to show that, because of his participation in the rescue operations on the day of the attacks and with the loss of a hundred of his colleagues and friends, and his ceaseless activity defending the memory of the victims of September 11, the destruction of this building would cause him injury in fact.[35] While recognizing the heroism of the former fire fighter and agreeing that he had an important stake in seeing the building preserved, the court accepted the argument of the commission's lawyers. The latter underscored that, from a legal point of view, it was impossible to establish with certainty that the destruction of the building would cause direct injury to the life of Brown, since he did not live in the neighborhood and his economic livelihood did not depend on the preservation of the building. Despite the announcement made some days later by Jay Sekulow, the American Center for Law and Justice director, that his client would seek to appeal, the decision by the New York State Supreme Court marks the end—for the time being, at least—to the Ground Zero controversy. However, it by no means puts an end to the national debate about mosques and the place of religious symbols in public space.

A GEOGRAPHIC EXTENSION

In rapid succession, the Ground Zero controversy gave rise to many similar disputes in Florida, Tennessee, and California, for example. Directly west of Manhattan on Staten Island, a dispute erupted in May 2010 over the purchase of the vacant convent of Saint Mary Margaret by the Muslim American Society. Very quickly, however, facing the opposition of the Catholic community of Staten Island, the pastor in charge, Keith Fennessy, changed his mind and the Muslim American Society agreed to search for another location to build its mosque. The debate about prohibiting Sharia law (see chapter 3) was taking place at the same time. The two stories fed off each other, and the two debates contributed to heightened tensions and disagreements provoked by the battle over the Cordoba project.

In July 2010, Terry Jones, an evangelical pastor in the fifty-member extremist Christian community known as the Dove World Outreach Center located in Gainesville, Florida, announced his intention to organize a public burning of copies of the Quran.[36] This author of the book *Islam Is of the Devil* was attempting to make September 11 into the "International Burn a Quran Day." Unlike the Cordoba Initiative, which is at the center of a true debate between sympathizers and critics of a construction project, Jones's initiative was almost unanimously criticized by the leaders of civic associations in Gainesville; by Jewish, Muslim, and Christian religious organizations; and by President Obama, then secretary of state Hillary Clinton, and General David Petraeus. Given the amount of opposition, the pastor at first called off his plan, but on March 20, 2011, he organized within his church an "International Quran Judgment Day." At the end of this mock trial, Pastor Jones, dressed in a judge's robes, condemned the Quran to death for crimes against humanity. His associate, Pastor Wayne Sapp, then carried out the sentence by burning the book inside the church. Some weeks later, Pastor Jones denied all responsibility for the reprisals committed by Afghan extremists against the United Nations compound in Mazar-i-Sharif that caused the deaths of some thirty people.

The Gainesville episode is in no way representative of the general American opinion toward Islam. It was sparked by the views of a small extremist sectarian group that does not reflect those of most evangelical churches. Nevertheless, this affair, with its grotesque and sinister dimensions, stands as a sort of parody of the more straight-laced disputes that have taken place in other states. By pushing to the extreme a certain number of arguments developed in more civil fashion in these other cases, it reveals their shared tragicomedy. The Gainesville story, with a nutty pastor dressed up like a judge organizing a mock trial and pantomime execution, resembles a vaudeville number that confusingly blends images associated with burnings led by German fascists, American slave-era lynching, trial by jury, and international tribunals. Even though the Gainesville pastor's attitude was widely criticized, one finds in all the mosque controversies the same mixture of normative registers and heterogeneous association of images and themes—notably the idea that Islam is not a "true" religion but a political ideology, that Sharia is a threat to the survival of the United States, and that the national territory or "homeland" is sacred. Thanks to its over-the-top character, the Gainesville affair indirectly and a posteriori exposes the parodic, theatrical dimension present in all the mosque controversies. Pastor Jones's statements are judged unacceptable by the same individuals who denounce mosque construction projects often for analogous reasons but expressed with greater reserve.

A LITTLE MOSQUE IN TENNESSEE

Around the same time, a violent dispute broke out in Tennessee over the construction of an Islamic community center in the town of Murfreesboro, with a population of 100,000. The only mosque in this town, which has 140 churches, had become too small for the 150 Muslim families that have lived peacefully there for the past forty years. Like many southern states, Tennessee is known for its strong attachment to remembering the Civil War and the Confederacy. Moreover, one of the buildings at Middle Tennessee State University (MTSU), a public school, still bears the name of Nathan Bedford Forrest, a Confederate general and early Ku Klux Klan leader. Despite efforts by some students to have his name removed, many Tennessee citizens insist on continuing to commemorate this Civil War strategist. Certain radical groups still claim that the goal of the war effort by the northern states had nothing to do with abolishing slavery but was intended to raid and steal southern property. Small racist groups, even though marginal, continue to argue in favor of white supremacy by organizing "white pride, white power" celebrations. They relay the ideas of hate groups such as the Creativity Movement, for whom Jews and blacks are defective copies of whites, the only true human beings. The state of Tennessee has the largest number of local chapters of the Council of Conservative Citizens, a white supremacist organization with many leaders who favor the return of segregation. Tennessee is one of the Bible Belt states known for the strong presence of conservative evangelical communities. The state capital, Nashville, has over seven hundred churches, several religiously affiliated universities, and a number of publishing houses specialized in producing Bibles.

Arguing about the place of religion in the public sphere is part of daily in life in this state. In May 2009, a family brought a suit against Rutherford Nashville County and its attorney, Jim Cope, who had refused to authorize the construction of a Bible theme park—Bible Park, USA—on property it had recently acquired. In April 2011, the Tennessee House of Representatives voted 70 to 23 in favor of a bill encouraging students to question the scientific theory of evolution. It's not enough to simply define Tennessee as a state populated by evangelical conservatives with racist tendencies. A number of organizations exist there and constitute an important ideological counterforce, such as the Southern Poverty Law Center and the American Civil Liberties Union. Moreover, many conservative churches do oppose the dissemination of racist statements and statements hostile to other churches. The differences in priorities between generations are also significant. Even though religious universities are numerous and are attended in high numbers by young white evangelicals or conservative Catholics opposed to abortion and gay marriage, other student associations, both religious and secular, actively oppose conservative initiatives to deny individual liberties, and they denounce racism and bigotry. The Muslims in Murfreesboro arrived at the end of the 1970s mostly as students enrolled at MTSU. While first making do with a small room at the university, they later rented an apartment and made it into a sort of improvised Islamic center. After using many spaces in different locations, including a garage and several apartments, all of which proved to be too small, they succeeded in collecting enough money to buy forty acres of land in a residential neighborhood of the city on Veals Road across from a small Baptist church. On this land, bought for $300,000, they planned to build a mosque along with a gymnasium, a cemetery, and a school. Up until 2010, the Muslim community had lived tranquilly and had not been discriminated against. Its leading spokesmen say that even after the attacks on September 11, 2001, they maintained good relations with the rest of the city. In fact, until 2010 the vast majority of the city's citizens knew nothing about Islam and had only a vague awareness of the existence of this small Muslim community. The controversy that broke out in 2010 is all the more surprising as it seems to have had no precedent. It is shocking for its virulence, its style, and especially one of the key arguments used by those against the mosque: Islam is not a religion.

"Islam is not a religion"

One morning in February 2010, a sign saying "Not Welcome" appeared on the land that the Muslims of Murfreesboro were interested in—a small foretaste of public opinion in the city. But it is the May 24, 2010, decision by the city's planning board authorizing construction that ignited the powder keg. As with the Manhattan Islamic center, the Murfreesboro mosque proposal met all the legal, architectural, and environmental conditions. In 1984, Rutherford County, to which Murfreesboro belongs, granted property owners permission to build religious institutions, private dwellings, and farms in residential neighborhoods located in the outskirts of towns without requiring them to file for a zoning change. Therefore, projects of these kinds do not have to be examined and publically debated by the county commission. They are approved as soon as they demonstrate conformity to state laws relating to architecture, safety, the environment, or the size of parking lots. Moreover, the Tennessee Religious Freedom Act, adopted in 2009, reaffirms the right of religious communities to build places of worship.[37] Taking inspiration from the RLUIPA, this law reasserts that local authorities must give "clear and convincing proof" that the construction of a place of worship threatens the state's compelling superior interest before they can block construction. The Tennessee Religious Freedom Act was largely supported by conservative state legislators who wished to facilitate the founding of churches in residential neighborhoods. It also received support from liberal lawmakers who viewed the law as a means to fight against the possible activism of religious extremists against other religious communities.

However, despite being in perfect conformity with the law, the decision made by the planning board in May 2010 triggered immediate anger among many inhabitants. In a tense atmosphere marked by three incidents of antimosque vandalism (in January, June, and August 2010), the mobilization against construction turned into a debate over whether Islam is a religion, and the debate was supplemented by a defense of "the will of the people" that the judges in the decision are said to have shoved aside. The scale of the controversy is explained by the fusion of a conservative minority in the city that knew nothing about Islam and leaders of conservative and ultraconservative organizations who saw the case as a political opportunity. But the case also highlights the capacity to mobilize a large portion of the city's population in defense of religious freedom and against aggressive behavior and Islamophobic stereotypes.

On June 18, 2010, at a weekly meeting of the Rutherford County Commission, Kevin Fisher, a resident of Murfreesboro and a conservative evangelical African American prison guard, complained that he and the other neighborhood residents were not consulted before the construction permit was issued to the Muslims. Fisher's former wife had converted to Islam, and her house was located about one mile from the future Islamic center. Fisher asserted that the people in the neighborhood "have the right to be present at the moment that a law is decided or when decisions are made by this honorable institution, and in this case clearly the law was shoved aside."[38] The law said to be infringed requires local authorities to publicly announce the holding of meetings by the commission, although it does not require announcing the precise agenda of discussions scheduled.[39] The leader of the planning commission rejected the accusation and recalled that an announcement of the meeting to be held was published in the city's daily newspaper, the *Murfreesboro Post*.[40] However, although the place and date of the May 24 meeting were indeed given, the commission did not specify the agenda of the meeting. The matter may seem nitpicky, but it speaks to the feeling held by a portion of the city's residents—that they were tricked by the commission and that this more than any fundamental hostility toward Muslims is at the origin of this mobilization.

Taking advantage of popular discontent, the Republican and Tea Party candidate for the U.S. Congress from the sixth district of Tennessee, Lou Ann Zelenik, published on June 24, 2010, a public statement holding Muslim Americans and the federal government equally responsible for the increase in extremism: "Until the American Muslim community finds it in their hearts to separate themselves from their evil, radical counterparts, to condemn those who want to destroy our civilization and will fight against them, we are not obligated to open our society to any of them."[41] Defining American civilization as Judeo-Christian, she goes on to condemn the naïveté of the federal government and denounces those who "bow before the throne of political correctness" installed by the Democratic elite in power.

Strengthened by this show of support, Fisher and three other plaintiffs filed suit against the planning commission of Rutherford County. On the opening day of the trial, September 27, the plaintiffs' lawyer insistently repeated their main claims, especially that Islam is a political ideology and not a religion and that, therefore, Muslims cannot invoke the First Amendment to justify their right to build a place of worship. Just as Zelenik stated that America has no social obligation toward Muslims, the lawyer declared that Muslims do not have "the right to cancel our rights"—that is, our rights as Americans: "Why should we grant to any old religion the right to cancel the rights guaranteed by the United States Constitution? If the planning commission had approved a project submitted by Osama bin Laden, would one still say that one can get by without organizing a public hearing?" On September 27, at the request of the plaintiffs, testimony was given by Frank Gaffney, a deputy assistant secretary of defense under President Ronald Reagan and president of the Center for Security Policy (see chapter 3). Heavily involved in the anti-Sharia movement, Gaffney made a detailed presentation of the reasons why Sharia is incompatible with American values. The county attorney, however, rejected Gaffney's statements, saying they had no bearing on the subject at hand: "This is not relevant and Gaffney himself admits he is not an expert on Islamic law." The diatribes and questioning of the attorney, Joe Brandon Jr., gave the Murfreesboro trial a particular air that blends the art of syllogism with absurd analogies and a hyperbolic rhetoric that slides toward buffoonery. With his loud yellow tie and checked shirts that remind one of brash comedians from the 1950s or 1960s, Brandon turned the courtroom into a stage. With leading questions, he tried to get witnesses to say that because some women have been buried alive in Pakistan, all American Muslims are necessarily a danger to the country. But because a fundamentalist Christian has participated in terrorist attacks, are all Christian evangelicals dangerous? Brandon expressed his outrage in a loud voice and with forceful gesticulations at the authorization granted by the commission to inter Muslims on the grounds of the future mosque. He asked rhetorical questions such as "How much stinking is possible?" and to further whip up the public's anger, he made statements such as "Allah Akbar is what terrorists cry!" without bothering to say what that is supposed to prove. The reasons why Judge Robert Corlew III decided to hold this public hearing and allow Brandon to manipulate witnesses in this way remain unclear, especially since this Republican, Presbyterian judge—mindful of the need for order and civility—was known for his intransigence when faced with such disorderly conduct. Nothing obliged him to step forward and organize a hearing. He could have waited for the plaintiffs to make the request. His initiative and the way he allowed it to be said during the hearing that Islam is not a religion leads one to suspect that he shared Brandon's views or was at least in sympathy with the ideas of the antimosque militants.

To cut short speculation about whether Islam is a religion, U.S. Attorney Jerry Martin filed an amicus brief on October 18 that reaffirms the position of the U.S. government: the United States recognizes and has always recognized Islam as a religion: "The plaintiffs' claim that Islam is not recognized by the United States is false and no authority sustains such an idea. Freedom of assembly and religion is literally the foundation of this country." The text cites in support of its conclusions the works of researchers and political leaders and cites numerous cases related to religious freedom. The brief insists also on the definition of Islam given by Thomas Jefferson: "Jefferson thus understood Islam to be a significant religion of the world, alongside Christianity, Judaism, and Hinduism, to which our principles of religious freedom would naturally extend."[42]

The amicus brief only exacerbated Brandon's anger, however, since for him the brief was an illegitimate intervention of the federal government in a local affair. Declaring Islam to be a sect and continuing his heavy-handed ways with witnesses ("Isn't it true that in the Qur'an Mohammad had a six-year-old wife that he had sex with? Is that your idea of what a religion is?"), Brandon was called to order several times by his fellow attorney and criticized for turning the courtroom into a circus. To delegitimize the intervention of the federal attorney, Brandon attempted to show via syllogism that the reference to Jefferson made in the amicus brief discredits the Department of Justice: Jefferson owned slaves; therefore, his words have no legitimacy unless one's aim is to legitimate a return to slavery: "Did you say that you want the federal government that supported slavery to tell this court that Islam is a religion?"[43] On October 22, Brandon launched into a virulent diatribe against President Obama and his administration. "How does it make you feel," he asked one witness, "to have a president who says, 'I will stand with the Muslims'?" A resident of the city opposed to the mosque went further in Brandon's direction; "It bothers me that the federal government comes here to Murfreesboro to tell us not to go over a certain line."[44] The trial thus makes apparent not just a conflict between Muslims and non-Muslims but a militant stand of those who claim to speak in the name of the interests of the local community against the federal government, which is presented as naïve, elitist, and authoritarian. Although many of the witnesses used by Brandon first appeared as authentic and disinterested members of the local community or as serious experts on Islam, the validity of their testimony and their disinterestedness was contested by the lawyers defending the commission. One witness admitted to paying an association for help preparing arguments based on Islamophobic assumptions such as these: "If the religion of Islam allows men to beat their wives and have sex with children, then it's against our law."[45] Another witness confessed to having received money from the plaintiffs' lawyer for finding information about Islam from explicitly anti-Muslim websites, and he shared this information with the court. Faced with protests from the defense lawyers that simple rumors were being admitted as expert testimony, the witness was forced to recognize that he could not "swear to the truth of the contents of any of the documents [he] presented or to the truth of what one finds on any website."[46]

Opposition to the mosque did not arise solely from the activism of the local population. Several associations and churches played an essential role in organizing the movement against the mosque, financing the costs of the trial, elaborating and disseminating arguments, and preparing demonstrations. These groups often take inspiration from the arguments proposed by organizations such as Frank Gaffney's think tank Stop Islamization of America. The trial in Murfreesboro was financed to a great extent by Sally Snow and Howard Wall, married residents of Murfreesboro who are among the richest and most influential property owners in the region. A small community of activists known as Proclaiming Justice to the Nations, a group close to currents of Christian Zionism, also helped with financing. One of the main goals of this group is to strengthen support for Christian Americans in Israel. Laurie Cardoza Moore, the group's president, produced several short films about the rise of anti-Semitism and the defense of Israel, and even though she is not a resident of Rutherford County, she was one of the first to declare her opposition to the mosque project and threatened to sue the city's mayor as early as July 2010. Similarly, the Reverend Darrel Whaley, a pastor at the Kingdom Ministries Worship Center, stated during the trial, "America's reason for being is to be Israel's partner and protect Israel."[47] This political stand rests on the belief in the theological superiority of Christianity. By deforming the text of Corinthians, the pastor teaches his followers that "Islam is a thorn" that must be gotten rid of. Bill French, a retired professor of Tennessee State University and founder of the think tank Center for the Study of Political Islam, was also one of the most active individuals within the movement resisting the mosque. At several demonstrations or at the end of the day in court, French would harangue the crowd wrapped in the American flag or explain to passersby that Islamic law is on the verge of destroying the foundations of American society.

Some churches played a big role in the protest against the mosque. However, even if many members of the Grace Baptist Church, located directly across from the plot of land where the mosque was to be built, were totally opposed to the project, the church's pastor, Russell Richardson, insisted on maintaining civil and friendly relations with the Muslim community. But the members and leaders of the Pentecostal megachurch World Outreach Church were unanimously hostile to the mosque, to Muslims, and to Islam. This church, situated on Salem Road, is a gigantic complex composed of many buildings surrounded by walls and with its own private police force. The current pastor, G. Allen Jackson, is the eldest son of Betty and George Jackson. The Jacksons were first Methodists but became followers of Derek Prince at the end of the 1960s and eventually converted to Prince's Pentecostal theology.[48] The theology preached by Derek Prince is notable first for its belief in the possibility of rescuing impure souls from the demons that possess them and second for its unconditional attachment to Israel—not out of interest for the rights of Israelis but because Prince was convinced that Jesus Christ would one day return to Israel. Shortly after first meeting Prince, the Jacksons settled in Murfreesboro, where they founded a small Bible study school of about thirty people in 1968. Today it has become a megachurch with over six thousand members.[49] As directors of the Derek Prince organization, George and Betty Jackson spend six months a year in Israel. Their oldest son, Allen, the senior pastor of World Outreach Church, organizes several pilgrimages of Christians to Israel each year for this community and has been honored by the group Christian Friends of Israel at the Knesset for his support of Israel.

Popular Will Versus General Will

The Muslims of Murfreesboro were not left to confront this opposition alone. A group of students from MTSU joined the association Middle

Tennesseans for Religious Freedom, created by the young Christian alter-globalization activist Jase Short. This association organized numerous demonstrations in support of the Muslim community as well as counter demonstrations when antimosque groups demonstrated in front of the city hall or the courthouse. Middle Tennesseans for Religious Freedom and other liberal organizations such as the American Civil Liberties Union chapter in Nashville and the leaders of the Southern Poverty Law Center played a decisive role supporting and advising the Muslim community. Thanks to them, several lawyers offered to work pro bono for the Murfreesboro imam and his associates. And even though many local journalists chose to cover the story with a sensationalist and anti-Muslim slant, others made efforts to do more balanced reporting, including patiently explaining the differences between Islam and terrorism. A notable case is the work of the *Tennessean* journalist Bob Smietana. A practicing Christian, Smietana speaks of his faith in the power of teaching and communication to resolve tensions between the city's residents. His views resulted in his being the object of numerous acts of intimidation and pressure. The Murfreesboro affair was thus not a case of an isolated Muslim community defending itself against a majority of hostile Christians. Many individuals and organizations of all religions sided with the Muslims. The strong turnout of MTSU students also reveals a strong generational divide when it comes to perceptions of Islam.

On November 17, 2010, Judge Corlew decided to not revoke the construction permit for the Islamic center. Thus the plaintiffs did not succeed in showing how building a mosque would constitute discrimination against them. The judge's decision also specifies, contrary to Kevin Fisher's claim, that organizing public hearings on such matters is not mandatory. "It does appear that a vast majority of our county is zoned residential and as such allows for religious use by right," Judge Corlew said. "We cannot find the county erred or acted illegally, arbitrarily or capriciously in granting the ICM approval under religious uses of right."[50] Despite this first legal defeat, the opponents of the mosque fought back in the spring of 2011 in a context marked by increased mobilization of public opinion around an anti-Sharia law. While agreeing to allow the new suit to go to trial, Judge Corlew announced before it even began that he would no longer accept any discussion on the question of whether Islam is a religion. The sole matter to be examined would be whether the commission broke the law by not correctly announcing the meeting during which the authorization to build the mosque was to be discussed. On August 29, 2011, he confirmed his earlier decision:

> We have a duty equally to treat those whose religious beliefs are similar to the majority beliefs and those whose beliefs are very different from the majority. . . . If the zoning laws are too favorable to those seeking to build places of worship, then citizens should prevail upon their elected representatives to change those ordinances, but until they do the Court must apply those laws equally to Protestant Christians, Roman Catholics, Muslims, Buddhists and others.[51]

However, outside the courthouse people continued to doubt the religious character of Islam. The Tea Party candidate Lou Ann Zelenik repeated her alarmist message about the infiltration of Sharia within Judeo-Christian territory. As cofounder of the Tennessee Freedom Coalition, she invited the Dutch parliamentarian Geert Wilders to the inaugural ceremony of her organization held on May 12, 2011, at Madison's Cornerstone Church for fundamentalist Pentecostals.[52] Wilders warned Muslims: "I have a message for all those people who want to rob us from [*sic*] our freedoms, and my message is, 'Stay in your own country!' "[53] The audience, which included members of the Center for the Study of Political Islam, Muslims who had converted to Christianity, and people associated with the Christian Zionist movement, took up in unison the key themes of the antimosque, anti-Sharia orthodoxy: Islam is not a religion; protections guaranteed by the First Amendment do not apply to Muslims; American civilization is Judeo-Christian, and its core values are threatened; and the federal government and Democratic elites are naïve and contemptuous of the popular will. The meeting, like the many demonstrations that took place since the fall and the many days in court, resembled a cross between a political gathering and night of stand-up comedy routines. A former Muslim who had taken the name Sam Solomon appeared wearing a cowboy hat and wide cummerbund and declared in a loud voice his desire to convert to the customs of Nashville. Herman Cain, the former chief executive officer of Godfather's Pizza and at the time a Republican presidential candidate, repeated several times that the Murfreesboro Islamic center would be a future training camp for terrorists. On Fox News, he also repeated that Muslim Americans abuse the rights guaranteed by the First Amendment, that Islam is not a religion, and that local communities have the right to oppose the construction of mosques that are in any case too numerous in the United States. Just like Kevin Fisher, he was outraged that Muslim Americans dare to claim they're being discriminated against. The civil rights movement, he said, was completely different, and Muslims turning to the vocabulary of discrimination is, he believed, insulting to the memory of the struggle by African Americans. Meanwhile, the Muslims of Murfreesboro were getting started on the construction of their Islamic center on Veals Road.

A final twist in the affair occurred when, to everyone's surprise, Judge Corlew imposed a halt to the construction even though the mosque was nearly built. On May 29, 2012, the judge published a memo that said Rutherford County had, in fact, violated the Tennessee Open Meetings Act, which requires a government agency to announce publicly its meetings before they are held.[54] The court recognized that the planning commission did announce its meeting in the local daily newspaper, the *Murfreesboro Post*, but went on to state that the matter of approving a construction plan for the Islamic center required a "higher degree" of vigilance because it concerned "a subject of very great importance for the citizens."[55] Immediately, the civil rights division of the Department of Justice and the Islamic center itself, supported by the Becket Fund for Religious Liberty, each filed an appeal of the decision. Leaders of many religious organizations lent their support to the Muslims of Murfreesboro. On July 18, 2012, one hundred religious leaders signed a letter that would be sent to the federal judge for the state of Tennessee to request that the Islamic center be permitted to open for Ramadan. The same day, Judge Todd J. Campbell of the federal district court in Nashville issued a temporary restraining order requiring that an inspection of the mosque be undertaken, which would allow it to be open for Ramadan. He declared that submitting the Muslims to a higher degree of vigilance, as Judge Corlew would have it, "imposes a heightened notice requirement regarding the mosque which substantially burdens the Islamic Center's free exercise of religion without a compelling governmental interest."[56] Respecting the RLUIPA, said the judge, and treating all citizens equally furthers the general interest.

This last turn of events (before the definitive judgment in district court scheduled for 2013) echoes the Manhattan controversy.[57] Like the opponents of the Cordoba project, the residents of Murfreesboro recognized the legitimacy of constitutional principles, but they affirmed that Muslims ought to be subject to a special regime with a superior degree of vigilance and constraint. The outcome of the affair also reveals significant tensions between different understandings of law and disagreements between the judges themselves. The local court judge suggested that popular will ought to be taken into account in this affair: as soon as the local population is afraid of the Muslim community, it has the right to demand that the mosque construction project pass through a more difficult and constraining application process. The federal judge, on the contrary, underscored the general interest, the equality of citizens, and the preeminence of constitutional principles. From the amicus brief of the Department of Justice filed in October 2010 to the July 2012 decision, the Murfreesboro affair expresses not only a controversy between partisans and adversaries of the Islamic center but also major differences between diverse interpretations of the law, the Constitution, and democracy.

This long controversy both strengthened and weakened the city's Muslim community. Students, journalists, lawyers, civil rights organizations, and religious leaders all spoke up for the protection of religious freedom and against the racist and bigoted attacks. This resistance was decisive, for in the neighboring town of Brentwood, a similar controversy took place, but there—without anyone speaking out and without that support from a block of citizens—the Muslims lost the fight and were denied the right to construct a mosque. If the Murfreesboro affair shows one thing, it is that anti-Muslim initiatives and fundamentalist arguments don't necessarily always win, even in the heart of the Bible Belt. But in the aftermath of the controversy, the city's Muslims also admit to feeling more exposed and on the defensive. Calm and resigned, Saleh Sbenaty, a professor of physics at MTSU who originally came from Syria and has lived in Murfreesboro for thirty years, has become the official spokesperson for the community. He patiently tells his story and the stories of other Muslims to all journalists, lawyers, and activists in a narrative that is now perfectly seamless. All the other members keep away from the media and have been encouraged to be cautious around people they don't know. Even the mosque's imam at that time, Oussama Bahloul, who came from Egypt some years ago, accepts requests for interviews with some reluctance. He recognizes that he wasn't "ready for this whole thing. I had to learn to manoeuver within all these politics." Lema Sbenaty, Saleh's daughter, admits to feeling trapped: "We have to be proving all the time that we're innocent. They behave as though we were guilty. . . . They are not interested in what I believe, but in what I am. I walk around all day with a big smile, because otherwise, no matter what I do, they'll say it's because I'm Muslim." Although she didn't wear a veil before the controversy began, she recently decided to do so: "If my intentions are pure, the people will see it. If we're ready to carry this burden, we can go one step further."[58]

This controversy also illustrates a tendency that can be found in many American debates about religion, a particular type of discursive exchange similar to what occurred during the Ground Zero quarrel. There is a striking, permanent disjunction between, on the one hand, the violence of certain statements and the staging of anti-Muslim performances and, on the other, the maintaining of relatively civil relations and respect for the law. Members of the Muslim community were certainly targets of intimidation, from the "Not Welcome" sign to gunshots, arson attempts, and multiple verbal threats. But relations never ended, and some new ones were created between the opposing camps. Kevin Fisher, whose pastor is the former drawing teacher of Saleh Sbenaty's three daughters and whose former wife converted to Islam, now makes regular social calls on Muslims. He goes mostly to share his criticisms, of course, but he does go and takes the time to always ask more questions about Islam. Every day in court during the trial, Sally Wall was seated next to Lema Sbenaty and was seriously concerned about the courses the young woman was missing that day in order to be present. In other words, it's as though everyone was playing the role of the Islamophobe for various reasons but without it being necessary to perform it with hostile or violent behavior. In its absurdity and incoherence, the acrimony of the antimosque activists is disquieting but ultimately also reassuring. It is astonishing that Judge Corlew would allow a lawyer like Brandon to go so far overboard with his caustic treatment of certain witnesses. But in the end, no transgression of the law or of the Muslims' religious freedom occurred—and for good reason, as Mayor Ernest Burgess's ironic remark underscored: "What law did they want us to break by denying Muslims the right to build a mosque?" In other words, the whole thing caused a lot of commotion, but respect for the rule of law won out.

TEMECULA, CALIFORNIA

Citizens in other towns who were opposed to mosque building looked to the Murfreesboro controversy as a test. They learned that doubting the religious character of Islam was not a winning strategy. The residents of

Temecula Valley in southern California also drew lessons from the relative failure of Brandon's tactics. In December 2010, the town council of this small city located fifty miles south of Los Angeles issued a construction permit for a 25,000-square-foot mosque to be situated next to a Baptist church. The request to build had been submitted in 2008 by Imam Mahmoud Harmoush, a Syrian refugee and self-described Ronald Reagan fan who had come to the United States in the 1980s. On January 26, 2011, the town council confirmed its decision to authorize an expansion of the city's Islamic center. The existing mosque, located in an old warehouse, was no longer big enough for the hundred Muslim families living in the area. The project was supported by the Muslim Public Affairs Council, a group that defends the rights of American Muslims, and by interfaith dialogue groups such as NewGround: A Muslim-Jewish Partnership for Change, but it nevertheless caused anger among many residents.[59] George Rombach, the president and founding member of the association Concerned American Citizens to Promote the Separation of Shariah from Spiritual Islam (CAC), organized several demonstrations to protest against the decision of the town council.[60] However, having learned the lessons of the Murfreesboro affair, the city attorney for Temecula, Peter M. Thorson, warned the commission that its decision was to be based solely on land-use criteria, and the question of whether Islam is a religion was not to figure in the debate. Rombach was also careful about convincing his allies opposed to the mosque to avoid launching into commentaries about the nature of the Muslim religion. If he's opposed to the mosque, he said, it's simply out of concern for negative consequences relating to traffic and noise. He also criticized the town council for having extended favorable treatment to the Muslim community by not requiring the architectural plans for the mosque to be inspected for conformity to current environmental norms. However, even though speculation about Islam was now excluded from the courtroom, the discussion continued much the same outside the courtroom. The fundamentalist pastor at the neighboring Baptist church, William Rench, said unblinkingly that, for him, Islam is not a religion: "We've always held the view that Islam is wrong—it's a false religion with which we disagree." He then added reassuringly, "We also think Mormonism is wrong and Jehovah's Witnesses are wrong and that the Roman Catholic Church has fallen away from the truth. So we're not saying that Islam is the only group that's wrong!"[61] Articles published by CAC remind the reader that America is a Judeo-Christian

civilization; Muslims are apostrophized, described as arrogant and insensitive, and ordered to publicly renounce all ties to radical Islamism and work
actively to reform their theology. The articles also denounce the gullibility
of local authorities and cast aside as irrelevant all references to the constitutional liberties guaranteed to Muslims.[62] Fearing an "infiltration" of suburban America by radical Islamists, the members of CAC were uneasy about
Imam Harmoush because he had been affiliated with the mosque in San
Diego whose imam was Anwar al-Awlaqi, an al-Qaeda activist originally
from Yemen and a naturalized American. The least word of support for the
Palestinian cause was interpreted as proof of complicity with Hamas. In
a small association of Republican Tea Party women, one hears the same
themes: "I don't want them here opening mosques in every city, trying to
open one up on Ground Zero in New York where they killed thousands
and thousands of people. And if their mosque was used for religious reasons, that'd be one thing, but they're not. This is where they do their little
powwow meetings. They don't belong here!"[63] One of the most active members of CAC is Mano Bakh, an elderly conservative Republican and former
officer in the army of the shah of Iran, who fled the country in 1979. In a
self-published book, *Escaping Islam*, Bakh describes how he was arrested
and tortured by supporters of the Islamic revolution. For him, certain civil
liberties should not be extended to Muslim Americans so long as they have
not undertaken a radical reform of Islam.

However, just like in Murfreesboro, the Muslim community in Temecula
Valley was able to commence building of their Islamic center. Those opposed
were unable to stop the project from going forward, but they did succeed, as
others did in Manhattan and Tennessee, in getting certain notions that are
hostile to Islam and the Obama administration into wider circulation.

CONTRACTS OF EMOTION AND PARODIES
OF REASON

One of the main arguments used by antimosque groups is that Muslims
don't "deserve" legal protection. This claim goes against a basic principle of liberalism, which says the law applies to all without exception. In
the name of respect for offended sensibilities or of threats to security,

participants in antimosque movements aim to show that the First Amendment does not apply to Muslims. This exceptionalist view is at the center of sloganeering in most of these conflicts: "It's not about rights, but about what is right"; "They don't have a right to cancel our rights"; "We have no obligations to Muslims." The antimosque camp underlines the legitimacy of the popular will on which the liberal argument about equality of rights rests. They complain they've been dispossessed by the county, the city council, and the Department of Justice of their right to participate in the process of deliberation. For them, the interpretation of constitutional principles is up to local communities and not representatives of the federal government, which is perceived as naïve, elitist, and authoritarian. In the context of debates over domestic policy that have been ongoing since 2008, this antiliberal argument has been mostly built by partisans of a theory of constitutional populism from ideas circulating within the Tea Party movement.

This theory, which says the power to control the interpretation of constitutional rights and law is not the job of judges but of the people, has inspired many American social movements. The feminist movement and civil rights movements, for example, invoked the right of the people to interpret the Constitution as a way to legitimate their claims. But the Tea Party enthusiasts have taken up this theme in recent years from a nationalist angle, presenting themselves as being in sole possession of true historical knowledge about the American nation. The three founding principles of their vision of the world—individualism, small government, and free trade—are threatened by foreign or anti-American forces, among them Islam, but especially the liberal (i.e., "Leftist" or "Socialist") ideology of the Obama administration. As the American philosopher and legal scholar Paul Kahn has observed, this understanding of the sources of democracy is not founded on the liberal idea of contract but on a political theology of sacrifice: "Liberal theory puts the contract at the origin of the political community; political theology sees sacrifice as the point of origin. Contract and sacrifice are two conceptions of freedom."[64] The opposition between these two ways of conceiving of the social pact is not organized along the lines of accepting or rejecting law. The political theology perspective accords the Constitution an essential place. In the mosque controversies, the two opposing camps both refer to constitutional rights. But whereas the constitutionality of a law is defended by liberals according to the principle of individual rights, from the political theology perspective it is defended in the name of popular sovereignty.[65] It is this reference to the will of the people and the community that one encounters over and over in the declarations of antimosque groups. For them, rights are earned. By conditioning the granting or withholding of rights according to one's subscribing to a certain conception of what a religion ought to be, the antimosque camp breaks with one of the essential principles of the liberal definition of the social contract. The latter affirms that the individual will agree to respect the rules and procedures of collective deliberation and justice, but one's participation in civil society is not conditioned by any allegiance to a particular definition of the common good. In the view of those opposed to Islamic centers, however, as long as American Muslims do not establish a clear line between "spiritual Islam" and "radical Islam" they cannot legitimately draw on constitutional protections.

[handwritten margin note: diff ideas of who is eligible for protection by the Constitution]

A CONTRACT OF EMOTION

Sometimes the exchanges that take place between the defenders and opponents of mosques sound more like lovers' quarrels than clashes of civilizations: "How can you do this to us?" "How can you be so insensitive?" These are criticisms that suggest a relationship if not of equality, at least one built on reciprocal duties and expectations, and not simply relations of domination, fear, or hostility. The argument based on moral offense reveals a specific attitude toward Muslims that is based less on fear or a desire to annihilate and more on blame. The foregrounding of matters of civility expresses a conception of a social contract founded more on behavior and conduct than on negotiated polemics. The act of blaming someone makes sense only in a relation where each party feels concerned by the judgment and emotions of the other.[66] What is expected of the Muslims is not the wholesale acceptance of the reasons given by Imam Rauf's opponents. It's more that they're being summoned to express compassion toward their compatriots. Therefore, they must not turn to abstract public principles offered by liberalism's ideal of justice but instead toward a language of the heart and the behaviors that are appropriate to those emotions. With this in mind, it's more fitting to speak not of a political accord founded on public reason but of a type of intimate contract based on politeness and appropriate decency.

The participants in the debate are not putting into question the universally and politically rational character of the First Amendment. However, by declaring their indifference to the question of what is politically reasonable, and by underlining instead the importance of what is tolerable in a specific situation, they make the feeling of offense into a source of truth and a principle of action that compete alongside the First Amendment but without seeking to invalidate it. The absence of emotion and consideration for the families of the victims of September 11—or for the fears of the neighbors residing near the proposed mosques in Murfreesboro and Temecula Valley—is not perceived as a threat to a liberal political order but as a form of civic incompetence, deficiency, or incapacity—in other words, a lack of civility. This imputation of insensitivity ascribed by mosque opponents brings with it a whole array of additional moral inferences: If the Muslims are incapable of seeing why a mosque at this particular location offends or bothers us, how can we be sure they're able to commit and integrate into American society over the long term? Here again the language register is more in keeping with a lovers' quarrel than with an intercommunity conflict or a war of opposed civilizations. The incapacity to show an expected or a conventional emotion—for example, sadness at a time of mourning—is in many social circumstances interpreted as abnormal.[67] From this supposed abnormality, a number of alarming conclusions can be inferred. In Albert Camus's *The Stranger*, the inability of Meursault to feel and, especially, to show any pain on the occasion of his mother's death is interpreted retrospectively as a sign of his predisposition to kill. Similarly, the lack of sensitivity shown by American Muslims to the suffering of the families of victims of September 11 is interpreted as proof of their capacity to harm American society. As soon as the expression of a specific emotion in a particular context is identified as the suitable form of engagement and inclusion in the community, it becomes a necessary condition for the ratification of that context. Here, what the mosque opponents reproach the Muslims for is precisely their refusal or incapacity to ratify the mainstream narrative of post–September 11 America and the whole host of emotions that this narrative authorizes. Muslims' demands for mosques are like a crack, a wrong note, or formal

wish for a mosque disregards light in [light?] of 9/11 of grief mistake that disrupts the mythical story. Their absence of emotion is not perceived as a repudiation of liberal democracy but as a violation of the rules of etiquette and the preconditions of social cohesion, and therefore as a gesture of disengagement from the majority group. Where liberal thinkers looking on would see simply a disagreement between two camps as a divergence of opinion, opponents of the Cordoba project see in the attitude of American Muslims proof of a real moral deficiency—an incapacity to comprehend and respect the majority group's rules for living—their way of life.

PARODIES OF REASON

"Not here, a little bit farther away"—this was one of the most frequently repeated comebacks expressed by opponents to the Cordoba project. It was also a key line in perhaps the most debated, criticized, and mocked argument of the whole controversy. Brows were furrowed over the question of establishing the proper criteria to define what constituted being "too close to" or "far enough away from" Ground Zero. Exhaustive lists of active businesses and other pursuits going on near the site were compiled to demonstrate that the construction of an Islamic center would in no way disturb the already heterogeneous patchwork of activities that coexisted in the neighborhood. In Murfreesboro, the antimosque lawyer Joe Brandon Jr. wondered haughtily how much stink could be tolerated. In 2004, discussions in France about the acceptable dimensions of crosses, beards, and scarves in public schools came in for some mockery, just as later in Switzerland in 2008 serious comparisons between minarets, church bell towers, and factory chimneys also gave rise to numerous satirical commentaries. Indeed, many of the arguments brought forward during the American mosque controversies and in the European debates about head scarves and minarets can strike one as parodies of the very act of producing reasoned public discourse. What type of reason lies behind proposing that the Cordoba center be built "not here, a little bit farther away"? Where's the border between "here" and "a little bit farther away"? How does one make "the cloud of dust that contains the ashes of the victims" into a rational and universally acceptable criterion for public action? Similarly, by supposing that because there is no democracy in the Middle

East and women's rights are shoved aside there, one must be against the Murfreesboro mosque, Lou Ann Zelenik and the city's Tea Party members establish a cause-and-effect relationship between two orders of reality (or fantasy) that have nothing to do with each other.

Even though untenable on the level plane of logical reasoning, this sort of parody of argumentation is undeniably effective in the context of such controversies. Arguments based on civility, safety, and religion are both an avowal of the impossibility for the mosque opponents to offer valid legal or material arguments and a rhetorical strategy that makes up for this impossibility by substituting others instead. The success of these alternative arguments, which are then copied from state to state, reveals the incapacity of those who hold to science and the liberal legal argument to convince their detractors.[68] In the minds of mosque opponents, every phenomenon is the sign of a threat, a culture, an intention, or a project. A mosque is not an assembly hall for Muslims who live in the same neighborhood to carry out religious rituals; it has to be the prow of a ship of conquest or the front window of an extremist recruitment and training center. In the paranoid grammar of this discourse, signs and symbols are linked to one another in a coherent, implacable way. Attempts made by liberal finger-raisers to prove with empirical evidence or sociological studies that a mosque is just a mosque are not enough to interrupt the production of inferences that rather crazily follow from one another once one believes that everything *means* something.

As unsatisfying as it may seem from the perspective of the ideal circuit of communication, this dialogue of the deaf does in fact produce effects. For one, it contributes to a definition in a given context of the rules of debate and the conditions of compromise. The mosque controversies demonstrate that the Islamophobic discourse and the liberal discourse are, in a sense, equally ineffective. The Islamophobic insults do not manage to turn Muslim Americans into second-class citizens. On the contrary, Muslim American organizations use all the resources of the legal system to defend the freedoms and civil rights of Muslims, and they are largely supported in their efforts by Jewish and Christian groups, civil rights organizations like the American Civil Liberties Union, and the Department of Justice. Founded on fantasies about a will to dominate or subvert, the Islamophobic discourse has nonetheless failed to establish much evidence for it. The homogeneous, white, Judeo-Christian community that the antimosque camp describes as threatened does not correspond to the demographic reality of the American population. The adjacent blame that accompanies the argument based on moral offense has a function analogous to what Judith Butler has analyzed in the context of pornography—that of being a "compensatory fantasy."[9] The call for recognition of an offense is an allegory of the impossible achievement of Islamophobic politics and of the unfounded—because unfindable—imaginary homogeneous majority it posits. The argument based on offense gets deployed in a register that is at once accusatory, parodic, and mimetic, but it expresses no cultural, affective, or psychological depth below its words or before politics. Likewise, the liberal argument based on equal rights is also not quite fully effective. It does not convince the mosque opponents who denounce as naïve and dangerous a social ideal that would give equal treatment to citizens subscribing to different visions of the world. In the wake of these mosque affairs, it has become more common to say out loud that Islam is not a religion, but an awareness that Muslims are claiming their rights and receiving a large measure of support from the general population for doing so has also spread.

3

THE ANTI-SHARIA MOVEMENT

On July 21, 2010, Newt Gingrich, a former majority leader of the U.S. House of Representatives and at the time one of the Republicans competing in the primaries to be the party's presidential candidate, gave a speech at the American Enterprise Institute, a conservative think tank, titled "America at Risk: The War with No Name." Gingrich argued notably for the creation of a federal law prohibiting any use of Sharia in U.S. courts. He warned his listeners about "a fundamentalist political, economic, and religious movement that seeks to impose Islamic law or Sharia throughout every society in the world."[1] In a documentary film with the same title produced by the group Citizens United, an organization "dedicated to restoring government to citizens' control," Gingrich decries the blindness of the federal government.[2] If the war is said to have "no name," it is because the members of the Obama administration now refuse to use adjectives such as "Islamist" and "Islamic" to describe America's enemies.[3] How does one win a war against an enemy that one refuses to name? To answer this question, the documentary offers testimony from people presented as recognized experts on Islam and terrorism, such as the oriental studies specialist Bernard Lewis; the neoconservative former ambassador to the United Nations, John Bolton; and neoconservative editorialists Frank Gaffney and Michael Ledeen. For all these witnesses, as for Gingrich, the enemy does have a name—radical Islamism—and its main feature is its devotion to Sharia.

Taking inspiration from this documentary, many political leaders, essayists, and activists also try to show how and why Sharia now represents one of the most urgent threats to the survival of the United States. The Oak Initiative is an organization of evangelical and charismatic leaders who seek to respond to the crisis they see traversing America by restoring "the core values that are based on biblical or kingdom principles and wisdom."[4] On September 24, 2010, it disseminated on its website an interview with one of its members, Lieutenant General Jerry Boykin, a former deputy undersecretary of defense for intelligence (2003–2007) and a born-again fundamentalist Christian. He stated, "We need to realize that Islam itself is not simply a religion, it's a totalitarian way of life. It is a legal system, the law of Sharia; it's a financial system, it's a moral code, it's a political system, it's a military system. Islam should not be protected by the First Amendment, especially when one knows that those who obey the diktat of the Koran are duty bound to destroy our Constitution and to replace it with Sharia law."[5] Starting in 2010, such statements were freely repeated in the media and at political meetings, especially those of Republican candidates. In unison with Newt Gingrich and Michele Bachmann, a Republican presidential candidate momentarily in 2012, the Catholic conservative former senator Rick Santorum (R-Pa.) asserted at a campaign dinner speech in March 2011 that "jihadism is evil and we need to say what it is. . . . Sharia law is incompatible with American jurisprudence and our Constitution."[6]

What is this so-called anti-Sharia movement that rose up in the United States around 2010 and where did it come from? It derives from the activism of a network of political actors, lawyers, conservative polemicists, think tanks, and lobbies all as hostile to the Obama administration as they are to Muslims and Islam. The antimosque movement was born from the encounter between grassroots organizers residing in particular neighborhoods and local communities and national conservative organizations. The anti-Sharia movement, though, was made out of whole cloth by a small team of individual players and organizations whose goal has been to push ever more rightward the political agenda of conservative Republicans. Newt Gingrich's speech may be considered the inaugural moment of this movement before the American people, but the double denunciation of both radical Islamism and the naïveté of the Obama administration's response to "global terror" has been a leitmotif of the Far Right conservatives since 2008. These alarmist themes were developed in congressional hearings held on March 10, 2011 under the direction of Representative Peter T. King (R-N.Y.), who served as chairman of the House Committee on Homeland Security. The hearings aimed to examine "the extent of radicalization in the American Muslim community and that community's response," with the goal of discussing forms of violence that are specific to Islam. Another goal was to denounce the inadequate commitment of Muslim Americans in fighting the war on terror. The anti-Sharia movement is defined by a precise objective: using legal measures in order to ban all reference to Islamic law from U.S. courts. But the stakes of this legal battle are, above all, political. The objective is to prolong the controversy over Islam in order to saturate the debate with arguments hostile not only to Muslims but, more importantly, to the Obama administration, the Democratic Party, and a certain conception of liberal democracy—and even toward certain conservative Republicans who are considered to be too moderate.

THE ANTI-SHARIA ORGANIZATIONS

At the base of this political and legal battle is a network of organizations that have been working for several years to build an argument hostile toward Islam and collect facts and documents likely to further their point of view.

One of the leading actors in this movement is the Center for Security Policy (CSP), a think tank created in 1988 and presided over by Frank Gaffney whose stated goal is "peace through strength." Praise of American exceptionalism, warnings against attacks on national sovereignty, and admiring references to the Reagan legacy are at the heart of the CSP ideology. Islamic extremism is the new enemy, replacing the Communist enemy of the Reagan era: "We as a nation must also work to undermine the ideological foundations of totalitarianism and Islamist extremism with at least as much skill, discipline and tenacity as President Reagan employed against Communism to prevail in the Cold War."[7] Gaffney, a deputy assistant secretary of defense under Ronald Reagan and an editorialist for conservative media such as the *Washington Times* and WorldNetDaily, also hosts a radio show on Secure Freedom Radio. Since roughly 2000, he has made the fight against "Islamist totalitarianism" a centerpiece of his campaign to protect the Reagan legacy from the Democrats—and also from certain Republicans who are deemed to be too soft on Muslims. Besides relying on a committee of counselors and a set of academic advisers, the think tank is rather exceptional for also having a military committee composed of about ten retired generals and admirals.[8] The job of these three committees is to define a strategy to win the battle against radical Muslims and their moderate allies who seek to weaken the vigilance of American public opinion by posing as victims. Nonie Darwish, currently a senior fellow at the CSP, is a key figure in the promotion of this narrative. An American of Egyptian origin and the founder in 2004 of Arabs for Israel and a member of Former Muslims United, she plays perfectly the role of the disaffected-Muslim-woman-converted-to-Christianity, and her biography lends an air of authenticity, legitimacy, and credibility to her criticism.[9] Darwish is the author of two books that play on the most common stereotypes about Islam, which is presented as a bellicose, violent, conquering religion hostile toward women; she publishes a blog that includes sensational stories of female Muslims burned alive and Christian women forced to convert; and she is a regular participant in televised debates on Fox News. In the area of foreign policy, the CSP relentlessly denounces the Obama administration's submissiveness toward international treaties and diktats of the United Nations and its inability to protect American sovereignty.

In 2010, the CSP published a detailed 177-page report that aims to explain why Sharia represents a grave threat to the survival of the United States. Directed by Frank Gaffney, its complete title is *Shariah: The Threat to America: An Exercise in Competitive Analysis: Report of Team B II*.[10] The title alludes to a "Team B" report prepared in 1976 by a group of international security experts on the request of George H. W. Bush, then director of the Central Intelligence Agency. That report's goal was to contest the "official evaluation" in intelligence circles concerning the offensive capacities of the Soviet Union as well as the politics of détente that it ostensibly defended. The authors of the Team B II report assert that, even though the Islamic threat has replaced the Communist threat, the credulity and incapacity of the Obama government to guarantee national security are analogous to the weaknesses of those in charge of the politics of détente a generation ago. Among the report's authors, besides the research associates of the CSP, one finds editorialists from the conservative press and self-proclaimed security consultants, Lieutenant General Jerry Boykin, former FBI agent John Guandolo, former CIA director James Woolsey, and former assistant U.S. attorney for New York Andrew C. McCarthy III.[11] To prove that Sharia is incompatible with the U.S. Constitution, the report asserts that Islam is not strictly speaking a religion but is actually a political and legal code that aspires to subvert every existing political order: "It is a political, military, legal doctrine, rather than a religion as defined by American standards. . . . In reality, Islam is a revolutionary ideology and a program that seeks to transform the social order of the entire world, and reconstruct it in conformity with its principles and ideals."[12] Adhering to Sharia is contrary to the spirit of America's Constitution because it implies submitting one's will to God and hence the renunciation of freedom: "Moreover, Sharia is a doctrine that imposes the rule of Allah over all aspects of society. More precisely, contrary to the Virginia Statute for Religious Freedom, and in a way absolutely incompatible with it, Sharia asserts that God did not create freewill but tied it to the will of Allah—the condition of human beings is submission to Allah and not freedom."[13] It is thus urgent, the report's authors believe, to protect the Constitution from Sharia. They also insist on the primacy of popular sovereignty: "Note that 'We, the people' create the Constitution; the Constitution does not create 'We, the people.' 'The people' as the founding entity was created by the voluntary act of consent to the principles in the *Declaration of Independence*. In creating the Constitution to guarantee natural rights and liberties, the people acted from its sovereign capacity."[14] This people, united and already constituted, may at any moment decide to suspend the guaranteed constitutional protections when faced with a threatening minority that is not part of "the people." Here one is far from the liberal approach to constitutional democracy, which affirms equal rights for all and extends legal protections to religious minorities to shelter them from the chance winds of popular will.

Many other organizations and media personalities joined the CSP's anti-Sharia campaign. Think tanks such as the Ethics and Public Policy Center (EPPC) worked on producing arguments and proof of the Islamic threat. Lobbies of conservative lawyers, such as the American Public Policy Alliance (APPA) and the American Center for Law and Justice (ACLJ) offer legal counsel and pressure politicians in various states. Grassroots organizations, both religious and nonreligious and of various sizes, seek to alert and mobilize local communities. Examples are the Concerned Women for America (CWA) and the Florida Family Association (FFA). These groups bring together former anti-Communist intellectuals and activists, diehard Reagan fans, American Copts and Maronites originally from the Middle East, and ordinary citizens still in shock after September 11, 2001, and the financial crisis of 2008. Despite their differences, all these organizations defend a single set of themes. Their aim is to protect America's heritage of "Judeo-Christian" values against the dual threat of Islam and liberal secularism by militating, for example, in favor of obligatory prayer in public schools, teaching creationism, and a larger place accorded to religion in public spaces. The theme of freedom—religious and economic—occupies a central place in their thinking alongside ferocious criticism of the policy objectives of the Obama administration. This means, for example, favoring a tough stand on immigration and expressing fierce opposition to health-care reform—that is, the Affordable Care Act, maligned as "Obamacare" by its detractors. These organizations favor a minimalist government and express with bitterness that the American people's constitutional rights are endangered by what they consider to be the antidemocratic legalism or "juristocracy" imposed by liberal Democrats. Within this discourse, a Europe invaded, terrorized by Islamic groups, and turned into "Eurabia" is cast in a central role as negative example. In order *not* to go the way of Europe, these organizations believe it's important to launch a preemptive war against the risk of Islamic infiltration. Organizations that defend Muslim American rights, such as the Council on American-Islamic Relations (CAIR) and the Muslim Public Affairs Council (MPAC), and are believed by the anti-Sharia camp to be in the pocket of the Muslim Brotherhood are thus a prime target.

Besides the network of anti-Sharia organizations, certain individuals have played key roles alongside Frank Gaffney—two of the most prominent being Brigitte Gabriel and David Yerushalmi. In 2003, Gabriel, an American of Lebanese Maronite-Christian origin, founded ACT! for America, an organization entirely devoted to the fight against "radical Islam." The American Congress for Truth (ACT!) has many chapters in different states and abroad (including India, Israel, Canada, Argentina, and Norway). Presenting herself as "one of the leading national security experts in the world," Gabriel perfectly fulfills the role of one who has known and undergone Islamic violence "from the inside" and whose testimony is thus all the more authentic. A former television news anchor, Gabriel arrived in the United States in 1989 after marrying an American. Since then, she has ceaselessly denounced America's political correctness, which she says causes it to be blind to the true nature of Islam. Besides telling whenever asked the story of her Lebanese childhood and how she lived in terror until the day she was rescued by Israeli soldiers, Gabriel repeats over and over on her website, at demonstrations, and as a frequent television guest her hatred for Islam and her support of Israel. She is the author of several pamphlet-style publications hostile to Islam and appears regularly on Fox News to support claims that violence and conquest are inherent characteristics of Islam. The ACT! for America website currently claims to have "280,000 members organized in more than 890 chapters nationwide and 11 countries worldwide." Gabriel has also hosted her own cable television show with Guy Rodgers, a former consultant to leaders of the Christian Coalition such as Ralph Reed, Pat Buchanan, and Pat Robertson.

On July 30, 2011, *New York Times* journalist Andrea Elliot published a profile of David Yerushalmi, a Brooklyn lawyer and Hasidic Jew, titled "The Man Behind the Anti-Sharia Movement."[15] Born in 1956, Yerushalmi lived until 2001 in the West Bank Israeli colony of Ma'ale Adumim and gained attention for his provocative remarks about women and blacks. In a 2006 essay, he lashed out at the culture of "political correctness" that prevents people from admitting the existence of genetically determined differences between races. Why, he asks, do "people find it so difficult to confront the facts that some races perform better in sports, some better in mathematical problem-solving, some better in language, some better in Western societies and some better in tribal ones?"[16] In the same essay, in a discussion of the American Founding Fathers, Yerushalmi seems to suggest that women and blacks should not have the right to vote: "There's got to be a reason if the Founding Fathers did not give the right to vote to women or to black slaves. You may not approve or like this idea, but the founders of this country . . . certainly took it seriously."[17]

Persuaded that the goal of Islam, unlike that of other religions, is conquest, Yerushalmi is particularly hostile toward two leading Muslim American organizations, CAIR and MPAC, which he believes are Trojan horses of the Muslim Brotherhood. He and his associates cite as proof of an alleged project to subvert the American Constitution a document made public during an investigation of the Holy Land Foundation for Relief and Development, a charitable organization based in Texas whose members were convicted in 2008 for sending funds to Hamas. This document explained that the strategy of the Muslim Brotherhood in the United States ought to seek "to eliminate and destroy Western civilization from the inside." A list of twenty-nine Muslim American associations, including CAIR, also appeared in the document.

Yerushalmi has been highly criticized as a fundamentalist bigot by the Anti-Defamation League, a civil rights organization defending especially Jewish Americans. But besides being a member of CSP and a coauthor of its Sharia threat report, he also created his own organization to promote anti-Sharia legislation: the Society of Americans for National Existence (SANE). Its goal is to "reinforce the national existence of America by leading a new and thorough discussion that others fear or avoid." Its website, the organization's principal mode of existence, is open to members only for a fee of $150 per month. It mostly disseminates editorials in which Yerushalmi asserts the danger of Sharia, attacks Muslim American organizations, decries and discards the criticisms of his work made by liberal organizations, and offers advertising links to sites inviting Muslims to renounce Islam.

If all these organizations are well funded and well connected to conservative media outlets, especially Fox News, their power to harm ought not to be exaggerated. For one thing, the notoriety of each group is linked more to the charisma and prolixity of one or two media-made stars (Gaffney for CPS, Gabriel for ACT!, the Sekulows for ACLJ) than to well-organized and sustained activism. Certainly each group claims to have a large number of members and an abundance of local representatives. In some cases, such as CWA, the local "grassroots" do in fact exist, but for others this is more bald assertion than proven fact. Their dynamism depends, above all, on their high decibel level and their talent for occupying considerable airtime with simple and frequently repeated arguments that are relayed by cutting and pasting from one to another. Wajahat Ali, an expert at the Center for American Progress (CAP), said about the FFA initiative of David Caton against the reality show *All-American Muslim*, "It's literally one dude with a poorly made Web site, one fringe individual with an e-mail list, but by parroting the talking points created by this incestuous network, he's triggered a national crisis."[18] In truth, the anti-Sharia

ANTI-SHARIA PRESSURE GROUPS

The Ethics and Public Policy Center (EPPC)

This think tank was founded in 1973 by Ernest W. Lefever, a specialist of moral and Christian philosophy, to be a guardian of the "Judeo-Christian moral tradition." It seeks to defend "the major Western imperatives" such as respect for human dignity, individual liberty, and minimalist government. Permanent members of the EPPC include conservative Christian intellectuals and researchers. George Weigel, a Catholic theologian and the author of several books including a biography of Pope John Paul II, has been writing since 2005 about the threat of Eurabia and radical Islamism. Michael Cromartie, vice president of the EPPC and a former member (named by George W. Bush) of the Commission on International Religious Freedom (2004–2010), is the author of many books on the place of evangelicals in American politics. Republican Rick Santorum, a former U.S. senator and one-time presidential candidate, was a member of EPPC up to June 2011. He created within the organization the Program to Promote and Protect America's Freedom, which is essentially a series of pieces by Santorum himself about radical Islam. Even though the EPPC is less virulent than the CSP in the anti-Sharia campaign, Santorum played a key intermediary role funneling ideas from the CSP to the EPPC in his numerous articles about the invasion of Europe by Muslim radicals, the danger of Islamic financing schemes, and the lack of religious freedom in the Muslim world.

The American Public Policy Alliance (APPA)

Created in 2009, this nonpartisan group says it wishes to work toward better protection of the Constitution and the sovereignty of the United States. A spokesperson for APPA, Stephen Gelé, a New Orleans lawyer, used his influence to get a law adopted in Louisiana that would prohibit all references to foreign law. For members of APPA, "transnationalism" is today the number-one threat to American security and sovereignty.* Supported by Frank Gaffney, James Woolsey, and Jerry Boykin, this pressure group played an important role promoting the template of anti-Sharia legislation developed by the lawyer David Yerushalmi. While appearing neutral, its main goal is to forbid all references to Sharia. The organization seeks to apply pressure on state legislatures to alert them about the danger that Sharia represents for subverting the U.S. Constitution. The APPA is also engaged in the fight against liberal organizations such as the ACLU and CAP as well as Muslim organizations such as Karamah, whose analyses it systematically disputes or discredits.

The American Center for Law and Justice (ACLJ)

This conservative pressure group, led by Jay Sekulow and his son Jordan, uses teams of lawyers to intervene in many trials about religious freedom, abortion, and immigration. Since 2008, the privileged targets of the ACLJ have been fights against Obamacare, abortion, and immigration. The group also strongly backs Israel and Christians in the Middle East. The ACLJ has taken a particular interest in the persecution stories of Christian Iranian pastors and Egyptian priests, and makes detailed use of these accounts as evidence of the barbarism of the Muslim world and the incompatibility of Islam with religious freedom. With close ties to conservative media stars such as Glenn Beck and Sean Hannity, the Sekulows are a regular presence in the media, often on Fox News. The ACLJ also has offices abroad in Israel, Russia, Kenya, France, Pakistan, and Zimbabwe. Through various intermediaries, the organization attempts to influence international debates on the topic of religious freedom. It played a notable role, for example, in the European controversy about the presence of the crucifix in Italian classrooms. The group participates actively in current debates in many African countries about homosexuality and puts pressure on governments to adopt laws hostile toward homosexuals.†

Concerned Women for America (CWA)

Part lobby, part grassroots movement, this conservative group was founded in 1979 around six major themes: defense of family, opposition to abortion, religious liberty, education, the fight against pornography, and safeguarding American sovereignty. Present in all fifty states, CWA claims to have 500,000 members in five hundred local chapters, which lends the organization credibility as a grassroots organization of day-to-day activism. The group was founded by Beverly LaHaye, the wife of Tim LaHaye, an evangelical pastor and the author of the apocalyptic series Left Behind,‡ originally to counter the feminist activism of Betty Friedan. The group lobbies members of Congress to maintain prayer in public schools; to discourage HPV vaccines (in the name of abstinence before marriage); and against rights for homosexuals, whom they consider to be morally deviant. CWA's engagement in the anti-Sharia movement is not based on an emancipation agenda like one finds among European secular feminists fighting against head scarves and burkas. CWA rejects Sharia in the name of its desire to defend America's Christian identity and its sovereignty. Liberal and republican (in the European senses of those terms) European feminists may attack certain Muslim symbols in the name of principles of secularism (in French, laïcité) and equality, but CWA women entered the anti-Sharia battle by way of a particular discourse about sovereignty and culture. More discreet than the APPA at the national level, CWA is nevertheless very active on the local level. In every small city or town in America, CWA women are present at any and all demonstrations against mosques and Sharia.

The Florida Family Association (FFA)

This group, originally named the American Family Association, was founded in 1987 by David Caton, a former accountant and, according to his own testimony, former pornography addict turned born-again Christian. After years of activism against pornography and rights for homosexuals, he began to target Muslim Americans. Publishing an endless stream of hostile articles against organizations such as CAIR, he gained prominence in 2011 for his attack against the reality series *All-American Muslim*, which features the daily lives of individual Muslim Americans. Caton's main criticism was that the show presents an overly normal image of Muslim Americans. The show's lack of alarming stereotypes is precisely the danger because it risks weakening the proper vigilance of the American public. The FFA thus pressured over one hundred companies to withdraw their advertising support for the show.

The Religious Freedom Coalition (RFC)

This Washington-based nonprofit organization was created in 1982 to save America's "Judeo-Christian heritage" by lobbying the public and members of Congress for the right to pray in public schools, and against abortion and gay marriage. On foreign topics, the group sounds alarms about the persecution of Christians in the Middle East and endlessly denounces the negative influence of the United Nations and Islamic law. The RFC's president, William J. Murray, was the leader of an anti-Communist organization in the 1980s called Freedom's Friends. In the 1990s, he established one of the first publishing houses to print Bibles in the former Soviet Union. The RFC was active in the fight against the Islamic center in New York and against the mosque in Murfreesboro.

The Sharia Awareness Action Network (SAAN)

This network is a coalition of individuals and organizations whose goal is to resist the threat of Sharia infiltration. The network includes most of the organizations just mentioned. In November 2011, SAAN organized the conference "Constitution or Sharia: A Freedom Conference" and invited the leaders of all its affiliated groups. Although the conference was originally to take place in the Hutton Hotel in Nashville, Tennessee, the hotel decided to break its contract with SAAN at the last minute out of fear of troubles that such a gathering might provoke. The conference was finally held at the Cornerstone Pentecostal megachurch in the small town of Madison, about twenty miles from Nashville.

*The APPA website's homepage states: "One of the greatest threats to American values and liberties today comes from abroad, including foreign laws and foreign legal doctrines which have been infiltrating our court system at the municipal, state and federal levels. This phenomenon is known as 'transnationalism' and includes the use of international law and foreign law in court opinions when those conflict with both Constitutional liberties and protections, and state public policy" (http://publicpolicyalliance.org/about/).

†On this point, see Kapya John Kaoma, *Colonizing Africa: How the U.S. Christian Right Is Transforming Sexual Politics in Africa* (Somerville, Mass.: Political Research Association, 2012).

‡The Left Behind series, published between 1995 and 2007, consists of sixteen volumes dealing with Christian dispensationalist End Times. It was a best seller in the United States and abroad.

movement is not so much a stable, broadly based network of powerful organizations with an uncontested capacity to mobilize overwhelming force as it is a patchwork of certain key figures within the world of Christian conservatism (such as the Sekulows) and more marginal figures such as Gabriel, Pamela Geller, and Caton. As famous as they may be, thanks to their thirst for media attention, the leaders of the anti-Sharia movement are in a way second fiddles within the Republican Party and the conservative movement. From one group to another, one finds the same names among its leaders (Gaffney, Woolsey, Yerushalmi, Boykin). The serial quotations and the ceremonial circular deference create the illusion of power and of access to diverse sources of influence, whereas in reality it's always the same small group of people who appear in every debate and at each conference. What's more, as we shall see, the anti-Sharia movement was in a sense the result of failure. It's because its leaders were unable to convince the true leaders of the conservative movement or those of the Republican Party or in federal agencies of the pertinence of their project that they were forced to turn instead to state-level legislative bodies and gamble on the anti-Washington reflexes of many state and local politicians.

Yerushalmi openly admits that he changed strategies in the spring of 2008 after having failed to convince the Treasury Department about the danger of banking practices according to the rules of Sharia.[19]

A PRETEXT: THE NEW JERSEY AFFAIR

Feeling confident about the strong support coming from these organizations, the proponents of anti-Sharia legislation seized on a case being heard in a New Jersey court in 2010. The judge in the case had refused to issue a restraining order against a man of Moroccan origin who was accused by his wife, also of Moroccan origin and married by force at age seventeen, of repeatedly raping her. According to the victim, the husband reportedly said that such acts were in accordance with the Muslim religion: "The woman, she should submit and do anything I ask her to do."[20] On June 30, 2009, the judge ruled in favor of the husband, who, he said, had acted without criminal intention but simply in conformity with his conscience and his religion. In June 2010, the first judge's decision was appealed, and the reference to religious freedom was rejected by the Superior Court as a nonpertinent criterion: "The defendant's behavior when he attempted to have nonconsensual sexual relations was undeniably intentional, no matter what his belief might have been about his religion permitting him to behave as he did."[21] The Superior Court judge ruled that the first judge "was mistaken" when he excused the husband's behavior out of consideration for his religious beliefs, and went on to issue the restraining order against the husband. For the anti-Sharia camp, this affair proved the reality of Sharia's infiltration into the American judicial system. Such a generalization is surprising. Since the error of judgment of the lower court judge was corrected and his decision reversed by the appellate judge, the case seems to illustrate the good working order of the American justice system and not, as alleged, its submission to Islamic law.

In fact, many cases involving Muslim individuals or families where explicit references have been made to Sharia or Islam had up until then been handled by American courts with the strictest respect for American law and without causing the least problem. Indeed, up to that point Islam had been accorded little attention in legal debates about the First Amendment, the most heated disputes having actually been caused by claims coming from Christian groups. Generally speaking, in resolving these conflicts, the pragmatism of American judges outweighs ideology. Thus in the many cases involving the *mahr* clause, a feature proper to Islamic divorce, one finds among American judges and lawyers neither Islamophobic presuppositions nor categorical refusals on principle to refer to Sharia but rather a concern to resolve the conflicts in each case individually by striking a balance between respect for the religious beliefs of the parties in conflict and respect for the First Amendment's establishment clause.[22]

In other words, the anti-Sharia bills appear as a solution to a nonexistent problem. But that was beside the point for the anti-Sharia activists. For them, the very act of pronouncing the word "Islam" in an American court is a problem, and even proof of an Islamic threat. Theirs is a preemptive war. The guiding thought in this combat is not "We should respond to repeated, verified infractions against individual liberties" but rather "And what if, one day, Islamism manages to subvert the American Constitution and justice system?" Many anti-Sharia activists admit that the starting point of their involvement was not a genuine infringement of individual freedoms but imagining the establishment of an Islamic legal system on American territory. If the anti-Sharia movement is somewhat baffling, it's more on account of its leaders' mode of reasoning than their Islamophobic statements, which are mostly garden-variety slurs. After all, if one is willing to say that a purely fictional threat requires a reaction as firm as a real threat, then why not ask for preventive measures against a hypothetical invasion from outer space or against the future domination of America by China? What is surprising is not so much the virulence or absurdity of the anti-Sharia arguments but the increasing blurriness of the border between fiction and reality in public debates and in courtroom proceedings. For Sharia opponents, what matters most is affirming the right of the American people to be the proper guardian of the Constitution—against the wishful thinking and dilettantism of overly liberal judges and lawyers. "It's wrong," says Stephen Gelé, "to just accept that the courts generally get it right, but sometimes get it wrong. There is no reason to make a woman play a legal game of Russian roulette."[23]

OKLAHOMA AGAINST SHARIA

The Oklahoma referendum constitutes Act I—the first test case—of the anti-Sharia movement. Shortly before the midterm elections in November 2010, two Republicans, Senator Rex Duncan and Representative Mike Reynolds, proposed an amendment to the Oklahoma state constitution that would prohibit any reference to Sharia in Oklahoma courts. On Election Day, November 2, in a state where Muslims represent less than 1 percent of the population and where Sharia had up until then never been mentioned in any court, 70 percent of the people voted in favor of the amendment. "Question 755," nicknamed "Save Our State Amendment," whose aim was to modify the state Constitution's article 7.1 (relating to the prerogatives of the courts), proposed the following changes: "The courts shall not look to the legal precepts of other nations or cultures. Specifically, the courts shall not consider international law or Sharia law."[24] The latter was defined very vaguely: "Sharia law is Islamic law. It is founded on two principle sources: the Koran and the teachings of Mohammad."

Why was such an amendment proposed when the authors themselves agreed that there had never been any conflict linked to Sharia in any Oklahoma state court? In fact, the New Jersey affair is routinely cited as the proof of the imminent reality of the risk of subversion of American law by Islam, regardless of the fact that the "mistaken" decision of the first judge was reversed on appeal. In this alarmist scenario, Europe plays a central role as negative example. In an interview on MSNBC on June 11, 2010, Duncan described his amendment project as a "preventive strike": "This is a war for the survival of America—it's a culture war." This war's goal is to reassert America's Christian values. Representative Reynolds, coauthor of the amendment, went on to add: "America was founded on Judeo-Christian values, it's the basis of our laws and some people are trying to deny that. . . . I think people are becoming aware of the fate of our Christian values in our country, and they're beginning to speak up."[25]

After the election, on November 4, Muneer Awad, the director of the local CAIR chapter, filed a lawsuit against the state's electoral commission. He asked that the amendment be declared unconstitutional on the grounds that it violates the First Amendment for several reasons.

The changes would prevent the state of Oklahoma from making regulations to guarantee that businesses were not selling fake halal products to their customers. Practicing Muslims would no longer be able to have written in their wills the desire to be buried according to Muslim tradition. A couple would no longer be able to be married, beyond a civil union, according to an Islamic marriage contract, or to borrow money to buy a home in conformity with Islamic economic principles. These restrictions, Awad added, are all the more unacceptable since they target only Muslims. It is not prohibited to refer to canon law or the Ten Commandments, only Sharia. In other words, by preventing Muslims from freely exercising their religious freedom in many instances of ordinary daily life, and by "specifically" taking Islam as its target and not other religions, the Save Our State Amendment violates both the free exercise clause and the establishment clause of the First Amendment. It also violates the clause relating to the supremacy of the American Constitution, which affirms the priority of federal law over the laws of the states and requires that they apply the international treaties entered into by the federal government.[26]

On November 29, 2010, after a day of hearings, the district court judge in Oklahoma City, Vicki Miles-LaGrange, issued a temporary injunction against the electoral commission to prevent it from enacting the amendment.[27] Her decision shows that we are faced here with two opposing approaches to law. Those in favor of the state constitutional amendment see themselves as defending the will of the people. The latter must assert its right to proclaim the Constitution and stand up against the liberal elite of incompetent judges who endanger the nation's sovereignty and the heritage of the Founding Fathers. On the other side, the judge reaffirms the principle of constitutional democracy, which protects the fundamental rights of minorities against the whims of the majority:

> Throughout the course of our country's history, the will of the "majority" has on occasion conflicted with the constitutional rights of individuals, an occurrence which our founders foresaw and provided for through the Bill of Rights. As the United States Supreme Court has stated: "The very purpose of a Bill of Rights was to withdraw certain subjects from the vicissitudes of political controversy, to place them beyond the reach of majorities and officials and to establish them as legal principles to be applied

by the courts. One's right to life, liberty, and property, to free speech, a free press, freedom of worship and assembly, and other fundamental rights may not be submitted to vote; they depend on the outcome of no elections."[28]

In reply to those who protested against the antidemocratic character of this overturning of the result of a democratic election, the judge made the following statement: "While the public has an interest in the will of the voters being carried out, for the reasons set forth above, the Court finds that the public has a more profound and long-term interest in upholding an individual's constitutional rights."[29] In other words, the claims of those supporting the Save Our State Amendment notwithstanding, the majority that appointed itself sole arbiter to define and represent who the "people" would be does not always get its way and does not have unlimited rights. The amendment's supporters immediately denounced the judge's decision, seeing in it but one more proof of the contempt of judges for the popular will.

The use by the amendment's supporters of notions of "injury" and "suffering" is characteristic of the populist mode of reasoning. As in the case of those opposed to the Manhattan Islamic center, the anti-Sharia activists refuse to countenance the rights of Muslims because it's not about rights; it's about the survival of America. In reply to Awad's oral arguments, the defendant counters that the plaintiff (Awad) did not undergo any "injury in fact." In other words, the imagined harm caused by Sharia in a hypothetical future on generations to come is considered as a more pertinent basis for action than the real and present harm caused to Muslims currently living in Oklahoma. In similar fashion, during the Ground Zero controversy, the painful memory of September 11 was presented as sufficient grounds for depriving Muslims of their right to build a community center. But ultimately this reasoning was rejected by the courts. The district court in Oklahoma City upholds, contrary to the defense's views, that the injury is "concrete, particularized, and imminent" such that one may accept the legal case of Awad.[30]

On December 1, 2010, however, the defendant's side appealed the decision. But on January 10, 2012, the U.S. Court of Appeals for the Tenth Circuit ruled that the amendment drafted by Rex Duncan and Mike Reynolds was indeed unconstitutional, and it decided to definitively block its ratification.[31] The decision handed down by the court reiterates the arguments of Vicki Miles-LaGrange: respect for election results is essential, but the constitutional protection of minorities must be defended unconditionally: "But when the law that voters wish to enact is likely unconstitutional, their interests do not outweigh Mr. Awad's in having his constitutional rights protected."[32] The judges also ruled that Question 755 is discriminatory because it explicitly singles out Islam and no other religion. The defense's claim that all religions were in fact implied but only Sharia was mentioned as an example was rejected as contradictory, given "the amendment's plain language, which mentions Sharia law in two places."[33] The amendment as proposed stipulated that "courts shall not look to the legal precepts of other nations or cultures." The defense was unable to convince the court that "other cultures" implies all religions and is not just targeting Islam. This reasoning does not stand up to scrutiny: "The amendment bans only one form of religious law—Sharia law. Even if we accept Appellants' argument that we should interpret 'cultures' to include 'religions,' the text does not ban all religious laws."[34] Unless the attorney general for the state of Oklahoma decides to appeal that decision, in which case the matter would be turned over for an eventual decision by the Supreme Court, the Save Our State Amendment may be considered definitively invalid.

AMERICAN LAW FOR AMERICAN COURTS

Although the Oklahoma controversy seems to end in defeat for the supporters of anti-Sharia legislation, they very quickly apply the lessons learned from this experience. Throughout this affair, legal specialists were elaborating a more presentable version of the legislation that does not specifically target Islam. David Yerushalmi, working on behalf of APPA, drafted a legislative proposal called "American Law for American Courts" (ALAC). The objective was "to protect the constitutional rights of American citizens against the infiltration and incursion of foreign laws and foreign legal doctrines, especially the Islamic law of Sharia." As with the Sharia report put out by the CSP, the preamble of ALAC insists on the necessity of safeguarding the true heritage of the Founding Fathers, protecting the Constitution, asserting the people's right over the Constitution, and strongly defending American sovereignty. In this combat, state legislative bodies "have a vital role to play to preserve these constitutional rights and the American values about liberty." America's exceptional status, recalls the preamble, rests on its dedication to freedom of religion, freedom of speech and of the press, the right to due process, the right to privacy, and the right to have and to bear arms. While holding back on making any explicit reference to Sharia, ALAC proposes the following declaration: "The [general assembly / legislature] finds that it shall be the public policy of this state to protect its citizens from the application of foreign laws when the application of a foreign law will result in the violation of a right guaranteed by the constitution of this state or of the United States."[35] This "model legislation," even if it seems less openly in violation of the First Amendment, remains problematic and is arguably senseless. One may ask what the point is of a law that reaffirms what exists already—the impossibility for any state to pass a law that would violate the Constitution. Furthermore, while the law first speaks simply of "foreign law," it goes on to specify in the second paragraph the interdiction of applying a "foreign law, legal code or system." The latter are more precisely defined as a "system of a jurisdiction outside of any state or territory of the United States, including, but not limited to, international organizations and tribunals." This wording seems, however, to be in conflict with the Constitution's supremacy clause and in contradiction with the last paragraph of the legislative proposal itself, which states: "This statute shall not be interpreted by any court to conflict with any federal treaty or other international agreement to which the United States is a party to the extent that such treaty or international agreement preempts or is superior to state law on the matter at issue."

The anti-Sharia camp immediately adopted this model legislation as the most effective instrument in the legal battle against an "Islamic invasion." Senator Michael Fair in South Carolina said he had learned the lessons from the Oklahoma case and was careful to leave out any mention of Sharia from his bill. Senator Phil Jensen, the initiator of a similar bill in South Dakota, did the same.[36] In Arizona, the wording of a first bill went as far as explicitly banning from its courts all reference "to principles of any body of sectarian religious law" including "the law of Sharia, Canon law, *halakha* and karma [*sic*]." After this early version of the bill was rejected, one with a more neutral appearance, modeled entirely on the ALAC template, was passed on April 12, 2011. A similar law, also following the ALAC template, was passed in Louisiana on July 2, 2010. In Tennessee, a bill that directly attacked Islam and Sharia was withdrawn and replaced with a more neutral one. The first bill, proposed by Senator Bill Ketron and Representative Judd Matheny, wanted to make referring to Sharia a felony punishable by up to fifteen years in prison. It defined Sharia as a major threat that "obliges all of its members to actively and passively seek to replace the constitutional American republic, including the representative government of this state, with a political system founded on Sharia."[37] The bill that finally passed was based on the model legislation proposed by David Yerushalmi.

As of January 2016, laws have been passed in the states of Louisiana, Tennessee, Arizona, Alabama, Florida, North Carolina, Oklahoma, and Texas—and bills that take the ALAC wording as their model are under discussion in more than twenty states, even if the anti-Sharia movement may appear to be losing steam.[38] An anti-Sharia bill was withdrawn in New Jersey after resistance from Muslim and civil rights organizations. In 2011, similar bills were set aside in Arkansas, Maine, Texas, and Wyoming. Others are near to being abandoned in Georgia, Indiana, Iowa, and Mississippi, although some could still return because the movement has proved to be quite resistant. In March 2012, South Dakota governor Dennis Daugaard, under pressure from anti-Sharia activists, signed a law that followed the ALAC model. And similar laws are on the verge of passing in Kansas, Oklahoma, Florida, and Alaska.

The debates that have taken place in all these states since 2010 and the changed strategy after the Oklahoma defeat demonstrate that the anti-Sharia movement is well organized if somewhat fumbling, and yet is capable of adjusting its strategy on the fly in reaction to its adversaries' moves. It also pursues multiple political, legal, and media objectives, all simultaneously. This is why the anti-Sharia legislation advocates do not shy away from bills as grotesque as the one in Arizona and consider the decision of the appeals court in Oklahoma as only a setback, not a defeat. For them, what counts is keeping the debate over Sharia and Islam front and center and having the fight continue. They also embrace the technique of first proposing extreme, far-out bills and then eventually backing down somewhat so as to more easily reach a compromise on legislation that is still problematic but looks more reasonable and acceptable in comparison. Thus it's always a winning strategy on all fronts—politically, legally, and in the media. What may look amateurish and clueless often turns out to be proof of their resistance and resourcefulness. Commenting on the appeals court decision on the Oklahoma referendum, Frank Gaffney simply reaffirmed the importance of the anti-Sharia movement. He concedes that the amendment as worded could only end up being rejected. But fortunately, he adds, the model legislation developed by Yerushalmi would allow the fight to continue and avoid such setbacks. What counts is "to pursue in Oklahoma and elsewhere across the country other means of achieving the same end—namely, protecting American citizens from foreign laws whose application in U.S. courts would violate their constitutional rights or state public policy."[39]

CHANGING THE CONDITIONS OF COMPROMISE

Asked many times to give concrete examples that prove the need for an anti-Sharia law during hearings of the North Carolina House of Representatives in April 2011, Representative George Cleveland ended up saying, "I don't have any precise examples in mind." In March 2011, in the House of Representatives in Missouri, Representative Paul Curtman gave the same answer to a similar question: "I don't have the details with me today. But if you go to . . . uh, I can't remember the name of the website. But any Google search on the use of International law in the United States in state courts will give you examples."[40] In almost every state where anti-Sharia laws have been discussed, senators and representatives in favor of the legislation have admitted that they know of no cases where reference to Islamic law in American courts had caused a problem. Thus as the ACLU and MPAC have noted, these bills offer "a solution in search of a problem."[41]

Not only are anti-Sharia activists often incapable of proving the reality of an Islamic threat, but the few cases they do put forward to strengthen their argument prove in fact exactly the reverse of what they allege. In a report published in May 2011, the ACLU considered one by one the cases cited by the APPA as proof of the existence of an Islamic threat.[42]

For example, the APPA cites the case of *Shaheed Allah v. Adella Jordan-Luster*. In 2007, a Muslim prisoner filed a complaint against the prison administration where he was held because halal meals were not served every day, which, he explained, prevented him from freely exercising his religion. The APPA sees this as a clear sign of the subversion of American law by Sharia. But according to the ACLU, if this case proves anything, it's exactly the opposite because, first, in this case the court rejected the prisoner's complaint and sided with the policy of the prison, which held that serving meals without pork was sufficient as respect for the religious constraints of the prisoner. Second, even if the court had sided with the prisoner, further accommodation would not have been contrary to American law. It would have been no different from measures that are regularly taken to satisfy certain dietary requirements of Jewish and Catholic prisoners.

But in the Sharia controversy, facts that actually prove the opposite of what they're supposed to show can nevertheless be cited as relevant proof. A fact becomes proof not because it corresponds to the concrete reality of what happens in courtrooms but because it solidifies a fantastical edifice constructed in advance. Thus the question of what Sharia truly is—a definition that Muslim and liberal organizations seek to establish—like the question of what exactly happens in courtrooms, is of hardly any importance.

For the partisans of the anti-Sharia movement, what matters above all is to win what they call the "lawfare." The term, derived from "warfare," literally means "the legal battle" but here refers to the battle that uses law for political and ideological purposes. The passage or not of anti-Sharia laws is practically a secondary matter. The first goal is to create, sustain, and amplify the controversy and thereby elevate ever higher the threshold of Islam's acceptability among the American people. David Yerushalmi stated in July 2010 that "if the law were to pass in all fifty states without any friction, it would not have fulfilled its goal. . . . The goal was heuristic; it was to push people to ask 'What is Sharia?' "[43] Similarly, in November 2011, he insisted on the decisive character of this lawfare, which opposes "American patriots" and "the union of the Muslim Brotherhood and progressives." Patriots must stand ready: "You're going to get bloodied, but at the end of the day you hope to draw more blood than you've lost."[44] The battle, he declared, will have negative consequences for Muslims and liberals no matter what the outcome. Because the more virulent and passionate the attack, the more difficult and costly will be the defense or counterattack of the opposing camp. If the general aim is to change the law, the specific tactics aim to change the behavior of the adversary:

> You have to get ready to pursue trials against the organizations of the Muslim Brotherhood. The latter will have to calculate the costs of such trials, and what impact it will have on their public image, how much it will cost in legal fees, and how long they will be held up in court. This calculation by the bad guys will force them to change their behavior, just as it changes ours. The good guys often give up writing a book, change an editorial, or use a different term, all out of fear of being taken to court. The same calculation will take place in the camp of those who adhere to Sharia.[45]

While most Muslim organizations and liberal groups are still motivated by the ideal of rational deliberation founded on a rule-governed exchange of arguments, the anti-Sharia camp has a warfare mentality where each side adjusts its strategy according to the moves of the opponent, and one speaks of spilling blood on behalf of the good cause. While Muslims and liberals organize conferences and debates about "what Sharia is," the anti-Sharia movement organizes aggressive coaching sessions where the goal is to develop, fine-tune, and deploy adequate tactics. Yerushalmi gives his audience advance warnings about the kinds of criticisms they will face: "You're going to be attacked by the Muslim Brotherhood and progressive liberals. They will unleash their propaganda machine decrying 'Islamophobia.'" The courts are a privileged site to counter this propagandistic narrative. They

> provide a unique opportunity to change policies in a way that is more effective than grassroots activism. . . . Nothing attracts more attention than the dramas and testimonies in the courtroom. . . . That is the biggest advantage of a trial. In court, even if you have a progressive judge, the facts create a playing field. And once they are in the record, even if you lose—and then you take it up on appeal and create your appellate record—that then becomes the facts of the case, the law of the case, and even if at the end of the day the opinion or the judgment is against your client, that survives and can always be pointed to later on.[46]

Even in defeat, the anti-Sharia movement is always a winner in such battles, since its aim is to establish a dominant narrative and not to lay out convincing arguments. Whether it succeeds in passing laws—and it has succeeded in several states—it always succeeds in radically altering the terms of compromise within the public debate. By working to impose such a radical and unfounded narrative—"Sharia threatens the survival of the United States"—the movement achieves its two main goals. First, on account of having to devote so much time and money to endless court battles over absurd arguments, Muslim American organizations are left with few resources to pursue other goals, such as encouraging Muslims to engage in politics or civic affairs and educating the public about Muslims and Islam. Second, by responding to the accusations made by the anti-Sharia movement, the liberals and Muslims inadvertently legitimize somewhat the narrative of their opponents. It hardly matters that the fight is over an imaginary threat founded on specious reasoning—it still remains very difficult for the liberal and Muslim organizations to win this battle. Any utterance, any action can become a piece of evidence. If the Muslims say they don't want to impose Sharia, it's proof of their deceitfulness and their hidden agenda. If they say they do want to follow certain aspects of Islamic law, it's proof of the reality of the Islamic threat. The general suspicion that the Muslim population has decided to subvert the very foundations of American law can only have a negative influence on more specific debates, such as over the building of mosques or over extending to Muslims certain accommodations similar to those granted to all other religious communities. The result is that the bar of acceptance of American Muslims has been placed much higher. They no longer only have to prove, like in 2001, that they are not terrorists; they must now answer to the widely held suspicion that being a practicing Muslim in and of itself represents a threat to the U.S. Constitution and American law.

ANTI-SHARIA OR ANTIGLOBALIZATION

At the base of the anti-Sharia project, one finds not so much a moral or religious vision but rather a set of defensive postures around a certain imagined conception of politics that combines constitutional populism, anti-elitism, "originalism" (i.e., legal literalism that believes the Constitution can and must be strictly interpreted the way it was first intended at the time of its ratification), and a binary approach to the world founded on the distinction between friends and enemies. The rhetoric about defending Judeo-Christian values failed to convince a number of Christian and Jewish leaders who denounced the negative effects for religious freedom in their communities of the anti-Sharia laws.[47] Nathan Diament, director of the Orthodox Union Advocacy Center, who earlier had contested the Islamic center in Lower Manhattan, expressed warnings about the negative consequences that ALAC's prohibition laws could have on the Jewish religious tribunals known as *beit din* and therefore the religious freedom of American Jews. These laws, he said, "are problematic particularly from the perspective of the Orthodox community—we have a beit din system, Jews have disputes resolved according to halachah. We don't have our own police force, and the mechanism for having those decisions enforced if they need to be enforced is the way any private arbitration is enforced."[48] Many organizations, such as the American Jewish Committee, joined forces with the ACLU to alert political leaders in various states about the liberty-killing effects that the anti-Sharia legislation would have on all religions.

The recurring link between Sharia and international law and then, in the ALAC template, the replacement of references to Sharia with "foreign law" reveal an antiglobal, antiliberal way of thinking as much as it does Islamophobia. According to the logic of the anti-Sharia movement's leaders, respecting international law is not an obligation but a voluntary matter. References to the American Revolution and the Constitution as exceptional founding moments play a decisive role that allows a fresh claim for the sovereign authority of the people (whether the issue is Social Security, gun ownership, abortion, or obeying international treaties). The authority that undergirds this claim allows those making it to fight better against "this modernist pathology of legal regulation."[49] According to this way of thinking, the politician's fundamental question is about identity and sacrifice ("Who are we, and what must we do to remain who we are?") and not about justice or contracts ("What should the law be?").[50] This is why the arguments put forward by those opposed to the anti-Sharia movement, which prove that such legislation would violate the rights of Muslims as well as those of other religious communities, are so ineffective. The anti-Sharia leaders are operating within a logic based on the affirmation of will instead of rational deliberation. As Paul Kahn observes, "Sacrifice is always an act of will, not of reason. Its logic is that of the gift, which can never be demanded."[51]

Within this mind-set, Europe plays an ambivalent role and is looked to alternately as a source of inspiration or as foil. The Old Continent is presented as the absolute negative example—what America risks becoming if it *does not* resist the Islamic menace. Deploying ideas developed by the "Eurabia" theorists, the anti-Sharia leaders, just like the antimosque groups, claim that America is on the brink of collapse. The United Kingdom is invaded by Sharia tribunals, extremist groups threaten national security in France on a daily basis, freedom of expression is threatened by Muslim bigotry in the Netherlands, and so on. During the conference organized in Tennessee in November 2011, an entire panel was devoted to painting an alarmist portrait of the European situation. One participant, Paul Diamond, a British lawyer and member of the Christian Legal Centre, described in detail the numerous victories of Islam over the secular state but especially over Christianity.[52]

There is a striking resemblance between the strategies and arguments developed by those participating in the controversies against minarets, mosques, and the *niqab* in Europe and the American arguments against Sharia and mosques. The Swiss campaign against minarets, led by the Democratic Union of the Center, was based on the same arguments used by Yerushalmi and his followers.[53] What mattered was creating a polemic and making noise, not engaging in argued debate. The Swiss artist who designed an Islamophobic poster was entirely frank about it when he declared, "We make posters and the other side goes to the judge. I love it when they do that."[54] The antiminaret campaign rests on a prevention argument, just like the anti-Sharia campaign. It does not matter that there are really only a handful of minarets in Switzerland—they are to be seen as the first sign of an imminent invasion. Similarly, the Northern League opposed the construction of a mosque in Milan in 2010, claiming that it was a secret training camp for terrorists. More surprisingly, the anti-Sharia argument and strategy bears certain resemblances to the French controversy over wearing head scarves at school and burkas in public spaces. Even though in 2004 many American commentators rushed to interpret the veil debate as a French idiosyncrasy—an obsession of authoritarian, secular republicanism with legislating behavior—the anti-Sharia movement seems to invalidate the idea of this being exclusively a French thing. American calls for legislation (remember that the whole movement began with Newt Gingrich's plea for a federal anti-Sharia law), for proper government action ("What is the state doing? We need laws that reflect the will of the people"), and the many declarations demanding that Muslim Americans "assimilate" all sound curiously "French." Thus the anti-Sharia movement can be seen to exhibit a mind-set founded on a properly American political history, but one also observes increasingly formatted discussions of Islam in Europe and the United States that use the same model.

CREATING A BETTER ENVIRONMENT FOR CONSERVATIVE POLITICS

The opposition between the theological-political mind-set and the contract-based, liberal model is not, however, a point-for-point face-off between liberals and conservatives or Democrats and Republicans. If the leaders of the anti-Sharia movement relentlessly denounce the Islamic-leftist alliance, they are no less critical toward a number of conservative and notably Republican politicians. They seek to keep the pressure on to maintain the conservative wing as far to the right as possible and fight against what they describe as a dangerous centrist or even liberal tendency. Even though they have access to major financial resources and an undeniable capacity to attract media attention, the anti-Sharia leaders are actually on the margins of the conservative movement. Having been unsuccessful at selling their argument to the elite within their own political family, they have opted for another strategy. With the success of the Tea Party as inspiration, they too turned to grassroots public appeals in search of easy explanations and solutions as a way to cope with the lingering trauma of September 11. In the media, the anti-Sharia activists may claim to speak in the name of the entire conservative movement, but utterances at conferences and meetings tell a different story of important internal divisions. For example, the position of the Federalist Society, an organization of conservative judges, lawyers, and law studentsm was denounced by activists as much too moderate. The latter reject arguments that make a distinction between Islam as a religion and political uses of Islam.

For the anti-Sharia movement, this distinction, defended by a large majority of conservative Republicans, is a trap. For them, Islam as a religion is intrinsically bad, dangerous, and hostile to America.

This explains why Frank Gaffney's speeches are mostly devoted to criticizing the Islamophilia within the conservative camp. Considering himself the sole true heir to the Reagan legacy, Gaffney is capable of harshly attacking much more influential types such as Grover Norquist, an important figure of the conservative movement thanks to his work as a lobbyist and the founder and president of the antitax organization Americans for Tax Reform. Norquist is married to a woman of Muslim origin and has been involved in many initiatives to improve relations between ethnic and religious communities in order to not lose the Latino and Muslim vote to the Democrats. He was a vocal critic of those opposed to the Islamic center in Lower Manhattan, and he also opposed the anti-Sharia legislation template developed by the APPA.[55] As a result, Gaffney labeled him a "useful idiot" and an "agent under Islamic influence" and close to the Muslim Brotherhood in the United States. The acrimony became especially harsh due to Norquist's support for his friend Souhail Khan, a Muslim American of Indian origin and professor of political science at the University of California, Berkeley. Khan had been an aide and spokesperson for Representative Tom Campbell (R-Calif.). In that role, he had worked on issues of religious freedom, the right to bear arms, and the reform of affirmative action policies. Khan is active in organizations such as the American Conservative Union and the Council for National Policy, a powerful network of conservative groups, but he's also an associate member of the Institute for Global Engagement in charge of Islamic-Christian dialogue. In February 2011, during the annual meeting of the Conservative Political Action Conference, a major gathering of American conservatives, Pamela Geller, David Horowitz, and Gaffney accused Khan and Norquist of working for the Muslim Brotherhood.[56] Thus, for these radical conservatives, besides their denunciation of the liberal Democratic establishment, they wage war on their own camp to extend the competition for the Reagan mantle and to keep the political agenda and the rhetoric of conservatives as far to the right as possible.

In the minds of many conservatives who occupy powerful positions, the Islamophobic tactic is destined to fail and, moreover, seems rather irrelevant. At the Conservative Political Action Conference, Norquist called on the Right to distance itself from the Islamophobic discourse, claiming that it went against the Reagan legacy and was politically counterproductive. Similarly, in a press conference in August 2011, New Jersey governor Chris Christie explicitly defended Sohail Mohammed, a Muslim American lawyer who he had nominated to be a state judge. This nomination provoked a controversy in conservative ranks, with a number of commentators accusing Mohammed of having links to extremist Islamic networks. Questioned about the anti-Sharia legal initiatives and the alleged links between the judge and radical movements, Governor Christie expressed his exasperation with Gaffney and his followers: "Sharia law has nothing to do with this at all. It's crazy. It's crazy. The guy's an American citizen who has been an admitted lawyer to practice in the state of New Jersey, swearing an oath to uphold the laws of New Jersey, the constitution of the state of New Jersey, and the Constitution of the United States of America."[57] There is no clearer way to say how annoyed many conservative Republicans have become with the anti-Sharia movement.

EFFECTS ON THE RELIGIOUS PRACTICES OF MUSLIM AMERICANS

This whole controversy has had immediate tangible effects on the daily life of Muslim Americans and their strategies to integrate into public, civic, and political life. Anti-Sharia activists force Muslim organizations like CAIR and MPAC to spend large amounts of their resources (time, money, expertise, energy) countering the efforts to prohibit Islamic law, answering accusations claiming affiliation with extremist groups, and correcting erroneous or caricatural representations of Islam. A Muslim American finds himself having to be the spokesperson for "the Muslim world" and forced to account for every negative news story associated with Islam anywhere in the world: an honor crime in London, the treatment of women in Afghanistan, female genital mutilation in Africa, polygamy, and so on. But in making statements on all these matters, Muslim Americans are indirectly letting stand a definition of Islam that they do not necessarily agree with, a vision of Islam that gives scant recognition to it as a religion defined above all by faith, interiority, sincerity, and where the Islamic community's symbols, customs, and habits are considered at most anecdotally. In fact, to contest the literalist, scriptural approach of the anti-Sharia activists, which seeks to apply over a diverse Muslim American population a single fan- tastical definition of Islamic law as a juridical and political code of conquest, Muslim Americans have ended up defending an opposite definition of Sharia as a simple spiritual moral code of personal good behavior. This explains why the legal scholar Intisar A. Rabb would say in an interview,

> We have never had a threat to our democracy from the long-time religious practices of Muslims in America. I think in part that stems from the nature of Muslim religious practice in this country—it is more of a private religious matter than a very public iteration. . . . There are many who claim to speak for Sharia. In Islam there is no church akin to the Catholic Church. There is no pope. With so little hierarchy, you get a very diffuse, Protestant-like view of what Islamic law means in the religious lives of individual Muslims and communities.[58]

To answer accusations made against them, Muslim Americans tend to reinforce the distinction between, on the one hand, political Islam or "Sharia Islam" and, on the other, "spiritual Islam" of a "Protestant" style that conforms to American culture. This opposition between a religion of faith and interiority and a political religion is at the heart of most debates about Islam since 2001. Muslim Americans have become trapped in a way by the terms of a debate that were defined by the anti-Sharia activists. Any effort to doubt the truth or usefulness of this opposition is also immediately seized on as proof of culpability or duplicity. But in trying to establish their good faith, in all senses, by proving that American Islam does meet the criteria of a good religion—spirituality, interiority, faith—the Muslims wind up adding to the weight of this type of argumentation in public debates. In a context of hysteria, it's impossible to have nuances be heard or to explain, for example, that one's attachment to a literalist reading of sacred texts or to a form of orthopraxy does not necessarily mean that one wishes to subvert the Constitution.

It should be noted that Muslims are not the only ones forced to submit to the hegemonic character of this argumentative strategy. Mormons, among others, are regularly the object of attacks and suspicion for the same reason as Muslims. Given this vision of the world founded on a distinction between good and bad religion, the association of faith with a certain number of obligatory practices and with a particular form of socializing is perceived as a danger. But because of the September 11 attacks, the more recent arrival of most Muslim immigrants, and the large amount of ignorance about Islam in the general public, Muslims have to put up with the negative effects of their approach to religiousness more than others.

Moreover, those who take the side of Muslims adopt the same perspective. To reject the argument of those in favor of the Oklahoma amendment, Judge Vicki Miles-LaGrange defined Sharia as a faith and a tradition disconnected from any obligatory legal dimension:

> Based on this testimony, the Court finds that plaintiff has shown "Sharia law" lacks a legal character, and, thus, plaintiff's *religious traditions and faith* are the only non-legal content subject to the judicial exclusion set forth in the amendment. As a result, the Court finds plaintiff has made a strong showing that the amendment conveys a message of disapproval of plaintiff's faith and, consequently, has the effect of inhibiting plaintiff's *religion*.[59]

By upholding this opposition between religion as faith and political religion, the discourse of intellectuals and liberal lawyers of all religious backgrounds reinforces a certain "teleological" conception of democracy and of the relation between religions in America. According to this narrative, all minorities were first the object of suspicion and attacks, but by progressively adapting to American culture, they were finally able to put these suspicions to rest.

Paradoxically, the anti-Sharia movement has also led to some good things for Muslims. If the strategy of seizing every occasion to blacken Islam and Muslims in the hope of gaining something by it brought the anti-Sharia movement a lot of publicity, it also seriously compromised what little credibility its leaders had. The anti-Sharia movement also contributed significantly to placing the defense of Muslim rights nearer the top of the agenda of many organizations, liberal or not. Given the extreme character of militant anti-Muslim criticisms, their adversaries were forced to stake out their position more clearly and engage more forthrightly in the defense of Muslim rights. Left-leaning think tanks such as CAP, important civil rights organizations such as the ACLU and the Southern Poverty Law Center, journalists, and ordinary citizens all took up the

Muslim cause. Within the Republican Party, certain influential figures such as Chris Christie and Grover Norquist denounced the excessive and unjust character of the whole anti-Sharia undertaking. Jewish and Christian religious authorities also lent their support to the Muslims.

But what this controversy reveals most of all is the striking contrast between the sphere of political discourse and activism and that of law. One may have witnessed an unfurling of verbal violence toward Islam, but one can also observe an unwavering attachment among American judges to constitutional principles and the legal protection of minorities. The role of the latter is all the more decisive and the court decisions all the more intriguing given that the populist mind-set bent on "originalism" and anti-liberalism seems to hold a privileged place in public debates. The word "liberal" seems most often to be an insult, and bringing up the notion of equality is enough to get one labeled a socialist. The American situation is in a sense the opposite of the European controversies over Islam. In the United States, the theological-political mind-set, founded on ideas of will and sacrifice, seems to dominate in the public sphere; yet it does not have a direct influence on the law and the justice system, which are the best allies of Muslim Americans. In contrast, the contract-based norms of liberal political theory in Europe are much more influential in public debates. Even if the attacks and criticisms against Muslim symbols and places of worship are numerous in Europe, one sees less tolerance in their public debates for the far-fetched arguments that American anti-Sharia activists resort to. The rejection of the display of religious symbols in public continues to be argued for in the name of principles such as equality, emancipation, freedom of expression, and the republic. But whether it is head scarves, burkas, or minarets, Muslims in Europe have not been able to use the law to defend their interests as effectively as they have in the United States. All the national legislatures may protect freedom of speech and religious practice, but European Muslims are much less likely than American Muslims to go to court to protect their rights. Beside the problems linked to the acceptance of religious symbols in various public spaces, disputes over discrimination in the workplace, for example, are numerous and often still unresolved. Given the wide diversity of situations that exist across different countries in Europe, the European Union continues to grant each member state considerable "freedom to choose" when it comes to applying the directives set down to protect the rights of religious minorities.[60]

4

THE FACE OF ANTI-MUSLIM POPULISM

THE POPULIST PERSUASION

The antimosque and anti-Sharia discourses are in a sense hardly original. Throughout American history, one encounters arguments where the populist denunciation of elites is mixed with the rejection of a religious minority that is perceived as a threat to the nation. American movements against mosques and Sharia have also taken much of their inspiration from ideas developed in Europe by politicians and Far Right organizations over the past fifteen years. The debates and demonstrations in America repeat a well-known script but also contribute to its modification.

There are certainly significant differences between each of these populist movements, between the contexts where they develop and the groups that are targeted. Nevertheless, it's important to situate the contemporary controversies over Islam within the frame of this discursive tradition of American history, even if it is not exclusive to the United States. Obviously, there are fears and prejudices linked specifically to Islam and the American context of the twenty-first century, but the populist themes and "paranoid style" are not exceptional to this time and place.

Instead of viewing it as a particular form of political organization or social activism, populism can be understood as a mode of persuasion.[1] By retracing the history of populist party movements, from the People's Party of 1892 to the conservative movement of the Reagan era, the historian

Michael Kazin shows how populism is not so much a political strategy or social collective as it is a type of rhetoric. Certainly the goals vary. The People's Party, led by William Jennings Bryan, wanted to defend the interests of southern farmers and farmhands against those of the banks, the railroads, and industrialists. In reaction to a drop in farm prices, the party called for the closure of national banks, the regulation of the railroads, and improvements in the working conditions of farm laborers. Subsequently, other movements would have recourse to populist rhetoric to pursue entirely different objectives. There was, for example, at the end of the nineteenth century the Women's Christian Temperance Union, under the leadership of Frances Willard, which fought to improve the moral character of the nation, win for women the right to vote, and ban the sale of alcohol. Persuaded that there was an industrial conspiracy among alcohol producers, the Women's Christian Temperance Union's militants demonstrated in favor of a "Christian patriotism" that would save the American people. Later still, George Wallace, then governor of Alabama, fought in the name of the people against the civil rights movement and for the continuation of segregation. Despite these different goals, the populist persuasion in American history organizes itself essentially along two vectors. As Kazin notes, "activists who blame an immoral, agnostic media for America's problems have little in common with those who indict corporations for moving overseas."[2] But even though some are insisting on purifying morals while others emphasize reforming the economy, these two types of militant employ the same vocabulary and style. Their mode of persuasion rests on four recurring themes that can be found in every populist's rhetoric: protecting America, defending the people, criticizing elites, and calling for mass mobilization. References to America and the use of the expression "We the people" are more incantations than descriptions of a precise collective. "It has been our fate as a nation not to have ideologies but to be one," Kazin underlines, quoting the political scientist Richard Hofstadter.[3] In the speeches of political leaders, the definitions of the people and of the nation's fundamental values remain remarkably vague. Working people, white shopkeepers, people put back on the straight and narrow by pious evangelical women, citizens, and activists hostile to the federal government—all these signifiers overlap, contradict one another, and mix together. Insofar as they are distinguishable, it's along the blurry and ever-changing borderline between the included and the excluded. The force of the populist persuasion comes from this imprecision. By remaining indeterminate, the signifiers "people" and "America" speak to everyone, since anyone can self-identify as belonging to these ill-defined entities. When a politician or an activist speaks in the name of the people or America, what exactly he is referring to with those words matters less than what this utterance allows the person to accomplish in a particular context.

Certain recurring features of this rhetoric can be observed since the nineteenth century. First, populist leaders owe their success to an ability to present themselves as the voice of common sense. This makes them all the more effective when it comes to disparaging the discourse of the "enemy"—be it trusts, the federal government, international socialism, the United Nations, and so on—as naïve, overly idealistic, and irresponsible. The prowess of populist orators comes from their skill at appearing to a large number of people as the single truly sensible voice, even though the solutions they propose are most often completely unrealistic and impractical. This is why, as Kazin notes, few actual policies in perfect conformity with populist currents have ever been adopted. The populist logic operates in a world that is essentially fictive and weak, a delusional world sustained by a belief in the possibility of a nonmediated relationship between the people and power, between imperatives and action. The populist discourse trades in malediction and catastrophic prophesy, not the logic of pragmatic action. This belief in the existence of such things as "the people," "elites," and "power," and in the possibility of magically granting power to the people without the mediation of any institution, does not stand up in the real practice of politics. As shown by Kazin, President Reagan, before coming into power and throughout his tenure in office, made frequent use of populist rhetoric when he presented himself as the hero of a strong America that would resist liberal-secular humanism while affirming its Judeo-Christian identity and as the defender of the nation's sovereignty against the Soviet Union—not to mention his opposition to tax hikes. But at the end of the 1980s, taxes on the middle class remained high, abortion was still legal, and the society was on the whole more secular than in the 1960s. The Republican Party, Kazin notes, "was after all, still the party of business, and the only priority of business (in an era distant from the days when John D. Rockefeller and Henry Ford denounced the saloon) was to sell products, not to worry about the spiritual health of its consumers."⁴ The same holds for the movement of the Christian Right: "At the stage of protest, a language of moral revival is enormously useful; it gives voice to people who feel the nation is slipping away from its righteous moorings. But the same language sounds mean and divisive when spoken by people in or close to power. It seems a peril to majority rights instead of a cry of outrage by the unrepresented."⁵

PARANOID RATIONALITY

At an early stage of their being, most religious minorities have had to face vigorous statements of rejection and fear on the part of the Protestant majority. These gestures of exclusion are not founded simply on a predisposition toward a conformist, inward-turning character but on a specific type of rationality that Hofstadter defines as "paranoid." It is marked by a strong belief in a conspiracy against the homeland and American culture. Those who hold this point of view never speak about their own interests but always in the name of the threatened collective. Moral indignation and a self-righteous attitude are key ingredients of this paranoid style. In many ways, the antimosque and anti-Sharia movements look like reruns of previous episodes in American history. In 1798, Jedidiah Morse, a Massachusetts preacher, affirmed the existence of a conspiracy by Illuminati and Jacobins against America. On the Fourth of July of that year, Yale University president Timothy Dwight IV gave a speech in which he warned against "the sins of these enemies of Christ and of Christians": "Will our sons become the disciples of Voltaire and the dragoons of Marat and our daughters the concubines of Illuminati?"⁶ In the 1830s, Freemasons were also suspected of plotting against the government and America's Christian values. Anti-Freemason journals and conventions spread rapidly. Anti-Jewish and anti-Mormon paranoia have been the object of many studies too numerous to describe here. What the anti-Muslim movements of today evoke most, however, is the violent anti-Catholicism in nineteenth- and twentieth-century America. In 1835, Samuel F. B. Morse, the son of Jedidiah and the inventor of Morse code, published a book entitled *Foreign Conspiracy Against the Liberties of the United States*, in which he describes Catholics as being irredeemable infidels and foreigners in America.

Another book published in 1836 by a mysterious "Maria Monk," allegedly a former nun who left her convent, remained very popular in the United States until the 1950s. The book, *Awful Disclosures*, revealed to the public the hidden side of convents, the debauchery of priests, the libidinous character of Catholics, and especially their lack of loyalty to the American homeland. "Anti-Catholicism," writes Hofstadter, "has always been the pornography of the Puritan. Whereas the anti-Masons had imagined wild drinking bouts and had entertained themselves with fantasies about the actual enforcement of grisly Masonic oaths, the anti-Catholics developed an immense lore about libertine priests, the confessional as an opportunity for seduction, licentious convents and monasteries."[7] Monk's book, while extremely violent, is nevertheless accepted by the public as completely plausible. In a similar vein, nativist anti-Catholic movements claim that Catholic immigrants steal jobs from Protestant Americans and seek to undermine the Constitution. A famous example is the Know-Nothing group, which started in 1843 as a secret society hostile to Irish immigration and even became a political party starting in the mid-1850s, calling itself the American Party; it favored prohibition, was very hostile to immigration, and expressed reservations about granting American citizenship to European Catholics who, they thought, took orders from the pope. In *Ten Great Religions: An Essay in Comparative Theology*, published in 1871, the Unitarian minister James Freeman Clarke claimed that northern (Protestant) Europeans were superior to southern (Catholic) Europeans:

> In the South of Europe, the Catholic Church, by its ingenious organization and its complex arrangements, introduced into life discipline and culture. In the North of Europe, Protestant Christianity, by its appeals to the individual soul, awakens conscience and stimulates to individual and national progress. The nations of Southern Europe accepted Christianity mainly as a religion of sentiment and feeling; the nations of Northern Europe, as a religion of truth and principle.[8]

Just like the anti-Islamism movement today, anti-Catholicism gave rise to major legal and legislative quarrels. In fact, the Sharia controversy bears considerable resemblance to the polemic around the Blaine Amendment, which aimed to reform the Constitution or local laws of many states so as to prevent the subversion of the federal government by religious institutions. In 1875, House minority leader James G. Blaine (R-Maine) failed in his effort to get his amendment through Congress. He and his followers then changed strategies and concentrated their efforts on the state legislatures, where they eventually succeeded in getting laws passed in several states that would prohibit the use of public money to finance so-called sectarian schools. Even if the Catholic Church was not explicitly singled out, supporters of the Blaine Amendment mostly belonged to evangelical protestant movements that were nervous about the Catholic menace. There are striking similarities between Blaine's supporters and the strategy of the anti-Sharia crowd, notably the shift from a national goal directed at federal law to one directed at the various states and, of course, the resemblance between the two arguments—the former anti-Catholic, the latter anti-Muslim.

In all these episodes, one finds the same stock figures and similar lines of reasoning behind the obvious surface differences. In each case, history is viewed as an extended conspiracy whose development can be arrested only in a brutal way in the manner of a crusade to defend civilization. The tone is one of urgency: time is running out, and the catastrophe is imminent—the subversion of the American Constitution by—take your pick—Freemasons, Catholics, Communists, or Muslims. In this apocalyptic vision of the world, the figure of the renegade or apostate plays an essential role. Nineteenth-century anti-Mason associations are composed almost entirely of former Masons, the revelations of the mysterious Maria Monk are all the more believable for having come from someone who suffered under the vices of the Catholic convent, and former Muslims are heavily courted by the anti-Sharia and antimosque movements. The self-proclaimed prophet is the only one lucid enough to effectively warn others and combat the invisible danger. In the debate over Islam in the United States, a Pamela Geller, Glenn Beck, or Frank Gaffney, or, in Europe, an Anders Breivik or a Geert Wilders incarnate the "megalomaniac view of oneself as the Elect, wholly good, abominably persecuted, yet assured of ultimate triumph."[9] In the local movements against mosques or Sharia, one also finds a large number of less mediatized figures but who also incarnate this worrisome stand of the self-proclaimed prophet of justice.

What's more, all these movements are notable for their unfalsifiable and perfectly coherent vision of the world. The smallest fact can be used as proof of the real and imminent danger that must be combated. Nuance or ambiguity cannot be tolerated—those precisely are marks of lily-livered concession to the insidious and false reasoning of "the powerful" who must be taken down. A whole interlocking set of self-confirming claims gets put in place such that one becomes convinced that only the incredible is credible. As Hofstadter remarks, what's distinctive about the paranoid style "is not, then, the absence of verifiable facts (though it is occasionally true that in his extravagant passion for facts the paranoid occasionally manufactures them), but rather the curious leap in imagination that is always made at some critical point in the recital of events."[10]

The anti-Sharia partisans list off a whole series of legal cases and conclude that Sharia is infiltrating the American legal system. But this conclusion is rather surprising, since the counter report by the American Civil Liberties Union shows that the facts (even those that are especially held up as proof) prove just the opposite. It is almost impossible, however, to have an argument-driven discussion with a populist orator because he's never wrong. This is also why populism remains, above all, a discourse of opposition and dissensus that is not easily translatable into actual policy: "The paranoid tendency is aroused by opposed interests which are (or are felt to be) totally irreconcilable, and thus by nature not susceptible to the normal political processes of bargain and compromise."[11]

This also explains the parodic quality of the populist-paranoid discourse that is fond of long reports by experts, rivers of analysis (either theological or political), and stacks of evidence and proofs. All this material constitutes a sort of parody of the social science research and public expertise produced by bipartisan think tanks and civil rights organizations. The populist discourse rejects that scientific research while also mimicking it. But the process of parodic imitation produces secondary effects on the field of scientific expertise. By forcing social science specialists, legal scholars, and theologians to answer them, if only to correct or deny their statements, the populist agitators succeed in creating a well-worn path that consists of *their* preferred questions and lines of analysis that frame the debate. For example, to refute the paradigm of a "clash of civilizations" or the idea of Islam as intrinsically a code of military conquest, one tries to bring nuance; one makes distinctions between diverse forms of Islam; one praises a moderate Islam, Sufism, or mysticism; one mentions examples of patriotic Muslims. And yet, claiming that all Muslims are not at base evil does nothing to unseat the seemingly legitimate presupposition that there is something fundamentally problematic about Islam itself. It's for this reason that, even though it is a minority phenomenon, the populist-paranoid discourse always has a hegemonic potential. Given their ambivalent attitude toward expert testimony that combines uncertain amounts of contempt, resentment, and fascination, populist orators contribute to a softening of the line between scientific discourse and counterfeit discourse. The debates on campuses and talk shows over the past decade lead one to ask if all participants in such controversies are not, to varying degrees, influenced by this populist-paranoid discourse when the focus is on Islam. More than the virulence of anti-Muslim diatribes broadcast by certain experts and self-proclaimed prophets, what's intriguing is the adoption of this mode of persuasion by a growing portion of the Western public. Again, to cite Hofstadter, "it is the use of paranoid modes of expression by more or less normal people that makes the phenomenon significant."[12]

THE INFLUENCE OF THE EUROPEAN RADICAL RIGHT

There are also strong ties between the leaders of anti-Muslim movements and the groups, intellectuals, and European parties that, since the turn of the century, have been developing the same type of project.[13] Anders Breivik's pamphlet, which was written before he massacred sixty-nine people on the Norwegian island of Utøya where the Workers' Youth League was holding its annual summer camp, represents the most dramatic example of this process of Euro-American transfer of Islamophobic arguments.[14] The apocalyptic style of the manifesto delivered by the "Justiciar Knight Commander of the Knights Templar of Europe" evokes a world that mixes together the esoteric views of the Knights Templar and Freemasons, the fantastic aesthetic of *Star Wars*, millenarian talk about the end of the world, and the culturalist conviction about a war of civilizations. Breivik is an extremely grotesque example of the style of polemicist that one sees in Robert Spencer or Frank Gaffney—someone who maintains the appearances of civil discourse but who has recourse to the same schematic fantasizing and use of fear. Breivik also belonged to the

Nazi group Nordisk, which claimed inspiration from the "Vienna school" and promoted "crusade nationalism" calling for the deportation of all the Muslims of Europe. Ultranationalist groups regularly refer approvingly to organizations such as Stop Islamization of America and Jihad Watch, which themselves are largely inspired by extreme-right parties such as the English Defense League, financed by a certain Alan Lake.[15] Breivik also evokes the "citizens' movement" Pax Europa, created by René Stadtkewitz (also the founder of the Liberty Party [Die Freiheit] in Berlin),[16] an active figure in the antimosque movements in Germany and who also influenced mosque opponents in America.

Warnings about the decline of Eurabia and the threat of "dhimmitude";[17] praise of Israel as the world's last rampart against the Islamic threat; a permanent denunciation of Muslims' duplicitous double language; and claims to an absolute right to freedom of expression are the essential themes of these anti-Muslim polemicists and activists on both sides of the Atlantic. In her book *Eurabia: The Euro-Arab Axis* (2005), Gisèle Littman, writing under the pseudonym Bat Ye'or, asserts that European and Arabic politicians have planned in secret to transform decadent Europe into an Arabian colony in order to destroy America and Israel. Europeans in this colony would have a subaltern status, protected only thanks to the reestablishment of a system of millets, courts under the Ottoman Empire that guaranteed certain rights and protection to "people of the book."

This theme of Eurabia and urgent calls to fight against Islamization have been taken up with varying amounts of crudeness or nuance by a number of essayists, notably in the United Kingdom. There is, for example, Melanie Phillips, an editorialist at the *Daily Mail* and the author of *Londonistan: How Britain Has Created a Terror State Within* (2006); Douglas Murray, the director of the conservative think tank Centre for Social Cohesion and the author of *Neoconservatism: Why We Need It* (2005); Mark Steyn, the author of *Lights Out: Islam, Free Speech and the Twilight of the West* (2009); and the prolific British historian Niall Ferguson, whose *Civilization: The West and the Rest* was published in 2011.

At the heart of these arguments is nostalgia for a strong Europe and fear of the demographic and cultural threat that immigration represents. In Germany, for example, Henryk Broder and Thilo Sarrazin assert that Turkish immigration risks lowering the country's overall level of intelligence. In his "declaration of European independence," Breivik explains that he singled out the year 2083 because that date would mark the four-hundredth anniversary of the last siege of Vienna by the Turks. He also cites the writings of Broder, who deplores the fact that "after winning in Poitiers in 732 and Vienna in 1683, Europeans are now being defeated by demography."[18] A large number of European activists and authors participate in conferences organized in the United States by anti-Muslim groups, but the theme of the cultural and demographic decline of Europe is reformulated in the United States as the themes of political subversion and destruction of the Constitution. In July 2010, Geert Wilders announced the creation of the International Freedom Alliance, whose aim would be to fight against the Islamization of the West and for the defense of Israel. In his speech at the Cornerstone Church near Nashville in May 2011, he declared that it was necessary to encourage the Israeli settlements because "if Jerusalem falls, Athens, Rome, Amsterdam, and Nashville will fall."[19] The denunciation of Muslims' double discourse, the naïveté of the Left, and the Islamic-leftist alliance is a constant within the discourse of anti-Muslim activists in Europe and the United States.

Another point in common is their outspoken claim to an unlimited right to free speech and their denunciation of the intolerance of Muslims and liberals. Thus Elisabeth Sabaditsch-Wolff, an Austrian academic and a member of Pax Europa, received a fine for incitement to hate and "denigrating religious beliefs" after having, among other things, referred to the Prophet Mohammad as a pedophile several times during a conference organized by the Freedom Party in Vienna in 2009. Lars Hedegaard, a former member of the Danish People's Party, the author of *Daughters of Mohammad: Violence, Murder, and Rape in the House of Islam*, and a member of the editorial board of the International Free Press Society (which also includes Geert Wilders, Bat Ye'or, and Robert Spencer), asserted in a 2009 interview that Muslims "rape their own children. . . . Daughters in Muslim families are raped by their uncles, cousins, or fathers."[20] Being tried for incitement to hatred, then, offers these polemicists a new opportunity to cast themselves as victims of the dictatorship of political correctness.

The denunciation of Islam holds an important place within the political strategy of many European populist parties since 2000. Oskar Freysinger, the leader of the Swiss movement "against the construction of minarets" and a deputy member of the Swiss People's Party, has described minarets as a symbol of the project to impose Sharia.[21] Similarly, as mentioned earlier, the Northern League opposed the construction of a mosque in Milan, asserting that it would serve as a terrorist training center. Valentin Kusák, the leader of the antimosque movement in the Czech Republic, has stated that Muslims are lying about their intentions when they ask for the right to build places of worship. The arguments of American anti-Muslim activists appear as more or less a collage and a pastiche of the ensemble of caricatures, insults, phantasms, and faulty reasoning developed in Europe since 2000.

LIBERALISM, SECULARISM, AND FEMINISM

The normative dimension of references to secularism and liberal feminism is, however, very different in the American versus European controversies.[22] The critique of Islam and of Muslim demands in Europe is most often rationalized with references to liberalism and secularism in all the European countries where disputes have broken out. In Italy, Germany, and England, the negotiated settlements between the religious and the political are based on different principles than the French notion of *laïcité*. In the former, one often hears talk of greater tolerance or even indifference to the display of religious symbols in public space—consider, for example, the crucifixes in Italian classrooms or the turbans worn by Sikh police officers in Great Britain. The populist parties in Denmark, Austria, and Switzerland insist much more than France's National Front party on the nation's founding Christian values. However, despite these differences, in every European country, the same liberal, secular argument dominates the discussion as soon as it's about Islam. Opposition to mosques, veils, and burkas has most often been pursued in the name of individual self-determination and the emancipation of women. Islam is denounced as a patriarchal, communitarian religion that obstructs the emancipation of the individual, oppresses women, and is incompatible with the principle of separation of church and state. This paradigm of an opposition between Islam and individual autonomy has also played a key role in French debates over head scarves and burkas and has been the subject of numerous studies and critiques.[23]

Although hegemonic in Europe, including among its Christian conservative groups, this form of justification has not acquired the same normative force in the United States, where such general arguments are used much more selectively. In a context where the labels "liberal" and "secular" are typically used as insults, even the selective use of these principles is rather counterproductive. Linking criticism of Islam with praise for liberal principles would sound strange coming from those who are endlessly denouncing the liberal, secular derailment of America under President Obama, and has seldom been effective even within anti-Muslim movements. The recent polemic surrounding the documentary film *The Third Jihad: Radical Islam's Vision for America* (2008) reveals the ambiguity of this use of liberal norms.

On January 19, 2012, the journalist Tom Robbins triggered a lively debate when he revealed that this Islamophobic film had been used in training courses by the New York Police Department.[24] This sixty-five-minute film presents a succession of violent scenes in which one sees bombs exploding, angry crowds burning churches, and fiery imams haranguing people. A series of interviews with "experts" such as Glenn Beck, New York Police Commissioner Raymond Kelly, and former CIA director James Woolsey reinforce the film's main message: Muslims are invading America. The film's narrator asserts that "people try and have Americans believe that most Muslim groups are mainstream and moderate, whereas in fact, if one looks closely, the reality is very different. One of their leading tactics is dissimulation." The film was directed by the Canadian-Israeli filmmaker Raphael Shore and produced by the Clarion Fund, a New York organization that also funded the Islamophobic film *Obsession: Radical Islam's War Against the West* (2005). *The Third Jihad* seeks to expose the secret plan of America's Muslim leadership: while presenting themselves as moderates, their ultimate goal is to subvert the law and Constitution of the United States and impose Sharia. The narrator is none other than Zuhdi Jasser, an intellectual Muslim activist who has specialized in the denunciation of the Islamist plot and has been a member of the U.S. Commission on International Religious Freedom since 2012. His testimony at hearings organized by Representative Peter King to examine the extent of radicalization among Muslim Americans was criticized by many Muslim organizations. Referring to the famous document written by a member of the Muslim Brotherhood and used in the trial against the Holy Land Foundation,

Jasser asserts, "It wasn't until I saw this document, written in America by American Muslims, that I understood what was really going on: a strategy to infiltrate and dominate America." One of the main criticisms that Jasser addresses to American Muslim leaders is that they refuse to subscribe to what he presents as the American model based on the separation of church and state. In rejecting this principle, they are not good "Jeffersonian democrats." In a radio broadcast on January 27, 2012, as a guest on *The Brian Lehrer Show*, Jasser develops his point of view:

> Not every Muslim has bought into the Establishment clause. Yes, they may believe in it as a minority, but when they are at home, or in their mosques, are they teaching the separation of mosque and state? Or are they saying "You know what, we follow the laws of the land as a minority, but Islam is a way of life as far as laws, as far as society, and we want, as a majority to have an Islamic state"? That creates radicalization. . . . People need to understand that Evangelical Muslim movements in the West are not about violence. It's about spreading the concept of political Islam within our communities.[25]

Muslim insistence on presenting Islam as a total way of life is interpreted as proof of the incompatibility of Islam with the liberal and secular principles of "Jeffersonian democracy." Chapters of the American Congress for Truth (ACT!) have since seized on this theme of incompatibility between Islam and secularism in meetings with local communities. Websites close to the Tea Party, such as the libertarian populist *Jefferson Review*, have also relayed these ideas.

Nevertheless, among the American people, the liberal-secular wedge argument has not managed to achieve the same broad normative force that it has in Europe. The reason is that most spectators who find the film convincing—members of ACT!, allies of Jasser, the Clarion Fund, and sympathizers with the anti-Sharia movement—consider secularism in America to be something evil, and they mostly use the term "liberal" to insult their enemies. They approve of Mitt Romney's criticism in April 2012 of the new "religion of secularism" that the Obama administration is said to have imposed. In a speech on April 3, 2012, Romney, then a leading Republican presidential candidate, expressed virulent condemnation of secularization in America: "I think there is in this country a war on religion. I think there is a desire to establish a religion in America known as secularism."[26] Along the same lines, on February 26, 2012, Republican candidate Rick Santorum, a Catholic, made this declaration in favor of greater inclusiveness of religion in public space: "The idea that the church can have no influence or no involvement in the operation of the state is absolutely antithetical to the objectives and vision of our country. This is the First Amendment. The First Amendment says the free exercise of religion. That means bringing everybody, people of faith and no faith, into the public square."[27] As a guest the same day on the ABC show *This Week*, Santorum stuck to his message: "To say that people of faith have no role in the public square? You bet that makes you throw up. What kind of country do we live in that says only people of non-faith can come into the public square and make their case?"[28]

Opposition to the visibility of Islam in the European "public square" gets going in the years 2000 to 2010 based on the postulate that religious symbols must be confined to private space. In the United States, anti-Muslim groups consider that secularism is bad and there's too much of it—except among Muslims, where there is too little. Thus despite the number of similarities in their Islamophobic rhetoric, in the United States the normative discourse of liberal secularism does not at all possess the same one-size-fits-all character that is has in Europe.

By the same token, the liberal feminist argument occupies a much more limited place, and a more incoherent one, in anti-Muslim declarations within the United States. The duty to emancipate Muslim women from the patriarchal tutelage of their community of origin is a central theme in Europe, especially France. In America, the essential drumbeat is fear of foreigners invading America and subverting the Constitution. Since the women in conservative movements such as the Conservative Women of America are contesting liberal, secular feminism, it's rather surprising to hear their indignation about the "pious Muslim woman," since in many ways that figure corresponds to the ideal woman—devout, conservative, family oriented—that they favor. But for these conservative groups, the main lens for viewing Islam remains the danger it represents for the survival of the American nation and not the duty to liberate oppressed women. The question of the rights of Muslim women comes up only secondarily within the big picture of fighting against the threat of Islamic subversion. The anti–Sharia law advocates applied pressure on the legislature in Kansas, saying that the law was necessary to defend women's rights. State representative Peggy Mast and state senator Susan Wagle, both Republicans, claimed that this was not discrimination against Islam. Mast said the bill "will help women know the rights they have in America."[29] Simultaneously, these two Republican women were engaged for months in the fight against Planned Parenthood, a family-planning organization partially funded by the federal government that provides women with access to information and resources about reproductive health.

The liberal argument is used, often in a caricatural, sensationalist way, by women who grew up in a predominantly Muslim country and who then turn their denunciations of the freedom-killing character of Islam into a kind of business. Nonie Darwish, Pamela Geller, and Brigitte Gabriel are three examples. Their declarations look more like a parody of the arguments of liberal-secular feminists than the expression of deep convictions about the value and validity of these principles. They speak less about self-determination, the individual's free will, or gender equality and more about the traumatic experiences of persecuted women. Violent, almost pornographic images of genital mutilation or Afghan women burned, buried, or disfigured take the place of analysis. It is an industry that trades in morbid distraction and catastrophist exhibitionism. The war between progressive feminists and conservative movements is not primarily about Islam, but is mostly over the positions of the Catholic Church and evangelicals on the issues of abortion, contraception, gay marriage, and the ordination of female priests.

A JUDEO-CHRISTIAN PEOPLE?

Even if evocations of Judeo-Christian values and traditions play an important role in anti-Muslim populist rhetoric, is there such a thing as a properly Christian or Judeo-Christian populism? The "Judeo-Christian" reference has an essentially performative function. Its reiteration reinforces the feeling of belonging to the same group, but it does not necessarily imply any strong or sincere commitment to practicing a religion or to its traditions—because the religion, so to speak, of the anti-Muslim populists is, above all, a form of nativism or, one could say, the religion of Americanism. Every religious minority perceived as heterodox with respect to mainstream Protestant norms has had to face the opposition of these nativist movements. Mormons, Freemasons, Amerindians, Catholics, and Jews have all been accused—long before Muslims—of wanting to subvert the American Constitution. All of them have been judged incapable of adapting to the American cult of the common man. For a long time, Catholicism was considered incompatible with democracy. Polygamy among Mormons was interpreted as a sign of their incapacity to assimilate into the American body politic. The historian Henry Adams believed that Jews were responsible for America's decline.[30] The people in each group were described as passive and gullible, living under the authority of malevolent leaders. Catholics were "too ignorant to act at all for themselves," according to Samuel Morse.[31] The Freemasons made vows without knowing exactly what they were getting into:

> To the nativist mind, the reliance of these groups upon the fear, superstition, and ignorance of their members partly accounted for their secretive nature. Not one of these groups would put their aims and ideals to the test of open discussion, from which "real" Americans assumed truth would emerge. In fact, the presumed isolation of these groups from the controlling force of public opinion—the sole moral arbiter in American society—further fueled nativist suspicions of subversive conspiracies.[32]

This nativist conception of religious minorities is founded on the religious doctrine of the Puritans and, in particular, on the theologians' seventeenth-century ideal of a covenant among an association of voluntary "saints" chosen by God. The association is conceived of as entirely voluntary, but after having assented to the covenant, each "elected" one must strictly obey the rules governing relations and the orthodoxy established within the community.[33] As the historian Michael Hughey explains, the distinctive feature of "America's covenant framework" first developed by the Puritans is "its insistence that ideological consensus and conformity form the primary basis of political and social order."[34] Any individual or group presenting a heterodox vision of the world was excluded from the community. The theocracy of John Winthrop tolerated no deviation in behavior or divergence in ideology. This Puritan ideal of the covenant was subsequently reworked so as to include other Protestant communities.

But the insistence on consensus and on the voluntary engagement of the contracting parties remains a key component of this covenant framework:

> Americanism was and perhaps still is a creed in a way that Britishism or Frenchism is not. As Tocqueville observed, the American republic exists "without contention, opposition, argument, or proof, being based on a tacit agreement and a sort of *consensus universalis.*" . . . For roughly a century after gaining independence, American political and social order rested to a significant and perhaps even unique degree upon a self-conscious ideological consensus, or at least upon the majority's fervent belief that such a consensus *should* exist.[35]

Although founded on Puritan theology, this ideal of the covenant was gradually secularized, but the ideas of voluntary engagement and public pledges of loyalty and rejection of heterodoxy continued to play a decisive role in the rhetoric of all nativist movements of the nineteenth and twentieth centuries. Today this rhetoric takes the form of a hypernationalism rather than that of a theological or religious project. The Protestant conception of what counts as a "true" religion plays an important normative role in the evaluation of Islam, just as it did earlier when it came to the exclusion of Mormons, Catholics, and Jews. But there is no concomitant evangelical Protestant awakening—the reference to Protestant lineage represents only part of the nativist ideology; the rest is composed of a mix of the ideals of equality (but only for the "elect"), popular sovereignty, civic engagement, and freedom. "Christian America" functions therefore as a floating signifier that refers to different conceptions of America and to diverse religious doctrines. The reiteration of allegiance to this floating signifier forges the unity of this movement. Events organized by the Tea Party, antimosque demonstrations, and anti-Sharia demonstrations are not experienced as forums where one comes to debate or lecture but as rituals through which one reaffirms solidarity with the group. One participates less out of a sense of belonging to a Christian doctrine and more to restate one's faith in America, in the sovereignty of "We the people," and in the Constitution:

> Precisely because American unity rests so heavily upon voluntary allegiance to its ideals, and because those ideals were acknowledged to be

fragile and vulnerable to corruption, Americans were rarely able to attain the security of taking their ideals for granted. American nationalism has always been something of an artificial creed—or a genuine faith—in that it was assented to by conscious choice rather than being assumed unreflectively. It is surely this self-consciousness of belief, for example, that accounts for the "irritable patriotism" that so annoyed Tocqueville and other visitors to nineteenth-century America.[36]

THE FEAR OF MUSLIM FREE RIDERS

Barack Obama's victory in the 2008 presidential election left the Republican Party almost moribund. However, two years later the Republicans won sixty-three seats in the U.S. House of Representatives, which gave them a majority. This success was due largely to the unprecedented mobilization orchestrated by the Tea Party's backing of Republican candidates and opposition to the Democratic administration. Although a Tea Party website was created in 2002 by Citizens for a Sound Economy and groups were organizing political gatherings, or "tea parties," in various states shortly after the 2008 election, it was the February 19, 2009, rant by the reporter Rick Santelli appearing on CNBC that marked the beginning of the media success of the Tea Party. From the floor of the Chicago Stock Exchange, Santelli spoke out vociferously against the Obama administration's proposed measures to help families suffering in the subprime mortgage crisis: "How many of you people want to pay for your neighbor's mortgage [for a house] that has an extra bathroom and [they] can't pay their bills, raise their hand. . . . If you read our Founding Fathers, people like Benjamin Franklin and Jefferson, what we're doing in this country now is making them roll over in their graves."[37]

The mortgage crisis was one of the central themes that galvanized diverse local associations starting in 2009 and led them to unite under the Tea Party name. Protests against tax increases and "big government" are the foundation of this relatively heterogeneous movement. There are significant differences within the Tea Party when it comes to social and moral values. If many of the adherents could be described as socially conservative, others take a libertarian view, and not just about the economy but on the issues of abortion, marriage equality, and the religious freedom of Muslims. According to the political scientists Theda Skocpol and Vanessa Williamson, the "conservative" ideological unity of the Tea Party rests more on fiscal and antigovernment positions than on moral or social stands.[38] In other words, it is incorrect to view the Tea Party as a reincarnation of the Moral Majority of Jerry Falwell. Its success is based on a paradoxical alliance between religious conservatives close to the Christian Right and libertarians. The fiscal and antigovernment conservatism of the Tea Party has nothing in common with traditional, philosophical conservatism inspired by the writings of the political philosopher Edmund Burke. While Burke viewed political reason as a principle of constant balancing and adjusting within an existing order, the Tea Party members operate from a typically populist approach to political action. They reject all ideas of institutional mediation, balancing, and compromise. For Burke, government and society are codependent, whereas the Tea Party ideology is constructed around a denunciation of government "tyranny."

The Tea Party's essential rhetorical tool, this general critique of "big government," often contradicts the actual positions of Tea Party members on issues like the government regulation of immigration or abortion. "At the grass roots," as Skocpol and Williamson observe, "Tea Partiers want government to get out of the way of business. Yet at the same time, virtually all want government to police immigrants. And the numerous social conservatives in Tea Party ranks want authorities to enforce their conception of traditional moral norms."[39]

A fondness for Medicare among the militants aged fifty and up (who compose the vast majority of Tea Party membership) is a perfect illustration of their ambiguous attitude toward the government. While strongly opposed to health-care reform (mocked as "Obamacare") or government measures to ease the debt burden of homeowners, Tea Party members are nearly all opposed to any tampering with Medicare, the government-funded health-insurance program for citizens aged sixty-five and older. Their explanation is that they earned the aid from the government, unlike those profiteers and free riders who prefer to receive assistance by stealing the labor of deserving Americans. This opposition between hard-working, deserving Americans and all those who fall into the category of free riders or assisted—including the young, illegal immigrants, and Washington politicians—is fundamental to the Tea Party ideology.

The power and success of the Tea Party depends on an alliance between three groups of actors: local militant groups; the right-wing media, especially Fox News; and foundations backed by millionaires who have lobbied for tax reductions and smaller government for years.[40] Membership in local Tea Party chapters tends to draw mostly from middle- and upper-class people aged forty-five and older.[41] All of them are not necessarily actively involved in organizing events, creating political action committees, or fund-raising. Some are simply regular supporters and spectators of Fox News and may occasionally attend a meeting in their city or county. The activism of these associations that spontaneously adopted the Tea Party label in 2009 not only gave an important jolt to American local politics but also unsettled the often very hierarchical arrangements between local constituents and the individuals and groups that claim to represent them on the national level. Even if these grassroots associations receive money from foundations and benefit from the attention given to them by right-wing media outlets, they operate relatively independently.[42] On one side, then, there are local organizations created more or less spontaneously and operating with relative autonomy; on the other side are families of millionaires (Richard Mellon Scaife, John M. Olin, Charles G. and David H. Koch, and so on) that are situated politically and ideologically on the Far Right and that have been working for decades to shrink government and lower taxes. The Koch brothers (sons of Fred C. Koch, a founding member of the John Birch Society, a conservative lobby that started in the 1950s to fight Communism and that also favors minimalist government and an originalist approach to interpreting the Constitution), the principal backers of the powerful antitax lobby Americans for Prosperity, have associated themselves with the Tea Party label and agenda.[43] The Koch brothers, who favor the elimination of nearly all governmental bodies except the army, are at war against Democrats but also against overly moderate Republicans. Think tanks such as the Cato Institute and the Heritage Foundation receive their support. Between these two groups, the Washington-based lobbies, think tanks, and foundations and the diverse local chapters, there exists a system of mutual service and exploitation. Local activists depend on the foundations for money and for publicizing their events to a wider out-of-state audience. In the other direction, the foundations rely on local networks to disseminate and reinforce their antitax and anti-Obama message. The two groups are motivated by a single objective besides their shared opposition to the Democratic Party: push the Republican Party constantly farther to the right and obstruct all attempts at compromise with the other side.

Since for them the defeat in 2008 was due to excess moderation and inadequate pragmatism in the Republican ranks, the Tea Party has aspired to melt down the Grand Old Party (GOP) and recast it on a much more radical foundation.[44] The group's intransigence worked in its favor in many state primaries in 2010, and several Tea Party candidates eventually defeated both Democrats and establishment Republicans. Tea Party activism allowed the Republicans to gain a majority in the House of Representatives in the 112th Congress but also led to a radicalization of that majority. A study of the positions and voting records of the Republicans in Congress reveals a significant shift to the right since 2010.[45]

THE NEED FOR COMMON SENSE

The Tea Party's members and sympathizers use similar arguments to justify their criticism of regulatory mechanisms implemented by the government. As they see it, Washington elites are contemptuous of the will of the people, arrogantly disregard the Constitution, and betray the principles of the Founding Fathers. This reverence for the past shows that behind their bellicose discourse lies a nostalgia for the America "of our grandparents" and fear about America's decline. It gets expressed in a rhetoric that is close to the "paranoid style" described by Richard Hofstadter. Incantatory praise of America's lost power is a mainstay of Tea Party worship. The group's members have a typically populist approach to the world of politics, with their rejection of institutional mediation, compromise, ambiguity, complexity, and heterodoxy. In their eyes, what's needed is an immediate, simple relation between the people and government where the latter executes the wishes of the former. Their attitude toward history is similarly direct, with no ambiguity or mediating interpretation allowed. The historian Jill Lepore defines the Tea Party attitude toward history as an antihistorical discourse:

> Antihistory has no patience for ambiguity, self-doubt, and introspection. The Tea Party had an answer: "We have forsaken the Founding Fathers." . . . What the Tea Party, [Glenn] Beck, and [Sean] Hannity . . . shared was a set of assumptions about the relationship between the past and the present that was broadly anti-intellectual and, quite specifically, antihistorical, not least because it defies chronology, the logic of time. To say that we are there, or the Founding Fathers are here, or that we have forsaken them and they're rolling over in their graves because of the latest, breaking political development . . . is to subscribe to a set of assumptions about the relationship between the past and the present stricter even than the strictest form of constitutional originalism, a set of assumptions that, conflating originalism, evangelism, and heritage tourism, amounts to a variety of fundamentalism.[46]

Every local Tea Party chapter is free to say that its goals—cutting taxes or banning abortion—are the true living expression of American constitutional principles. With their originalist approach, they refuse to recall, much less consider, the numerous debates and political compromises that preceded the eventual ratification of the Constitution. Especially interesting, as Skocpol and Williamson also note, is that their vision of history is paradoxically closer to that of anti-Federalists and secessionists than to the Founding Fathers' views that they claim as their inspiration.[47] Their relation to the Constitution is the same as their relation to the Bible, and in fact Constitution study groups were initiated in imitation of the traditional Bible study model. Besides the Constitution, a book that became very popular in these discussion groups was *The Five Thousand Year Leap* (1981) by W. Cleon Skousen, a Mormon specialist of political science and constitutional law with ties to the John Birch Society. Skousen explains the creation of the United States in biblical terms. The book went unnoticed until 2010, when its sales skyrocketed thanks to the endorsement it received from the Fox News conservative journalist Glenn Beck, who frequently quoted from the book on the air. "In the far right," Lepore explains, "where originalism has slipped into fundamentalism, where historical scholarship is taken for a conspiracy and the founding of the United States has become a religion, it's not the past that's a foreign country. It's the present."[48]

By calling for the suppression of all mediating instances between the people and the government, and with their fundamentalist approach to the Constitution, the Tea Party maintains a fantastical relation to politics and history. Their wished-for universe—one that is simple, pure, transparent, and coherent and where compromise is unnecessary—is pure fiction. And yet they have been forceful and successful in large part thanks to their ability to present themselves to the American people as champions of "common sense"—indeed, the very oracles of common sense battling the convoluted, manipulative circumlocutions of elite Washington insiders. A work frequently cited is the 1776 revolutionary pamphlet by Thomas Paine, *Common Sense*. In fact, Beck often compares himself with Paine, as can be seen from the title of his indictment of the Obama administration, *Glenn Beck's Common Sense: The Case Against Out-of-Control Government, Inspired by Thomas Paine.*[49] It is not the first time in the history of American populism—both Left and Right—that this book and its author have been shoehorned into legitimating attacks against the federal government.[50] But rarely has this rhetoric of "common sense" been so effective in public debates and such a winning strategy for those who use it.

The invocation of common sense is all the more ironic since it ends up opposing the very possibility of a *common* shared space for debate and social relations. For Tea Party members, debating with Democrats is a waste of time. What's important in their minds is rooting out free riders and other stowaways and firmly refusing to share anything with those found to be undeserving. "Common" to them means the unique space that the Tea Party wants to protect—that is, the way of life and principles that *they* have in common. Here one is reminded of the argument used by those opposed to the mosque at Ground Zero—the common-sense call to do "what is right," which seeks to counter the building owner's claim to rights of private property and personal freedom. As in the Manhattan controversy, the point is to make "common sense" appear more legitimate, more democratic, and more binding than the principles of liberty and equality, which here end up getting labeled antidemocratic. The Tea Party's deployment of common sense in this way is not at all a turn away from politics, however; nor is the use of moral sentiments in the Manhattan example antipolitical. The effort to present common sense as a principle morally superior to and politically fairer than the sophisticated arguments of Washington elites takes place on a battlefield that is entirely political. Even if they claim to refuse the framework of negotiation and political haggling, local Tea Party chapters have been forced to play by the parliamentary rules that would allow them to promote their cause within state legislative bodies.[51] They have mastered the complex technical procedures of the legislative process that are as far as can be from the simplicities of common sense. Moreover, although they regularly attack the elitism of inside-the-Beltway Washington politicians, the Tea Party activist base also relies on elites—in their case, conservative foundations and their millionaire backers. "There is a certain irony in these newly formed ties. FreedomWorks, for example, is not any sort of insurgent force. As a multimillion-dollar ideological organization advocating 'Lower Taxes, Less Government, More Freedom,' Freedom-Works operates out of Washington D.C."[52] As in the Manhattan affair, here the liberal principle of equality before the law is replaced by another criterion that its defenders try to define as morally superior: "what suits a particular group" here and now is submitted as the only legitimate incarnation of the single public sphere.[53]

Another similarity between the Tea Party activists and the Manhattan antimosque activists is their tendency toward ritualized inversion of the roles of victim and oppressor. Both groups make it a point to portray themselves as victims and display with pride their victim status. In the Manhattan polemic, Imam Rauf's opponents deftly managed to turn things so that the Muslims were to blame: "we the people" aren't intolerant; it's the Muslims who are insensitive to our suffering. The Tea Party's common-sense rhetoric relies on the same form of victim status seizing—"the federal government is taking advantage of us"—and the ability to play the *legitimately* frustrated loser. The first pages of Beck's book express very clearly this strategy of undoing the stigma typically associated with the antiheroic figure of the "average American"—the one that liberals are said to relentlessly tease as ignorant, uncouth, intolerant, poorly dressed, and badly nourished:

> I think I know who you are. . . .
>
> You try to do the right thing every day. You work hard, you always try to do your best, and you play by the rules. You have credit cards, but you can make the payments. You have a home, but with a loan you can afford. . . .
>
> You don't hate people that are different than you, but you stopped expressing opinions on sensitive issues a long time ago because you don't want to be called a racist, bigot, or homophobe if you stand by your values and principles.
>
> You believe in treating people justly and honestly but there is a difference between right and wrong. . . .
>
> You thought that the politicians you supported and defended cared about the issues you do. Then you began to realize that you were wrong—they only care about themselves and their careers. You feel used and betrayed. . . .
>
> Now our government, the instigator of our problems, is telling everyone that they have to start sacrificing. *Don't they understand that I already have been*, you think. You weren't the one spending too much or living on money you didn't have. . . .
>
> Yet, despite all of that, you're still willing to sacrifice more because you want America to succeed. But you demand a plan based on common sense and that actually has a chance to work.[54]

These lines summarize well the central themes of common-sense populism: the feeling of having been tricked all one's life, the feeling of not being able to express one's views freely, the feeling that some earned their house and other possessions but others cheated to get theirs, and the feeling of nostalgia for the past and a willingness to sacrifice more for America's success.

THE TEA PARTY AND ISLAM

The Tea Party is not a repeat of the Moral Majority of the 1980s and cannot be defined simply as an instrument of the Christian Right. As shown in a Pew Research Center study from February 2011, its members and sympathizers have various beliefs when it comes to religion. While those people who say they belong to the Christian Right are mostly sympathetic to the Tea Party, the reverse is not always the case. Half of Tea Party sympathizers say they have never heard of the Christian Right.[55] While many in the Tea Party denounce liberals and secularism, other members apply to moral and social issues the same libertarian grid that they use to decide economic questions—and many take a "free to choose" stand on gay marriage and abortion. Certain members, such as Tom Mullen, even try to combine Christianity with the libertarian ideology. Mullen, a Florida composer, blogger, columnist, and admirer of Ron Paul and his libertarian views, published on his blog in 2010 a text titled "Jesus Christ, Libertarian."[56] Mullen, who is also the author of *A Return to Common Sense*, a book critical of the federal government, attacks social conservatives for trying to impose certain ideas of good and evil in spite of Jesus's true teaching.[57]

Among the Tea Party's evangelical sympathizers who insist on the Christian identity of the American nation that must now be reconquered, one finds sincere religious convictions intermixed with political activism. Glenn Beck has been a major force behind the redefinition of the protest in religious terms. In August 2010, he organized a large gathering in Washington that aimed to "restore America's honor" and called on Americans to reunite around faith in God. He sees the Tea Party protests as the beginning of a third "Great Awakening" in the tradition of the evangelical revivalism of the eighteenth and nineteenth centuries.

Despite these religious overtones, which have received heavy media coverage, the Tea Party is, above all, a protest movement against tax increases. The invocation of Christian values strengthens the nationalist, patriotic, populist message and reaffirms the true American identity with Americanism itself as its true religion. Even Beck's "9/12" project, launched in March 2010, to return America to its economic standing on September 12, 2001, is not, strictly speaking, a religious manifesto, despite appearances. Its list of nine principles (the first being "America is good") and twelve values (honesty, moderation, charity, work, and so on) is mostly a soft set of references to the Founding Fathers centered on a vague consensual moralism.

Islam is not a central concern within the Tea Party and certainly not one of the leading themes of its public demonstrations. The denunciation of the totalitarian character of Islam and warnings about Muslim projects to subvert the American Constitution certainly can be found often enough in its discourse. However, as with the praise of Christendom, the rejection of Islam does not derive from a will to defend a particularly religious world view. It's more just a corollary of the adherents' chosen nationalist, populist rhetoric. The barely disguised racism of many Tea Party members suggests that their attacks against Islam are for them a way to give free expression to racist attitudes without being too overt about it. Openly racist remarks are generally rare because the organization is careful about maintaining a respectable image. Criticizing Islam is considered more acceptable than racist statements about African Americans, and one could say that Islamophobic remarks are a way to vent other self-censored racist feelings. That said, Islam has not become a mobilizing issue outside of those places where a controversy existed already concerning mosque construction or anti-Sharia legislation. In other words, in the cities and states where part of the population has become stirred up against Islam, the members and politicians close to the Tea Party have joined forces with it in opposition to mosques and Sharia. But there is more a convergence of interests, discourses, and strategies than any real anti-Muslim populist project. Thus, in Murfreesboro, Tea Party candidate Lou Ann Zelenik tried to take advantage of the discontent in the neighborhood of the planned mosque to win voters by showing herself sympathetic to their complaints.

Anti-Muslim demonstrations with an intermingling of Tea Party activists, upset local people, and anti-Sharia networkers have regularly taken place in Georgia, Virginia, Ohio, Texas, and Florida. The criticism of Islam is a recurrent theme at Tea Party events but always put forward by the usual suspects—Pamela Geller, Frank Gaffney, Brigitte Gabriel, Nonie Darwish, and a few others—and one cannot say that there is a specifically Tea Party version of anti-Muslim rhetoric or argumentation. One finds the usual style of invective and imprecation and the same alarmist arguments about projects to subvert the Constitution or invade the United States that one hears at the antimosque and anti-Sharia demonstrations. Given the importance of defending the Constitution as a theme within the Tea Party ideology, it's obvious that the arguments of the anti-Sharia militants fall on sympathetic ears at Tea Party events.

The Tea Party's future in American politics now seems ambiguous and uncertain. In certain respects, it seems to be losing steam. In 2012, many

Republican candidates preferred to keep their distance from the Tea Party. At a Tea Party event in Florida in the fall of 2011 to which many Republican candidates had been invited, the number of no-shows was noted with stern criticism by the militants.[58] The group's calling to account of respected GOP figures such as Senator John McCain, who had publicly denounced the Islamophobic hyperbole within the party, seems also to have backfired on the movement.

One cannot say, however, that the Tea Party has been defeated. In a context of an ongoing reconfiguration of the radical Right, which involves both fragmentation and radicalization, the Tea Party may yet play a role that corresponds to certain expectations and a certain conception of political engagement. In any event, no matter what its future political power may be, its recuperation of anti-Muslim rhetoric has produced three notable effects. First, the Tea Party has won the semantic battle to impose terms such as "megamosques," "stealth jihad," and word–idea associations such as Sharia–Constitution and Muslim Brotherhood–terrorism. These terms, syllogisms, and conflations have become commonplace in the public debate. Not everyone subscribes to this lexicon and this logic, but they constitute the grid in relation to which everyone's position gets defined. An activist or a public intellectual who defends Muslim rights or an academic who takes part in the public debate all find themselves obliged to participate in something whose very structuring framework they disagree with. Despite the resistance of a few moderates, anti-Muslim activists within the Tea Party apply pressure on the Republican Party to keep it as right wing as possible. This pressure to radicalize has effects on the public debate—for one thing, it contributes to rendering increasingly tolerable and tolerated the hate speech toward Islam and Muslims that otherwise might have been considered unacceptable. It is now unacceptable, or politically incorrect, to insult someone in the media—and in public discourse generally—for the color of her skin or because she is Jewish or gay, but invectives against Muslims and hate speech toward Islam seem to be less unacceptable.

This normalization of clichés and insults is not necessarily accompanied by an increase in physical violence, but it does create a context where such acts appear increasingly plausible and justifiable. Attacks against Muslims have multiplied significantly since the shooting at a Sikh temple in Oak Creek, Wisconsin, on August 5, 2012. Just two days later, after a failed arson attempt a few months earlier, a mosque in Joplin, Missouri, was burned to the ground. The same day, pigs' feet were found on the building site of the future Al-Nur Islamic Center in Ontario, California. On August 10, shots were fired against the façade of a Muslim school in Morton Grove, Illinois. On August 13, paint bombs were splattered against the walls of the major mosque in Oklahoma City. On August 17, Muslim tombstones in the cemetery of Evergreen Park, Illinois, were damaged and covered with hateful graffiti. The suspects in all these cases are local residents in the neighborhood or city in question—individuals known for their opposition to the presence of mosques and Muslims and who frequently admit what they have done out of pride and bravado.

Anti-Muslim groups reject the alarm whistles sounded by groups such as CAIR and claim that Muslims are not being targeted with hate crimes any more than other communities. What is certain, and disturbing, is the generalization of the idea of a certain acceptability of such attacks against Muslims. Because of the emotions stirred by the shooting at the Sikh temple, the singularity of the comments provoked by this event were overlooked. A number of journalists and other commentators rushed to say that the attacker, Wade Michael Page, had mistaken Sikhs for Muslims, who were probably his real target. But saying that Page made a "mistake" in attacking Sikhs, or that Sikhs were "unfairly" targeted, as was said on CNN, comes close to saying that he would have been "correct" in attacking Muslims.[59] Thus the recuperation of anti-Muslim rhetoric by the Tea Party and the radical Right is nothing original, but it has had the dramatic effect on the general public of representing violent actions against Muslims as normal and deserved.

And yet this recuperation probably signals more a feeling of powerlessness, nostalgia for a mythical past, and fear of decline than a true sense of superiority. Beyond the question of Islam, these populist movements contribute to the affirmation and popularization of a particular mode of political engagement that has nothing to do with the ideal of argument-driven, rational, civilized debate. The Tea Party gatherings and anti-Muslim demonstrations resemble rituals of inversion where the participants celebrate their rough-edged, bad-boy qualities and ostentatiously thumb their noses at liberal niceties. Insofar as this is the case, their liberal opponents would be mistaken to simply mock the folkloric and monstrous carnival-like atmosphere of these gatherings. That atmosphere is more than just an incidental ornament to the debate. It expresses a will to engage in politics differently than through the method of polite exchange of reasoned arguments while still resisting to fall into open violence. It is an atmosphere that allows the articulation of a certain discontent, occupies space on the playing field, and offers an emotional outlet—a relatively restrained one—for feelings of frustration and incomprehension.

5

FORCING THE FIRST AMENDMENT

American Exporting of Religious Freedom

What place does Islam have in American foreign policy? To what extent does the foreign policy debate over Islam differ from domestic policy discussions? Controversies inside the United States reveal big differences between the logic of law, on the one hand, and the logic of public debate and political mobilization, on the other. I have shown how different normative frameworks clash: on one side, liberal principles of equality and contract; on another, notions of merit, sacrifice, and convenience. One does not find such sharp contrasts in foreign policy debates. On the contrary, the latter are characterized by much crisscrossing between the discourses of liberalism, security, and morality.

Since the end of the 1990s, Islam is viewed in American foreign policy in terms of either national security or religious freedom. The main objective is to put in place programs that prevent radical Islam and radicalization and that promote a moderate Islam—in countries such as Iraq, Saudi Arabia, Pakistan, and Yemen—with the aim of pacifying the region and protecting American interests. At the same time, in parallel with this realist security perspective, there has also been a liberal approach to promote religious freedom in the world through the efforts of diverse lobbies and political figures. For example, the International Religious Freedom Act (IRFA) was adopted in 1998 during the Clinton presidency as a tool to exert diplomatic pressure to defend individual rights to religious freedom.

For many intellectuals, diplomats, and political figures, the Muslim world is now a major focus of this policy initiative. Because this supposedly unified cultural area is often described as oppressive and intolerant, it functions as the ideal terrain for this mission. This policy of exporting the American concept of international religious freedom is obviously closely linked to the defense of the United States' interests in Muslim-majority countries. Thus the realist, culturalist paradigm of national security, on the one hand, and the liberal, idealist defense of religious liberty, on the other, appear as two sides of the same coin when it comes to understanding and managing Islam outside its borders. This is what leads Elizabeth Shakman Hurd to speak of "securitization" when talking about the use of religion in the American conception of international relations.[1]

Since 2001, many studies devoted to America's policy in the Middle East have been published, and they are often very critical of the United States' imperialism and its will to be the dominant power in the region. A complete account would go beyond the scope of this book. The goal here is to analyze how in American foreign policy a legalist perspective intermixes with a moralistic civilization argument when treating the category of religion, and more specifically Islam.

IS RELIGION A PERTINENT FACTOR IN FOREIGN POLICY?

There is not an official American foreign policy regarding Islam, or any foreign policy toward religion in general. Rather than being an operative category of recognized concrete action, Islam and religion are topics within the discourse of public diplomacy.[2] American international relations specialists are in disagreement over the importance that ought to be given to religion as a factor in world conflicts and their resolution. For some, conflicts are to be explained, above all, by looking at the material conditions and the unequal distribution of wealth and symbolic powers.[3] They do not consider differences in religious affiliation to be a leading cause of violence. Thus it is useless to have religion be a central theme in public diplomacy and international treaties. It's more important to encourage economic development of conflict-prone areas. However, there are also divisions among researchers who consider religion to be a factor that needs to be taken seriously. Some of them, in the tradition of Samuel Huntington, claim that there exists an irreducible difference between the Muslim world and the West, the former being, in their view, naturally more disposed toward violence than the latter. One of the leading representatives of this line of thinking is Monica Duffy Toft, who, on the basis of a comparative study of forty-two conflicts between 1940 and 2000, concludes that Islamic culture is characterized by great difficulty adapting to other cultures and by a more militaristic attitude. From her point of view, the resolution of conflict necessarily requires reforming Islamic culture. Other researchers come to similar conclusions but without sharing the same negative, culturalist vision of Islam. For them, there is no inherent problem with Islam—rather, religion and the religious are important vectors of communication and negotiation that have for too long been neglected in diplomacy and foreign policy. They claim that it is possible to find common ground around religious values and to take better advantage of the resources offered by religious communities for building peace. The idea of religion as an essential tool of "state-building" and the resolution of international conflicts is the thesis of the essay collection *Religion: The Missing Dimension of Statecraft* (1995).[4] One of the volume's editors, Douglas Johnston, went on to found the International Center for Religion and Diplomacy in Washington, a think tank devoted to promoting these ideas to politicians and the general public.

These disagreements over the role of religion in international relations are a leading symptom of the indeterminate status of the category of religion itself. "Religion" floats between meaning individual belief, a set of practices, and an organized collective with institutional hierarchies. When analyzed in relation to conflict resolution, it is understood as either a tool for pacification or a cause of radicalization. These conceptual uncertainties appear clearly in a report published in April 2010 by the Chicago Council on Global Affairs titled *Engaging Religious Communities Abroad: A New Imperative for U.S. Foreign Policy*. The thesis of the report is that religion in general (and not just Islam) ought to be considered as an asset and resource. Most of the study evokes the positive force of individual faith that leads people to act in the world. But one of its footnotes proposes another definition of religion, the only explicit effort at definition in the entire study, and it insists more on the collective and institutional dimension of religion: "We define religion as an established system of belief, practice, and ritual based in a collective affirmation of a transcendent or otherworldly reality that encompasses and gives ultimate meaning to earthly existence."[5]

Whether the insistence is on individual faith or on a social institution, religion for the Chicago Council is defined by its capacity to act immediately on conflicts in ways that other types of actors, actions, and institutions fail to do: "Religion—through its motivating ideas and the mobilizing power of its institutions—is a driver of politics in its own right."[6] Such an approach is problematic not only because of its tendency to essentialize religion as a "distinctive logic" of practices, representations, and discourses but also because it in no way explains the mechanisms by which religion allegedly shapes behaviors. Thus the category of religion understood as a resource functions in the reasoning of the Chicago Council experts as a sort of deus ex machina, thereby producing the illusion of an explanation and a strategy for global conflict resolution.

IS BUILDING A MODERATE ISLAM ABROAD IN CONFORMITY WITH THE CONSTITUTION?

The debate about the role of Islam in international relations is not merely an academic discussion among professors and think-tank experts. There is something concrete and immediate at stake, since it concerns an essential question of American foreign policy: To what extent does the First Amendment apply to the actions of the United States outside its sovereign territory? Legal scholars, diplomats, and civil servants of governmental agencies question the constitutionality of initiatives that relate explicitly to religious communities or to a theological approach. For example, to what extent does a program that seeks to promote a particular interpretation of Islam in a Muslim country or that favors one religion over another represent, indirectly, an attempt to "establish" a religion and stand therefore in violation of the establishment clause of the First Amendment? This question is closely linked to the larger question of the extent to which this amendment ought to constrain American actions abroad. Up until now, neither of these questions has received a clear and consensual answer.

The report of the Chicago Council on Global Affairs takes note of this uncertainty and its consequences: "Legal uncertainty about the extent to which the Establishment Clause applies to government action overseas has seriously undermined the effectiveness of U.S. foreign policy."[7] The Chicago Council "calls upon the president of the United States, advised by executive branch offices and agencies who have studied the problem, to clarify that the Establishment Clause does not bar the United States from engaging religious communities abroad in the conduct of foreign policy, though it does impose constraints on the means that the United States may choose to pursue this engagement."[8]

The Center for Strategic and International Studies, a think tank specialized in questions of security and international relations, began a similar discussion of the problem in 2007 with its own report that laid out the same questions. The authors note that "government officials remain concerned about developing and implementing religion-related policies abroad in part because legal guidelines on the applicability of the Free Exercise and Establishment Clauses to foreign policy are still evolving."[9] According to the Center for Strategic and International Studies, even if government agencies are increasingly aware of the religious factor since 2001, most government officials remain highly skeptical about the grounds and legality of such an approach. Many say they fear legal proceedings for acting in violation of the establishment clause. John Hanford, former United States ambassador-at-large for international religious freedom, is quoted in the report as stating that those fears are exaggerated and unhelpful: "There is a concern—I see as excessive— about the separation of Church and State that has led to a lack of comfort in dealing with religion."[10] Nevertheless, neither the report nor any of the meetings and conferences held since its publication have come up with a clear response.

And yet the question does not simply concern hypothetical policies. In 2015, Brookings Institution expert Will McCants raised this question again. He reported that the lawyers in the State Department opposed a project he had submitted when he was working there as a senior adviser for countering violent extremism. While the project sought to compile Islamic scriptures advocating for tolerance, the State Department lawyers objected, saying that such a document was meant to "promote one interpretation of a religion over another" and, as such, was in conflict with the establishment clause.[11] Likewise, some programs sponsored by the U.S. Agency for International Development (USAID) have been criticized for their violation of the establishment clause. Since fostering moderate Islam has become a key theme of policies aimed at building stability in the Middle East in the name of advancing both American interests and the ideal of democratization, several programs have been put in place by American governmental agencies in Iraq, Pakistan, Afghanistan, and Nigeria, but they would be judged unconstitutional if they were operating in the United States, according to Jesse Merriam, a constitutional law specialist. One example is the Islam and Civil Society (ISC) program launched by USAID in Indonesia on the idea that Indonesian political reform necessarily presupposes a reform of Islamic doctrine. "Religious terminology is more effective than secular discourse in winning popular support for democratic values," say the authors of the summary assessment of the program.[12] In order to build stronger ties between the United States and Muslim nongovernmental organizations, the program offers financial and logistical aid to different religious organizations—notably, a conservative association of Muslim students that has recently begun promoting themes of pluralism and democracy. The ISC supports civil studies education projects in universities such as the State Islamic University of Jakarta and the private Muhammadiyah University of Magelang in Central Java, Indonesia. The ISC also financed the publication by State Islamic University of the manual *Democracy, Human Rights and Civil Society* as well as the creation of the course "Democracy, Human Rights and Gender Equality in an Islamic Perspective." The USAID program encourages reaching out to and supporting organizations that defend a certain theological approach to Islam judged favorable to advancing American interests. The agency also finances "democracy education workshops" aimed at preachers who speak at Friday services. The program has sought to finance the distribution of roughly two thousand manuals and brochures on "democracy and pluralism" as well as the training of female preachers to lead debates on equality of the sexes. According to USAID, this collaboration with women allows them to fight against "harsh interpretations of Islamic (sharia) law."[13] In similar fashion, the radio show *Religion and Tolerance* financed by the ISC aims to promote the idea that the "true" interpretation of Islam is tolerant, pro-democratic, and favorable to American interests.

To what extent are such initiatives compatible with the establishment clause? For Merriam, similar programs financed by government agencies would never be able to operate inside the United States:

> Imagine an analogous domestic program, such as a federal program that sought to mediate our current culture war by encouraging evangelical professionals and leaders to become more tolerant of homosexuality. Also imagine that to achieve this goal, the United States funded evangelical organizations to teach courses in the most conservative evangelical universities, such as Jerry Falwell's Liberty University or Pat Robertson's Regent University, and that these courses focused on how good Christians must tolerate homosexuality. Or imagine that the United States designed and disseminated a university textbook that focused on this theme. Such domestic efforts to use evangelical Christianity as a political vehicle would violate the Establishment Clause by singling out gay-friendly evangelical organizations for preferential funding and by engaging in the interpretation of Christian doctrine.[14]

If it were certain that the establishment clause applied as strictly outside as inside the United States, most ISC programs sponsored by USAID would have to be declared unconstitutional. But for now there is no clear position on the matter.

USAID members themselves hold divergent opinions. Some years ago, a conflict erupted between the legal counsel for USAID and Clifford Brown, then an employee of an agency based in Kyrgyzstan.[15] USAID's lawyers prohibited Brown from carrying out his project of translating moderate Islamic writings into the Uzbek and Kyrgyz languages on the grounds that USAID's financing of that project would violate the First Amendment's establishment clause. Brown rejected this interpretation, however, claiming that the clause did not apply outside the United States. The question came up again in a July 17, 2009, audit by the inspector general of USAID.[16]

The investigation focused especially on the funding of two projects that were judged problematic: one to pay $325,000 for repairs to four mosques in Iraq, and the other a program to fight the AIDS virus that also encouraged young people to learn passages from the Bible. The leaders of the mosque restoration project in Iraq admitted that they were unable to give a clear answer as to whether their work was in conformity with the First Amendment and federal regulations. Federal regulations prohibit using USAID funds to restore structures devoted to "inherently religious purposes."[17] But the legal counsel for USAID-Iraq did not apply because the principal aim of the construction project was to provide work for masons, plumbers, electricians, and gardeners: "For example, some of the expected benefits from rehabilitating the Al Shuhada Mosque were stimulating the economy, enhancing a sense of pride in the community, reducing opposition to international relief organizations operating in Fallujah, and reducing incentives among young men to participate in violence or insurgent groups."[18]

USAID leaders were confronted with the same sort of dilemma with the funding of an AIDS-prevention program in Africa called the "Abstinence and Behavior Change for Youth Program." This project included optional use of Bible stories and memorizing religious verses with the aim of helping young people better resist sexual exploitation. USAID's financing of this program represents an indirect official endorsement of Christian principles and even a preference for Christianity. But the local USAID authorities were not certain that the establishment clause applies as strictly outside as inside the United States, especially when an American foreign policy objective as important as the fight against AIDS is at stake. They also insisted on the idea of "cultural differences"—arguing that recourse to religious themes in the African context is "useful for connecting with the target audience."[19] The report decries the fact that the Department of Justice never replied to USAID's leaders who asked for clarification about which projects the agency could or could not fund. One of the report's major recommendations is that the director of USAID's Center for Faith-Based Initiatives obtain a clear response from President Obama and the White House Office of Faith-Based and Neighborhood Partnerships.

One of the first American legal scholars to have closely examined this question is John Mansfield, a former law professor at Harvard University.[20] For Mansfield, the Constitution does not apply the same way abroad and on American soil, first, because of the necessity of adapting to constraints of the foreign context and, second, out of respect for "the rights of foreign nations to follow their own customs." That said, Mansfield does not give a definitive answer to the debate. He simply invites one to make the distinction between cases that involve what he calls "a core Establishment Clause value" and others that do not. According to Mansfield, one can accept that the federal government would finance a religious school in a foreign country to develop science education as long as religious schools are the only ones available for receiving financing in the country. Even if in this case the financing scheme is contrary to the establishment clause as it applies to domestic policy, such a program would still be acceptable because it serves the interests of the United States. But if the federal funds were to permit not science education but the school's development of certain theological interpretations, that, says Mansfield, would be an unacceptable violation of the establishment clause: "For the United States directly to embrace the doctrines of a particular religion, albeit for political ends, might conflict with the values of the religion clauses to an extent that cannot be outweighed by foreign policy considerations or the importance of respect for other cultures."[21]

To resolve the question of the applicability of the Constitution in foreign policy contexts, Jesse Merriam proposes two criteria: the "anomalous" and the "impracticable." In other words, one has to consider that the Constitution always applies to American foreign actions, except in cases where it would be anomalous or practically impossible to do so. Similar criteria have been used implicitly since the Insular Cases, a series of disputes treated by the Supreme Court between 1901 and 1914 that had to do with the status of territories, including islands, acquired by the United States in the aftermath of the Spanish-American War of 1898. During the proceedings, the Supreme Court argued that all constitutional rights did not automatically extend to all regions under American control. That discussion contributed to the development of the theory of territorial incorporation, which holds that the Constitution applies in its entirety to only incorporated territories (such as Alaska and Hawaii) but only partially to new, non-incorporated territories (such as Guam and Puerto Rico). Despite the explicit use of this criterion in the cases *Reid v. Covert* (1957) and *Boumediene v. Bush* (2008), the matter remains highly ambiguous.[22] The Supreme Court gave very little guidance that would help define the "anomalous" and the "impracticable."

The first step in evaluating the case of USAID's funding of mosque repairs in Iraq is to define clearly what the goals are of the U.S. mission in Iraq. If one accepts that the mission's goal is to build stability and economic development there, one could ask how the strict application of the establishment clause would obstruct progress toward those goals. For Merriam, this is not the right question. The reasons given by the USAID leaders to justify the reconstruction of the mosques—that is, creating jobs, restoring a feeling of community pride, stimulating the economy, and reducing the risk of youth turning to violence—are reasons that could justify building all sorts of structures and not only mosques. This is why "it seems entirely practicable to apply the Establishment Clause to this funding of mosques in Iraq."[23] The situation is different in the case of the funding of the African AIDS prevention program. That mission, according to the USAID audit, is "devoted to improving the self-awareness and self-worth of young people so that students of the program might become less vulnerable to sexual exploitation and thus less at risk for HIV."[24] In this case, the U.S. government cannot carry out this mission if it strictly applies the establishment clause—in other words, by refusing to include any and all theological references in the sex-education manuals. In short, for Merriam, the criterion of what's "impracticable" brings some clarity to the debate: in the case where the strict application of the establishment clause renders realizing an essential foreign policy objective impracticable, one can take the view that the Constitution does not apply.

To this day, however, no clarification has come down from the Department of Justice or from the White House Office of Faith-Based and Neighborhood Partnerships concerning the application of the establishment clause outside the United States. After the publication of the audit, the agency proposed changing its own regulations in order to pursue more easily a certain number of activities that would be potentially limited or prohibited if the establishment clause were to be strictly enforced. In a circular published on March 25, 2011, in the Federal Register, USAID deplores "that some provisions in the Final Rule go beyond the requirements of the Establishment Clause and other Federal law, are not supported by Establishment Clause jurisprudence, and constrict USAID's ability to pursue the national security and foreign policy interests of the United States overseas."[25] USAID proposed modifying the final rule such that "USAID funds may be used for the acquisition, construction, or rehabilitation of structures that are used, in whole or in part, for inherently religious activities, so long as the program for which USAID assistance is provided (i) Is authorized by law and has a secular purpose." Numerous specialists immediately opposed this attempt to soften the restrictions relating to the financing of religious programs. A group of six First Amendment experts sent a letter to Ari Alexander, the director of USAID's Center for Faith-Based and Community Initiatives, warning him about the flaws of this new regulation. The latter might prohibit the flagrant establishment of a religion, but it nevertheless authorizes actions that the establishment clause jurisprudence as it currently stands before the Supreme Court also forbids. Notably, the direct financing of explicitly religious activities is prohibited.[26] Also prohibited is using government money to finance the construction of buildings where religious cultural activities or religious instruction are to take place.[27] The six experts also reject the argument that considers funding a religious activity to be acceptable as long as it serves a secular purpose. This criterion is totally inadequate to justify direct aid from the government.[28]

USAID's proposed rule change was finally withdrawn, but the discussion it provoked revealed once again the disagreements and uncertainties that exist around the application of the First Amendment abroad. Given the massive American presence today in countries with Muslim majorities, it is unlikely that these questions will just go away. Neither the White House nor the Department of Justice have provided any clear answers. In 2009, President Obama tried to clarify the relation between the government and religiously inspired nongovernmental organizations with an executive order that defined more precisely what it was permissible to fund.[29] "Explicitly religious" activities were excluded. And yet foreign policy officials are still wondering what the exact constraints are on U.S. action in the Muslim world. The question of what exactly the establishment clause permits remains unresolved. The distinction between "rights" and "what is right"—so central to the domestic controversies, as we've seen—is not as effective in these foreign cases. There is considerable confusion between the legal argument and the moral, cultural narrative. This gray zone constitutes what Elizabeth Shakman Hurd describes as a "nonseparationist" landscape of religious engagement and reform.[30] It has complex and problematic consequences in the politics of promotion of international religious freedom: "It gives an edge to those religions that conform to an American understanding of what it means for religion to be free."[31]

EXPORTING RELIGIOUS FREEDOM

The International Religious Freedom Act was the outcome of a campaign led jointly by Christian activists and secular human rights activists as a way to place the fight against the persecution of religious minorities at the center of foreign policy.[32] In the mid-1990s, violence against Christians in Sudan and against Muslims and Christian minorities in China was a growing preoccupation for these lobbies. In the fall of 1997, Representative Frank R. Wolf (R-Va.) and Senator Arlen Specter (R-Pa.) sponsored the Freedom from Religious Persecution Act, which imposed automatic sanctions against governments found guilty of persecuting religious minorities. Secretary of State Madeleine Albright rejected the idea of sanctions and criticized the very principle of such a law, which in her view implied a dangerous prioritization of human rights. The State Department was generally hostile to the idea, which was perceived as largely an initiative of the Christian Right. The business community also worried about the consequences of such a law, fearing the negative repercussions on commerce in the event of such sanctions. Therefore, a slightly modified version, IRFA, was proposed and eventually signed into law by President Clinton in October 1998 after having been approved in the House of Representatives in May 1998 by a vote of 375 to 41.[33] The law calls for the creation of the Office of International Religious Freedom within the State Department and an independent bipartisan commission headed by a special counselor to the president that would be part of the National Security Council. The commission is charged with making recommendations to the president, the secretary of state, and the head of the National Security Council. Its job is to prepare reports that provide essential information about religious freedom in the world and to identify "countries of particular concern" (CPC). Section 402 gives a series of possible sanctions to be imposed against countries that do not respect religious freedom, ranging from public condemnation by the American president to the elimination of university exchange programs or other cultural cooperation activities. Economic sanctions, such as the suspension of economic aid, are also enumerated.[34]

As the IRFA supporters see it, the legal norm of religious freedom places the accent on individual liberty. This norm is founded on the presupposition that considers personal experience, faith, and sincere beliefs as the essence of religion—to the detriment of other approaches that emphasize being faithful to certain doctrines or social practices. Many detractors of IRFA criticize this propensity to present as universally true and timeless a definition of religion that in fact has a particular situated history. The historian Donald S. Lopez Jr. denounces this wish to erect as a universal legal norm a value that is "an assumption deriving from the history of Christianity that religion is above all an interior state of assent to certain truths."[35] The definition of religion as belief has the effect of making religious practices that are defined differently appear as abnormal or dangerous—for example, those that insist more on ethics, orthopraxy, and community. As Elizabeth Shakman Hurd has noted, the international dissemination of the American norm of religious freedom, far from guaranteeing the survival or emergence of plural ways of life and ethical orientations, works instead to reduce differences to a uniformity: "In its strongest forms, the story of international religious freedom globalizes the secular state's power over the individual. Appearing as a guarantee of the worth of the individual's own desires, it is actually a story of telling people who they are, what to do and how to be. It privileges particular ways of doing and being as deserving special protection by the state or associations thereof, leaving others behind."[36] The IRFA policy makes apparent a confusion between a liberal emancipation register of rights and a register of nationalism and security. These two narratives, explains Hurd, "justify intervention to save, define, shape, and sanctify parts of people's (religious and non-religious) individual and collective lives."[37]

This paradigm of international religious freedom, founded on the idea of the primacy of sincere belief and individual conscience, is consistent with what the anthropologist Webb Keane has described as the "moral narrative of modernity."[38] This narrative is founded on the essential distinction between sincere belief and all practices defined as nonessential—alimentary prohibitions, icons, rituals, and the like: "The moral narrative of modernity is a story about human emancipation and self-mastery. According to this moral narrative, modernity is a story of human liberation from a host of false beliefs and fetishisms that undermined freedom in the past."[39]

Part of the established foreign policy discourse on international religious freedom seems to presuppose that Islam does not make any distinction between the religious and the political. This suspicion toward

Muslims' alleged incapacity to produce political decisions independently from Islam appeared more recently with the questions raised about the neutrality of the members of the U.S. Commission for International Religious Freedom (USCIRF). The commission was criticized on several occasions for its treatment of Muslim employees. In June 2012, Safiya Ghori-Ahmad sued the commission for having reversed its decision to hire her after learning that she was Muslim. This trial, which followed a complaint filed by the commission concerning equality of opportunity in hiring, focused on a particular member of USCIRF, Nina Shea. She is said to have remarked that "hiring a Muslim like Ghori-Ahmad to analyze religious freedom in Pakistan would be like 'hiring an IRA activist to research the U.K. twenty years ago.'"[40] Leonard Leo, a conservative lawyer and longtime president of the commission, in addition to being vice president of the Federalist Society and a former adviser to George W. Bush, also came in for questioning during this trial. Serious reservations about the commission's neutrality and its anti-Muslim prejudice that had been expressed long before the Ghori-Ahmad affair led certain lawmakers to propose terminating its mandate at the end of 2011. The mandate was renewed for three years, but five commissioners were forced to resign, including Nina Shea. The nomination of Zuhdi Jasser to be a member of USCIRF by Senator Mitch McConnell (R-Ky.) did nothing to calm the critics of IRFA's orientation. As mentioned earlier, this Muslim doctor and founder of the American Muslim Forum for Democracy had gained public attention for his participation in the hearings organized in March 2011 by Representative Peter King (R-N.Y.) about the radicalization of American Muslims, for his opposition to the Manhattan Islamic center, and for his support of the anti-Sharia movement and of the New York Police Department's surveillance program directed at Muslims. After 2001, he became famous for his media appearances in which he explained that Islam can be compatible with democracy only if it is purified, reformed, and Americanized. On April 12, 2012, a total of sixty-four associations, mosques, and Muslim intellectuals sent a petition to Senators Daniel Inouye (D-Hawaii), McConnell, and Dick Durbin (D-Ill.), calling on them to withdraw Jasser's nomination on the grounds that he is a puppet of Islamophobic groups and opposed to the religious freedom of American Muslims.[41]

The IRFA is inspired by a vision of the world that began during the Cold War, when an evangelical rhetoric and a liberal-secular discourse in defense of human rights intermingled in an unprecedented way. Since the end of the 1970s, evangelical lobbies have pushed for a moralization of American foreign policy. According to Joshua Green, there has been development over the past three decades of a "movement of Christian solidarity" in the United States that wishes to make opposition to persecutions of Christians in Sudan, Saudi Arabia, and Pakistan become a foreign policy priority. And criticism of Islam is said to be an inseparable part of this combat. Thus Steven Snyder, a member of the association International Christian Concern, could assert in September 2001: "We are at war with an unseen enemy that has demonstrated its resolve to launch a *jihad* (holy war) on Americans, Christians, and Jews."[42] Grace Bible Church in Virginia, of which the Republican representative Frank Wolf—one of the authors of the International Religious Freedom Act—is a member, is active in this movement. Its pastor, Chris Robinson, seeks to convince his congregation, most of whom are engaged in projects to protect Christians in Burma or Sudan, that there is a symmetry between the fate of American Christians since September 11 and that of persecuted Christians in the Muslim world. Since the end of the 1970s, these conservative Christian groups have appropriated the secular discourse of human rights to add more gravitas to their combat. The IRFA is the outcome of this grafting of the secular humanist norms of human rights onto the conservative evangelical program. The career path of Nina Shea, a longtime member of the Commission for International Religious Freedom, is exemplary in this regard. She began to take an interest in religious freedom during the Cold War. After having been involved in the fight against the Sandinistas in Nicaragua, she helped found the Puebla Institute, a watchdog group opposed to religious oppression.[43] Today she is the director for religious freedom at the Hudson Institute, a conservative think tank, and a leading figure in the campaign against the persecution of Christians around the world. In a *Wall Street Journal* editorial published on July 5, 1995, Michael J. Horowitz, former head legal counsel to President Reagan at the Office of Management and Budget, denounced the persecution of Christians in Muslim countries, enumerating a series of atrocities: pastors assassinated, children kidnapped, churches burned. In the wake of the emotions stirred by this declaration, the first International Day of Prayer for the Persecuted Church was organized in 1996 and received massive support from many evangelical churches. Also in 1996, Shea published *In the Lion's Den: Persecuted Christians and What the Western Church Can Do About It*, a pamphlet filled with horrible tales intended to show the extent of Christian persecutions in Muslim countries. Many of those close to the IRFA who came of age in the Cold War context continue to have a Manichean and polemical approach to international relations, and for them the United States must play the role of the exceptional country. The image of Christians persecuted by Muslims is the updated version of Christians under siege from godless Communists.

An entire media industry has thus been developed that stages what the historian Melani McAlister calls "the spectacle of persecution." Since the passage of the IRFA, "there was a remarkable proliferation of materials that constructed a particular image of 'the persecuted.' In books and magazines, and increasingly online, believers could consume vivid stories and images of suffering."[44] Many organizations—Voice of Martyrs, Open Doors, Christian Freedom International, Compass Direct—have specialized in disseminating narratives of the martyrdom of Christianity by Islam.

The recrudescence of violence against Copts in Egypt after 2011 and the spread of expulsion and oppression against Christian minorities perpetrated by ISIS have reinforced the polarizing and asociological narrative of the clash of civilizations.[45] A coalition of self-appointed representatives of the Egyptian Coptic and Middle Eastern Christian diaspora, pro-IRFA politicians, intellectuals sympathetic to neoconservative causes, and evangelical leaders turned the Coptic cause into a key component of the international religious freedom campaign. Saba Mahmood has demonstrated how, to demand the protection of the international community, the American Coptic diaspora evokes not only the necessity of protecting freedom of conscience but also the defense of article 27 of the United Nation's International Covenant on Civil and Political Rights, which defines religious freedom as it relates to the right of a minority.[46] This strategy of referring to religious freedom and to the concept of a minority is another chapter in the continual history of Protestant missions in Egypt that originated in the nineteenth century. As the historical study by Heather Sharkey illustrates, Presbyterian missionaries in Egypt were ardent defenders of the cause of religious freedom in arguments to the U.S. State Department, the British Foreign Office, and the League of Nations.[47] Saba Mahmood argues that the

IRFA exemplifies the same imperialist will as the Protestant missionaries of the nineteenth century who viewed the promotion of religious freedom as a necessary condition for the success of their proselytism.[48]

> The recent passage of the International Religious Freedom Act by the U.S. Congress (1998) to promote the right of religious liberty (particularly Christians) in the Middle East must be placed within this long geopolitical history in which Western powers have often violated the principle of state sovereignty under the guise of promoting religious tolerance. No non-Western nation-state in modern history has been able to exert the same pressure to advocate the rights of religious, racial, or ethnic minorities living in the Western world.[49]

In the end, the efforts of Protestant missionaries to divide Christians and Muslims produced little result in Egypt. Unlike many other Christian communities in the Middle East, Coptic Egyptians long rejected the offers of European protection. They refused to be transformed into a protected "minority," and they sided with anticolonial nationalist movements, placing the accent on the importance of national unity. The authoritarian regimes of first Gamal Abdel Nasser and then Hosni Mubarak did, however, contribute to the polarization of Muslims and Copts. As the church came to be defined as the sole legitimate interlocutor of the Egyptian power elite, the identification via the religious marker replaced all other forms of identification for the Egyptian Copts. The Egyptian revolution of 2011 put an end to this equilibrium and this situation where the Copts lived a de facto minority status protected by a strict hierarchy, which was itself subject to the structures of an authoritarian government. The role played between 2011 and 2013 by the Muslim Brotherhood and the advances of the Salafist movement have been serious concerns to the Coptic community.[50] As Mahmood shows, a lively debate is ongoing among intellectuals and Coptic leaders as to whether they should now embrace the status of protected minority.[51]

It should be noted that the members of the Coptic diaspora in the United States practice a less nuanced discourse, more anti-Muslim and pro-American than their Egyptian coreligionists. They largely supported the 2008 initiative of Frank Wolf, who introduced legislation in the U.S. House of Representatives that would make the allocation of American aid conditional on respect for the religious freedom of Copts.[52] Michael Munier, an admirer of Representative Wolf and the founder (in 1996) of the U.S. Copts Association, is a leading defender of the thesis of Coptic persecution. He collaborates regularly with the Hudson Institute, where Nina Shea and Michael J. Horowitz have organized numerous conferences directed at diplomats and politicians who take up the fate of Egypt's Copts.

Nevertheless, even if the IRFA paradigm is founded on an orientalist conception of the Muslim world, it's important not to exaggerate the thesis that religious liberty is actually working as a tool of political imperialism. Researchers and activists may speak of a hegemonic project by analyzing the origins and implications of the IRFA from a theoretical perspective, but those practically concerned with this policy deplore instead its ineffectiveness, lack of coherence, and absence of real results. Thomas Farr, a former director of the Office for International Religious Freedom, has described in detail the failure of this policy.[53] Not only is the secular culture of American diplomacy slow to change, but the absence of clear directives concerning the application of the establishment clause overseas also discourages the few diplomats who might be willing to accord more importance to the religious factor. Isolated as it is within the State Department, accomplishing the goals of the IRFA is impeded by the unusual feature of having an ambassador-at-large. Paradoxically, the latter is subordinate to the assistant secretary of state for democracy, human rights, and labor.[54] This situation is different from the usual hierarchy within the State Department because normally the rank of ambassador-at-large is superior to that of assistant secretary. In 2003, the inspector general of the State Department released a very negative report about the organization of IRFA policy: "The current structure that places the congressionally mandated office of the Ambassador-at-Large for International Religious Freedom within DRL [democracy, rights, and labor] is at odds with the Department's organizational guidelines and has proved to be unworkable. . . . As a consequence the purposes for which the religious freedom function was created are not being adequately served."[55] On account of all these difficulties, promoting religious freedom is not perceived by young diplomats as an attractive field to enter but more often as a dead-end to avoid. Most IRFA reports evoke the ongoing tensions between the methods of the commission and that of the majority of State Department civil servants, who generally stick to a secular orientation and are even wary of the approach taken by the commission. According to Farr, the commission's recommendations are more often shelved rather than being used to serve any real imperial policy. He writes that this mix of disinterest and mistrust when it comes to religion can be found among liberals as well as realists. "Whereas realists see religion as relevant only to understanding the drive to power, liberals tend to see religious communities—especially traditional religious communities—as obstacles to the adoption of liberal policies."[56]

The nonbinding character of the IRFA program also contributes to its weakness. The principle tool of the USCIRF is the denunciation of a government's abuses against religious minorities and the place of certain countries on a list of CPCs. But imposing concrete sanctions on the basis of USCIRF recommendations has rarely happened. The IRFA report published in 2007 suggests that the policy of designating CPCs may sometimes even be counterproductive. After listing Saudi Arabia as a CPC in 2004, a nonbinding accord was signed between the Saudi and American governments that stipulated that the Saudi government would agree to stop paying for the studies of radical preachers, terminate the dissemination of Wahhabi literature abroad, and remove language judged overly intolerant from certain school manuals.[57] Four years after signing this accord, none of these promises had been kept, and the report even notes further stiffening in the language of the school manuals.[58] In similar fashion, notes Farr, China first expressed displeasure at being classified as a CPC, but very quickly it simply ignored the rhetoric coming from the commission: "[A]s the CPC designations recurred year after year, duly accompanied by a reaffirmation of the ban on control equipment, even the Chinese began to yawn."[59] Of the three leading goals of the IRFA bureau—the fight against religious persecutions, the liberation of religious prisoners, and the promotion of religious liberty—the third remains the vaguest and least achievable for the State Department. Implementation of the International Religious Freedom Act consists in identifying problem zones and condemning them verbally more than it does developing concrete measures that are suitable in a particular context. In 2011, Farr summarized the absence of resources, coherent organization, and interest when he described the policy for promoting religious freedom as anemic and ineffective: "Notwithstanding their internal inconsistencies, the combined weight of these arguments has fed a kind of paralysis in U.S.

international religious freedom policy, which, on balance, has been anemic and ineffective in Muslim-majority countries."[60]

In short, after starting off as the pet project of a small network of evangelical activists, the policy to promote international religious freedom has yet to gain wide acceptance. While all foreign policy leaders agree in principle to opposing the persecution of religious minorities, many have reservations about the IRFA's policies, its presuppositions, and its way of going about things. The incoherence of this program, the lack of resources at its disposal, and the low level of interest it has attracted are regularly deplored. The International Religious Freedom Act may be the instrument of an imperial vision of the world, but the practical successes of this policy have so far been limited. And yet, regardless of the number of sanctions it has been able to impose or other successful pursuits, the activists, intellectuals, and networks sympathetic to IRFA have managed to reinforce among the American people an image of an intolerant Islam and a Muslim world that persecutes Christians.

THE AMBIGUITIES OF RELIGIOUS FREEDOM AT HOME AND ABROAD

Those sympathetic to IRFA and those who support Christian causes in the world turn to the principle of religious freedom in very different ways, depending on whether it's in the context of foreign or domestic policy. When the focus is the Muslim world, religion gets defined in accordance with the liberal Protestant tradition as faith and belief. In order for all to be able to freely practice their religion and coexist, it's important to disseminate the idea that the essence of religion is interiority and sincerity, and not to insist on a social order or dogmas that one wishes to impose on others. The important thing is to plead in favor of a sort of "disestablishment" of the religious, and to insist on individual liberty as opposed to doctrines and religious, statist institutions. In national debates, however—notably, those involving the Catholic Church—one can observe the increasing pressure on the part of certain religious and political figures who speak out in favor of an implicit "reestablishment" of religious institutions and greater recognition of the role of Christianity in the public sphere: "While some national and international human rights regimes may have moved toward a more individualistic model of protecting religious freedom, one that focuses on the sincerely formed consciences of individuals, religiously motivated groups in the United States may be moving the other way, back toward what in the United States used to be called establishment—that is, government support of "pervasively-sectarian" institutions."[61]

The case of *Hosanna-Tabor Evangelical Lutheran Church and School v. Equal Employment Opportunity Commission*, which was decided by the Supreme Court in January 2012, offers a clear illustration of this contrast. On the basis of a principle termed the "ministerial exception," which prohibits the government from interfering in the internal affairs of religious institutions, the Court handed down its ruling on January 12, 2012, in favor of the Hosanna-Tabor Lutheran School and against its employees, notwithstanding antidiscrimination laws of the Equal Employment Opportunity Commission. Cheryl Perich, a teacher in a school belonging to the Evangelical Lutheran Synod (the second-largest Lutheran denomination in the state of Missouri), was obliged to go on sick leave for several months after being diagnosed with narcolepsy, a sleep disorder. Upon her return, her employer encouraged her to resign; in response, she threatened to file suit against her employer, whose next step was to fire her on the grounds of "insubordination and disruptive behavior" because she improperly sought outside support, whereas it was said such conflicts ought to be treated from inside the community. Even though she mostly taught nonreligious subjects (art, science, social studies, music), Perich did also teach a religion class, led students in prayer, and was considered part of the religion faculty since she had received religious training within the organization. By claiming that Perich's activities fell within the ministerial category, the school directors could legitimately invoke before the Court the ministerial exception, which prohibits secular courts from interfering in the internal discussions within a church. The Supreme Court's decision was considered a big victory for the leaders of religious organizations. Bishop William E. Lori, chair of the Ad Hoc Committee for Religious Liberty within the U.S. Conference of Catholic Bishops (USCCB), expressed his pleasure with the decision in a prepared statement: "This decision makes resoundingly clear the historical and constitutional importance of keeping internal church affairs off limits to the government."[62] Chief Justice John Roberts defended his opinion by underlining that "the church must be free to choose who will guide it on its way."[63] The *Hosanna-Tabor* case thus marks a victory for the principle of religious liberty, not as matter of freedom of conscience, but the freedom for a church to choose, govern, and fire its employees.

In a similar vein, Catholic and Protestant universities rose up to fight the provision in President Obama's health-insurance-reform legislation that requires reimbursement for contraceptive services, using as their main argument the principle of their religious freedom. Many schools filed suits against the Obama administration, asserting that the obligation to provide free access to contraception for their students and employees was a violation of their constitutional right to religious freedom. Republican candidates at the time immediately seized on this affair as a way to radicalize the public's opposition to the Democratic president. Mitt Romney, in his blog, encouraged his supporters to sign a petition to protest against "using Obamacare to impose a secular vision on Americans who believe that they should not have their religious freedom taken away."[64] According to Timothy M. Dolan, archbishop of New York and then president of the USCCB, "Never before has the federal government forced individuals and organizations to go out into the marketplace and buy a product that violates their conscience. This shouldn't happen in a land where free exercise of religion ranks first in the Bill of Rights."[65] Michael Galligan-Stierle, president of the Association of Catholic Colleges and Universities, also denounced this rule as a violation of religious freedom: "It's the first time in history that the federal government is legislating or prioritizing something over religious liberty. . . . This law is saying we are no longer free, that we don't have a choice. We are paying for things that we don't believe in."[66] In short, opponents of Obamacare—the Patient Protection and Affordable Care Act, which became law in 2010—succeeded in turning the reimbursement for contraception services into a constitutional debate over religious freedom, which is understood here in the particular sense of acknowledging a religious community's freedom to supervise and constrain the consciences and bodies of its employees.

This indirect call to establish the right for religious institutions to regulate the behavior and preferences of their members was clearly formulated by the USCCB in November 2011, and in particular by the Ad Hoc Committee for Religious Freedom chaired by Bishop Lori. The bishop denounced what he called the establishment of nonreligion as a religion in the United States, and he encouraged his colleagues to resist this. He does not speak of nonbelief but of nonreligion. The Founding Fathers, Lori recalls, wanted to create a legal system that ensured citizens the liberty to believe but also the freedom to have "churches and clerical institutions." For him, it is urgent to demand "the freedom of religious entities to provide services according to their own lights, to defend publicly their teachings, and even to choose and manage their own personnel."[67] This indirect plea for the establishment of the autonomy of (Christian) religious institutions is part of a wider movement in favor of a bigger role for Christianity in public life. Coalitions of Catholic and evangelical groups are increasingly using the term "public Christianity," which they oppose to the idea of a "naked public square." In the area of international relations, the idea is to strangle the threat of political Islam by insisting on the idea of religious liberty as meaning no freedom of conscience, and by opting for a nonestablishment perspective. In the domestic national debate, however, the idea is to fight to promote another sense of religious liberty so as to permit the development of public Christianity—therefore, one calls for a form of state recognition of certain religious institutions to the detriment of others. A joint declaration by Catholic and evangelical leaders was published in the March 2012 issue of the magazine *First Things*.[68] This manifesto opposes the reduction of religious freedom to a simple liberty of worship and belief, and denounces the secular influence of human rights discourses. Whereas IRFA sympathizers turn adroitly to the liberal-secular discourse of human rights to better communicate a moral- and security-oriented vision for the Muslim world, in the domestic political debate one notices, on the contrary, a clear opposition between liberal and religious references:

> Proponents of human rights, including governments, have begun to define religious freedom down, reducing it to a bare "freedom of worship." This reduction denies the inherently public character of biblical religion and privatizes the very idea of religious freedom, a view of freedom such as one finds in those repressive states where Christians can pray only so long as they do so behind closed doors. It is no exaggeration to see in these developments a movement to drive religious belief, and especially orthodox Christian religious and moral convictions, out of public life.[69]

A UNIVERSAL PARADIGM?

The will of IRFA supporters to make their understanding of religious liberty universal comes up against not only domestic opposition but also skepticism from a number of European countries. For IRFA, the rights that religious liberty must defend are individual rights. They are in conflict, however, with a concept of right to religion that the Organization of Islamic Cooperation (OIC) has sought to put forward since the end of the 1990s. Several resolutions to fight against "defamation of religions" were adopted within the United Nations between 1999 and 2005 by the UN Commission on Human Rights and, starting in 2007, by the body that succeeded it, the UN Human Rights Council.[70] The UN General Assembly also adopted similar resolutions starting in 2005. These nonbinding resolutions denounce the defamation of religions as a form of violation of human dignity and of religious liberty. They raise a warning about the negative consequences of such defamation for public order and collective harmony. They are regularly proposed by OIC member countries and sometimes passed with no vote, but never unanimously. The United States, Canada, the European Union, and several Pacific Ocean countries have always opposed them. For most Western countries, the OIC project is not only unnecessary, because there already exists a form of protection against inciting hatred in international treaties, but, above all, contrary to the principle of free speech.[71] IRFA supporters refuse the pertinence of OIC reasoning to justify the antidefamation resolutions. Religions cannot be rights-holders; only individuals can be. The idea that religions could claim rights in the same way as individuals would have dangerous implications. It would require individuals to compete with religions for the recognition of rights. Another dangerous consequence would be an easier restriction on individuals' freedom of expression.

In March 2011, after a decade of discussions and lobbying by human rights organizations and conservative lobbies such as the American Center for Law and Justice, the UN Human Rights Council passed resolution 16/18, which definitively invalidates earlier efforts to criminalize the defamation of religions. American human rights organizations (notably, the International Commission for Religious Freedom) considered this outcome as a victory for the principle of free speech and individual rights.

If this debate has revealed a consensus among Western countries, there still exist important differences between Europe and the United States when it comes to defining religious freedom. The American paradigm that asserts religious freedom equals individual freedom and the American tradition of court cases and jurisprudence to deal with religious conflicts are not easily accepted by European countries. Even if the discourse of individual rights also plays a central role in European debates about religious freedom, the approach founded on the recognition of the cultural heritage of religions competes with the individualist perspective focused on the protection of rights. In Europe, the state has historically played a key role in negotiating relations with churches and religious communities. Churches still proclaim with no compunction their status as culturally dominant or established churches, and states frequently maintain close ties with churches and religious institutions and communities. Discord has emerged on several occasions between the U.S. Commission for International Religious Freedom and the State Department, on the one hand, and European countries, on the other—for example, on the question of recognizing the Church of Scientology as a religious denomination or on the elimination of "religious affiliation" as a required item on Greek national identity cards.

European Union politics and policy tend to privilege the right of states over the rights of individuals when it comes to religious freedom. The European Union does not generally intervene in managing the neutrality of member countries' public space. This does not mean that the European Union recognizes the rights of religions to the exclusion of individual rights. However, it appears relatively hesitant about systematically applying the American paradigm of individual religious freedom. The legal scholar Ronan McCrea explains that

> the Court has repeatedly held that individuals cannot rely on claims of religious freedom to demand exemptions from generally applicable government regulations in areas such as employment. However, . . . Strasbourg institutions are sympathetic to the granting by Member States of precisely such exemptions to certain religious institutions. . . . The recognition by the Court of Human Rights of the rights of religious institutions in the public sphere can be seen, not [as] a matter of the assertion of religious rights against the authority of the state in the public sphere, but

rather as a matter of recognition of the right of states, within limits, to define their own identity and relationship to religion, including the right to treat certain denominations, by virtue of history, as constitutional status and institutional reality, in some way part of the state's cultural identity and broader public order.[72]

The difference between the European approach and the American approach based on the paradigm of individual rights appeared clearly in the "*Lautsi* affair" over the crucifixes in Italian classrooms. In November 2009, after legal proceedings before seven judges of the European Court of Human Rights, it was decided that the obligatory presence of a crucifix in the classroom was in violation of the European Convention on Human Rights. However, in March 2011, after a lengthy debate that roused public opinion all over Italy, the European Court reversed its decision. In this second decision, the Grand Chamber of the Court decided, 15 to 2, that the crucifix was not a violation of the convention. The position of the Italian government was supported by a coalition of central and eastern European states as well as by many law associations and religious organizations.[73] The European Center for Law and Justice, in association with an American group, the American Center for Law and Justice, submitted to the court an amicus curiae brief in favor of the Italian government. In reference to the first *Lautsi* decision, the director, Grégor Puppinck, strongly denounced Europe's secularization politics and the destruction of its Christian heritage: "Lautsi thus epitomizes the paradigm held by those who seek to secularize Europe and sanitize the public sphere of its Christian heritage."[74] The patriarch of the Russian Orthodox Church also spoke out in favor of maintaining crucifixes in schools. Indeed, the *Lautsi* affair mobilized the resistance of a powerful coalition of lobbies in Italy, eastern Europe, and the United States to oppose giving priority to the principle of individual freedom (here the freedom of atheists from being bothered by the sight of a crucifix) to the detriment of the notion of the long-standing cultural implantation of the Catholic Church. Despite attempts by IRFA supporters to present the paradigm of individual religious freedom as universally valid, one sees this approach contested not only in the Muslim world but also in Europe and even in America, as these recent campaigns by evangelical and Catholic leaders demonstrate.

In the final analysis, a number of questions concerning the applicability of the First Amendment in foreign policy contexts remain unanswered, and the constitutionality of government financing of diverse initiatives with a religious dimension is still open to debate. The Arab Spring revolutions did not give rise to any notable changes in the American foreign policy conceptions of religion and Islam. One still finds the same opposition between an approach that seems to largely discount the religious factor, even though Islamic parties now occupy a central place in current political conflicts, and an idealist, essentialist conception that makes religion into the determining factor behind present-day changes. In the pragmatic perspective of the Obama administration, Islamic parties are, above all, political parties with which one must negotiate. Religious dimensions are considered from a strategic point of view as either helping or hindering democratization and the protection of American interests. But they are not given any particular power outside the concrete logic of political competition. Conversely, neoconservative experts or those close to the Christian Right adhere to the logic of the IRFA and assert that the complete secularization of the Muslim world is a necessary precondition to the establishment of democratic regimes. Thus American foreign policy in the Muslim world appears deeply ambiguous—standing neither entirely with religion nor entirely on secular principles. Its discourse is, indeed, permanently exceptional since the clear distinctions between rights and morals that result from domestic controversies are constantly being blurred in foreign contexts.

CONCLUSION

The increasing number of controversies over the practices and symbols of Muslims in Europe and the United States shows that Islam continues to be perceived as an unthinkable and threatening Other.[1] The global spread of Islam is accompanied by a surprising standardization of the anti-Muslim argument.[2] But this standardization is not, strictly speaking, the continuation of the "clash of civilizations" model. To believe in that paradigm, one would first have to grant the existence of antithetical civilizations. But today Islam is no longer perceived as a menacing *culture* but as a form of barbarity and inhumanity. During the years 2000 to 2010, America went from being obsessed with a war on terrorism toward a more general habit of questioning the behavior of all Muslims and deploring their lack of sensitivity and compassion. Over the same period, a similar shift took place in Europe, where the debate about the Muslims' capacity to integrate as fellow citizens morphed into doubts about their aptitude for civility and even about their humanity. In France, in particular, one of the major consequences of the burka controversy was the way it radically changed the public debate over the criteria of Muslim acceptability. Until 2004, the disputes over head scarves at school were centrally about defining what counted as Muslim adherence to the rules of French citizenship. Since 2008, however, it is in a way the very humanity of Muslims that is being called into question. Whereas before people asked about the compatibility of Islam and citizenship, now they're talking in a completely different way about the disgust and physical revulsion provoked by the mere sight of a burka or minaret. The figure of the citizen-in-training has been replaced by a monstrous silhouette. Many supporters of a total burka ban claimed that women covered in this way were refusing a fundamental rule of human exchange—the reciprocity of gazes, the idea that one sees the other on condition of accepting to be seen. Thus wearing the burka started to seem like a negation of the humanity both of the person who wears it—now reduced to an object—and of the person who sees it being worn. In Europe and the United States, Muslims are now regarded by many as not just uncooperative citizens but as morally deficient and somehow inhuman.

These changes in the motives for rejecting Muslims are accompanied on both sides of the Atlantic by growing resistance to the ideals of liberal secularism. As Raphaël Liogier observes, the success of the myth of Islamization is due in no small part to the rise of a new European populism that glorifies the exceptional status of Europe and plays on people's feelings of frustration. Anti-Muslims in Europe and the United States are convinced that they're being had. In 2012, the extreme right National Front Party in France launched a campaign against halal products, complaining that it was unacceptable to force people to consume such products without their knowledge. Similarly, some French people were outraged by the polygamy of Abdelkader Bouziane, not because he was Muslim but because he looked like a shiftless unemployed person taking wrongful advantage of social-assistance programs.[3] Initiatives such as the occupation of the future mosque of Poitiers in October 2012 by nativists of the group Bloc Identitaire, the wine-and-sausage happy hours in the eighteenth arrondissement of Paris, and provocative caricatures of Mohammad all express a reactionary and ritualistic response of the community and are not unlike the indignant reply articulated by antimosque demonstrators in the United States. This is reflexive behavior: the threatened territory of the nation therefore becomes sacred space, and the ideas of "people" and "community" are understood in a particular sense that is more reminiscent of Charles Maurras and Maurice Barrès than of Jean-Jacques Rousseau and Jules Ferry:[4] "It's the Barrès motif of the soil and the dead that is returning with the aim of objectifying the country's identity within an orderly nature and time, and thus of suppressing the will of individuals who are then no more than the product of a *terroir*, a plant grown from a given earth."[5]

In short, for a majority of Americans and Europeans, Islam remains an opaque object that one is unable to think of in any way other than as a problem, threat, or retrograde legal code. This difficulty can be found to varying degrees among all the participants in today's controversies. Even intellectuals, activists, and experts who intervene to counter anti-Muslim words and deeds often remain prisoners of the warped paradigms that have become hegemonic. It is no longer possible to discuss Islam's place in Western societies without systematically invoking a series of normative oppositions: good/bad, moderate/radical, faith/law, West/Muslim, modernity/tradition, and so on. To intervene in the debate to "defend" Muslim rights—"No, not all Muslims are violent"; "Yes, Islam is compatible with democracy"; "No, they're not secret agents"—may help improve Muslims' conditions for a time, but it does nothing to change the terms of the debate. Today most analyses that seek to explain the practices and beliefs of Muslims oscillate between two types of argument: "Islam is everything" or "Islam is nothing." Either one starts off from an orientalist, culturalist perspective and considers that Islam is the essential determining factor that regulates all phenomena in Muslim communities and societies, or one begins from what one hopes is a more emancipated and less essentialist starting point and says that Islam is nothing but one language among others by means of which discriminated individuals and groups claim an identity, rights, and dignity. In both cases, Islam remains an opaque object either because of the omnipotence assigned to it or because of the invisibility to which it has been reduced. That Islam might simply be "something" between "all" and "nothing"—something both banal and specific that can be described ordinarily without drama—is something that Western societies always seem to have a hard time accepting, even leaving aside the particular differences that distinguish European countries from North America or the distinct discursive fields of academia, politics, and the media.

Are the controversies destined to grow ever larger? The different episodes recounted in these pages suggest that even if the determination of leading anti-Muslim activists never subsides, there does seem to be a sort of lifecycle to each affair: they lose steam, slow down, and always risk coming to a complete stop. Cranking things up again requires a plan and some imagination. When it becomes less easy to oppose mosques, a new target has to be found, such as Sharia. When the anti-Sharia movement begins to slow down, a new threat will have to be found and a lot of resources invested in reports, lectures, and demonstrations to convince the public of the reality of this danger. The leaders of the anti-Muslim movements have to work all the harder to keep the mobilization active, since the controversies have the paradoxical effect of producing their own undoing through the very communal processes of more meetings, mutual awareness, and adaptation that each controversy generates between the ostensibly opposed camps. The law also constitutes an important barrier against the unimpeded expansion of these controversies. Commenting on the outcome of the affair in Murfreesboro, Tennessee, and the decision handed down by Judge Todd Campbell on July 18, 2012, the Muslim American association CAIR declared, "It wasn't pretty, but it worked." This remark is an apt summary of the way Islam is being built in the United States: the public debate is characterized by verbal violence that is more intense than in Europe, but the law also plays a more decisive role in protecting Muslims. In France, Germany, the United Kingdom, and elsewhere in Europe, people are fixated on Islam's oppressiveness toward women and denounce the communitarian character of this religion. But arguments such as "Islam is not a religion" and "Mohammad is a pedophile," even if they may exist on the edges of public discussion, have not gained the same currency in Europe as in the United States. However, Muslim Americans seem to have been much more effective than European Muslims at using the law to their advantage. As a recent Council of Europe report shows, in the past few years European Muslims have become the favorite target of populist parties and the extreme Right, have been on the receiving end of restrictive policies and laws, and have been the victims of repeated discrimination often without the power to defend themselves as well as can Muslims in the United States. The report encourages member governments to "stop targeting Muslims through legislation or policy, and prohibit discrimination based on religion or other beliefs in all areas where it is taking place." It insists especially on the weak capacity for Muslims to use legal tools and goes on to recommend the empowerment of "independent equality bodies or ombudsmen to review complaints, provide legal assistance and representation in court, provide policy advice and conduct research on discrimination against Muslims and other religious groups."[6]

In the United States, the most decisive opposition to anti-Muslim movements will likely come not from the Department of Justice or progressive groups or Muslims themselves but from conservative Republicans. In July 2012, some Republicans raised their voices to complain about the neo-McCarthyism of certain of their members. When Representative Michele Bachmann (R-Minn.) accused Huma Abedin, a Hillary Clinton aide of Muslim origin, of having ties with the Muslim Brotherhood, Senator John McCain objected strongly to these allegations: "When anyone, not least a member of Congress, launches specious and degrading attacks against fellow Americans on the basis of nothing more than fear of who they are and ignorance of what they stand for, it undermines the spirit of our nation, and we all grow poorer because of it."[7] Edward Rollins, Bachman's former campaign chief, published an editorial on the Fox News website denouncing Bachman's McCarthyist tactics: "Her unsubstantiated charge against Abedin, a widely respected top aide to Secretary Hillary Clinton, accusing her of some sort of far-fetched connection to the Muslim brotherhood, is extreme and dishonest. Having worked for Congressman Bachman's campaign for president, I am fully aware that she sometimes has difficulty with her facts, but this is downright vicious and reaches the late Senator Joe McCarthy level."[8] Thus even if the radical right's pressure on the Republican Party remains strong, there are important figures in the party who are capable of pushing back and resisting the development of Islamophobia.

The 2012 elections seem to have strengthened the hand of these more moderate voices. Many of the most extreme candidates when it comes to the rejection of Islam (but also the rejection of the rights of women, the poor, the LGBT community, blacks, and Latinos) lost. For example, Representative Allen West (R-Fla.), one of the leading defenders of the idea that the Muslim Brotherhood is invading America's suburbs, lost to the Democratic candidate, Patrick Murphy. In Arkansas, state representative James McLean defeated his Republican opponent, Charlie Fuqua, who had proposed deporting all Muslims as a solution to "the Muslim problem." In Minnesota, Republican representative Chip Cravaack, an enthusiastic supporter of the inquisitional hearings organized by Representative Peter King (R-N.Y.) on Muslim radicalization, was also defeated. As for King and Bachmann, they managed to retain their seats, but by slim margins. Some candidates known for their anti-Muslim attitudes got better results; however, the "anti-Muslim caucus" in the U.S. Congress became weaker and more circumscribed after the 2012 elections than it had been in 2008.[9]

All the same, these results have not translated into better daily lives for American Muslims. Controversies over Islam, on both the national and local levels, continue and remain a lot alike. The American Freedom Defense Initiative, an anti-Muslim group directed by Pamela Geller, launched many provocative advertising campaigns in subways and on buses. In October and November 2012, for example, one could see posters in the New York subway that read: "In any war between the civilized man and the savage, support the civilized man. Support Israel. Defeat Jihad." Similar posters appeared in the Washington Metro and on San Francisco buses. Although they didn't necessarily have the same nationwide impact, there have been debates nearly every week in different American cities over a mosque, the sale of halal meat, or whether to recognize Eid al-Fitr and Eid al-Adha as holidays.

How do Muslims react to the persistent verbal and physical attacks that target them? Their attitude has remained mostly the same since September 11, 2001. They continue to fight against the misrepresentations of their practices through educational campaigns and other forms of communication. With the help of civil rights groups and the courts, media, and local associations, they are working to defend their rights and their image. The narrative of the "good Muslim American"—an active citizen and a pleasant neighbor—is not just a rhetorical strategy deployed by leading Muslim American organizations. It actually corresponds to the day-to-day reality of most Muslims today. This is especially evident among younger Muslims for whom the reference to Islam adds a certain cachet to political, artistic, or commercial ambitions but who otherwise declare themselves to be completely American. Certain Muslims, of course, remain skeptical about this feel-good narrative of American Islam. Some mosque-goers and members of conservative organizations believe the young leaders of organizations such as the Muslim Public Affairs Council or Muslim artists and public intellectuals are too eager to collaborate with the American government and chime in with their praise of American "values." One could, of course, worry about the danger for democracy of these conservative individuals who are less inclined to join the chorus in praise of these values. Such questions, however, inevitably degenerate into a circular, normative discussion that ends up asking if Islam is compatible with democracy. This question entirely skirts the true problem, which is not the alleged opposition between Islam and democracy, or between conservatives and liberals, but the striking mimicking and mirroring that takes place between conservative Muslims and non-Muslims and between conservatives and liberals.

Beyond their different practices, normative references, and symbols, anti-Muslim activists in the West and antiliberal Muslim activists have recourse to the same behavioral and mimetic conception of the social contract. All of them conceive of the social contract as the function of the capacity for each person to conform to a stereotype. The contract model proposed by liberal political theory is a hypothesis, not a code of behavior. It designates no particular society, group, individual, tradition, or conduct. Western anti-Muslim groups, and illiberal Muslim movements are founded on a different idea of the social contract. Both consider that what makes a political community hold together is, rather than the liberal *fiction* of the social contract, conformity to a stereotype. The person of common sense or, what amounts to the same thing, the devoted believer who scrupulously adheres to all alimentary and vestimentary codes are expected to act properly rather than justly.

The blaming and demands associated with the recriminations voiced by Americans opposed to Sharia and mosques is a displacement of the Puritan ideal of the covenant to which only the elect have the right of way. In this respect, it's not all that different from the project of the Salafist movement that seeks to re-create the ideal community of the Prophet's companions. In both cases, the notions of merit, suffering, and sacrifice count for more than do the criteria of equality, reason, and contract. Only the deserving belong to the community—those who have been elected. For anti-Muslim activists, all free riders—that is, all imposters and profiteers—must be excluded; these may be future beneficiaries of "Obamacare," people living off the labor and taxes of others, or Muslims who exploit to their advantage the First Amendment, which should really protect only Christians.[10] Similarly, for radical Salafists, the exploiters, the impure, and the corrupt must be excluded or eliminated.[11] For both groups, the norm of "what is right" is superior to respect for "rights." The relation to the other in this conception of community is defined, fundamentally, by a suspicion of having been tricked and the need to reestablish a just order. The covenant that unites participants and sympathizers of anti-Muslim or antiliberal movements is not based on the idea of a reunion of saints elected by grace or by the sincerity of their faith. It's more a uniting of the resentful that brings together all those who feel like losers or who at least have the firm conviction of being in the process of losing something dear—their identity, their safety, their America of "glory days," the "true" Islam, and so on. And this is indeed what is so scandalous for them: the elect have become the losers, or they at least perceive themselves that way. The feelings of rage expressed in all these controversies erupt from this contradiction that seems to go against the order of things—for some, the divine order.

This explains the constant need to show one's own merit, a posture of permanent indignation of "the righteous mind." The controversies over Islam cannot be reduced to an opposition between two visions of the world or two opposed ideologies. Undoubtedly, some among the anti-mosque and anti-Sharia leadership defend an illiberal vision of democracy, speak of the primacy of popular sovereignty, and argue for the suspension of constitutional rights for certain categories of the population deemed dangerous or deviant. But beyond these few stock traits from the populist handbook, the philosophical and legal reflection within these movements is rather poor. It's no accident if, up until now, they've lost the most important legal battles. What motivates the rank-and-file members of these movements is, above all, a form of political affect. The conceptual discourse paired with this fundamentally reactive political affect is stitched together from various hand-me-downs, with remnants from the Crusades, the Knights Templar, *Star Wars*, disaster movies, science fiction, the War of Independence, the Bible, and the Constitution. Likewise, the young Tunisians and Egyptians who join radical Salafist groups often have very little background in theology. What attracts them and interests them more than anything, and certainly more than theology, is a form of affect and a particular political performance defined by clear codes and rules of behavior.

In this behavioral approach to the social contract, belonging to the community does not fall to each citizen as a right. Anyone who wishes to enter must agree to follow the rules and prove their good faith. Proofs of loyalty and sincerity are what matter, not arguments. To be included, discreet approval of the community's principles is not good enough. Inclusion requires a public declaration of faith, a visible sincerity, and a clear willingness to submit and commit—hence the importance accorded to places and practices of high symbolic significance. The visibility of

Muslims is scandalous for anti-Muslim Americans. In symmetrical fashion, and for the same reasons, the insufficient visibility of Islam is scandalous for the Salafists and some illiberal Muslim conservatives. Each individual has a choice between simple loyalty or simply leaving. Multiple points of view or divergent behaviors are perceived as threats to the stability of the group. The social contract here means consenting and adhering to the common-sense view. And here common sense no longer means just the ensemble of shared opinions but the acceptable way to feel: a shared, common affectivity; a repertoire of required emotions. The other is thus doubly guilty and excluded—because she doesn't share the same opinions as the true elect, who deserve to belong to the national community, and especially because she does not feel the same feelings.

Even so, we cannot content ourselves with this opposition between, on the one hand, a behavioral approach to the social contract based on demands to conform to a certain stereotype and, on the other, a liberal perspective based on the presupposition of an ideal individual or citizen because, to a great extent, current disputes in the United States and Europe reveal a behavioral turn to the liberal approach itself. In a context of growing radicalization and polarization of perspectives, liberal ideals of equality, neutrality, secularism, and consensus seem to have turned into stereotypes themselves. To be liberal no longer means simply to believe in principles of justice and fairness but to exhibit certain acceptable behaviors, feel emotions that are expected of you, and repeat certain stock phrases. Put another way, to be liberal now means to laugh at a caricature of Mohamed, to feel worried about a mosque at Ground Zero, and to be disgusted at the sight of a burka—in other words, to conform to a stereotype.

Must one then conclude that liberalism and secularism constitute a double failure, and should one attribute all the present-day conflicts over Islam to their downfall? The critique of liberalism and secularism has been approached by various schools of thought ranging from communitarian to postmodern to postcolonial.[12] Secular liberalism is reproached for its abstract, disincarnated, ahistorical, and unsociological character. It is also denounced for its propensity to turn into an ideology of domination. While presented as the most suitable theory for guaranteeing equality and justice between citizens and the neutrality of the state when it comes to defining the good, it is said to be necessarily informed by a religious tradition, values, and history. In other words, behind the mask of neutrality a particular religion would always be hiding, and behind the pretense to ensure equality would always be a project of domination. The controversies over Islam and the curious mirror effects that they reveal between the different argumentative strategies proposed (liberal versus antiliberal, Muslim versus anti-Muslim) all suggest that the fundamental crux is not the opposition democracy/Islam or religious/secular or liberalism/antiliberalism. The real problem has more to do with the tendency to codify, render explicit, and transform the ideal type into a stereotype—and this across all theoretical and religious currents. For anti-Muslim activists who claim to be defending the Christian heritage of the West and for the antiliberal Salafists, belief is no longer "a social practice of difference" but, on the contrary, a mimetic constraint and a practice of exclusion.[13] A symmetrical process is under way among many proponents of secular liberalism. The ideal of justice and fairness is no longer that theoretical fiction that, precisely because no one can recognize themselves in it entirely, makes mediation possible. Instead, it is also becoming a model for exclusion and the constraint of assimilation. In both cases, living together is reduced to a matter of respecting a code and an etiquette. The social contract is no longer an accord over the possibility of disagreement based on equality of rights but the permanent constraint of good manners and consensus. The contract is reduced to the obligation to consent or, literally, the obligation to feel certain authorized emotions in a given context—disgust at a burka in Europe, fear of a mosque in the United States, anger at a church in Egypt.

The liberal-secular response to the current controversies over Islam essentially makes use of two tools—law and education—neither of which appears very powerful or capable of convincing the discontented and pacifying these conflicts. I have shown in these pages that there is a large tendency to adjudicate when these conflicts over Islam arise. However, this willingness to turn to the courts also accentuates the propensity toward codification and a transformation of liberal-secular ideals into stereotypes. This is what happens with the frequent slide of law toward theology. Since the U.S. Constitution does not define religion but only the freedom to exercise it, the challenge for judges consists in judging without "establishing," so as to guarantee religious freedom without defining religion. This challenging dilemma is not new, but it has taken on new intensity in the debates over Islam. The Department of Justice has had to intervene several times and take on the role of a quasi-theological official in order to underscore that the American government does consider Islam a religion and does think of mosques as places of worship. Similarly, the Oklahoma judges assert that Sharia is not a legal code but a type of ethical and spiritual guide. Through a series of declarations and programs directed at Muslim communities, and through its support to Muslim leaders who preach values of moderation and patriotism, the federal government constantly runs the risk of establishing an official Islam.

This theological-political process of constructing a moderate American Islam represents a big constraint on American Muslims. In order for their rights to be respected and protected, they find themselves ordered to conform to acceptable behavioral norms that are often decided against their will for the simple reason that they are not in a powerful bargaining position to define the terms of the debate. Most of the participants in the antimosque and anti-Sharia conflicts denounce the simplistic and reductive oppositional models between good and bad Muslims, political Islam and spiritual Islam, or faith and Sharia. Yet on account of their relative weakness in the media, in the courts, and in political parties and local civic organizations, they are always constrained to adopt and in a sense authenticate these stereotypes whether they like it or not. Lacking the ability to contest the pertinence of the very question, they are reduced to demonstrating that they are indeed good Muslims, that their religion is above all a form of spirituality and faith, and that they harbor no ambition to change the culture of American politics. The slightest attempt to suggest that adhering to Islam is a way of proposing an alternative conception of the world or way of life is immediately inflated into proof of anti-Americanism. For Muslims, to appear different means to be perceived right away as the enemy. This is why the leading Muslim organizations and the two members of Congress who are Muslim—Representatives Keith Ellison (D-Minn.) and André Carson (D-Ind.)—all send the message of the utter ordinariness of Muslims. An entire media industry is rapidly developing with the aim of reinforcing the idea of the good Muslim through books, reality-television shows, films, music, T-shirts, and various foods.

In all the court proceedings, it does seem that the law—independent of its pretense of neutrality and universality—is elevating to the status of concept (for example, the concept of "acceptable" versus "excessive" practices, or "reasonable" accommodation) a collective feeling of fear or a shared wish for exclusion. The law is practicing "savage ontology"; in other words, it is changing "this One of feeling into One of concept."[14] It thus permits arriving at a consensus, as Jacques Rancière understands that term, of "convertibility between the object of feeling and the object of the law, and in particular . . . convertibility between an object of fear and the Other which the law must first identity before expelling it."[15] The rule produced by the law is not determined on the basis of the neutral principles of justice and fairness but in relation to contextual codes of manners and acceptability. The convention follows from consent and not the reverse: "Behind the reference to the law and the universal, it is then a strange knot that gets tied between *phusis* and *nomos*, the one determined as the power to consent, the other as the power to suit and to contract."[16] The law becomes the consecration of consensus and the status quo rather than the guarantee of equality. From this point of view, one must ask about the hegemonic inclination of this model to regulate by law conflicts that relate to the religious. Turning to the courts to settle the question of religious freedom is all the more disturbing in that it excludes from the discussion all those who neither possess the requisite legal knowledge nor have mastery over the techniques of the law. It contributes in this way to a worrisome depoliticizing of the debate even though the stakes of this hegemonic ambition are undeniably political.

It is worth reflecting on the rapid standardization of the discourse on international religious freedom that is developing in North America and Europe at the same time as a parallel standardization of the anti-Muslim line of argument. If inside the United States the courts have so far shown themselves to be careful about respecting the First Amendment and the protection of Muslim rights, the reference to law in the realm of foreign policy is much more ambivalent. The entire policy to promote international religious liberty as led by the American commission dedicated to that cause (the Commission for International Religious Freedom) clumsily mixes together with problematic results a legalist discourse with one that is all-out culturalist and orientalist. Throughout the West associations are being founded to defend religious freedom in the world. At the same time as the American commission finds itself increasingly criticized at home, another commission created along exactly the same lines and with the same goals has appeared in Canada. The European External Action Service, a European Union department created in 2009 and launched in 2010, is also in the process of implementing something very similar, notably through the European Instrument for Democracy and Human Rights Regulation for 2014 to 2020.[17] But the effect of these initiatives is a triple depoliticizing of these conflicts and the powers opposed in each one. First, the question of Islam in the West and of religious liberty in the world gets turned into a legal and technical matter that can be treated outside of all considerations for the power relations on the national or international levels. Second, the hegemonic claim by a Western discourse over international religious freedom creates the fiction of a unified Western world opposite a Muslim world that is also artificially represented as a homogeneous cultural entity. Third, the standardization of this recourse to the category of religious freedom, which would be treated as essentially a legal matter, has the effect of making the opposition between religious freedom and Islam into the fundamental paradigm for understanding world conflicts, thus replacing the opposition between democracies and authoritarian regimes. So, for example, the attacks suffered by religious minorities in Pakistan, Iraq, or Iran are thought through from an abstract and typically orientalist perspective as an effect of Islam and not as a consequence of the undemocratic character of the regimes under which these attacks take place. Similarly, the ongoing revolutions in the Arab world and the arrival in power of Islamic parties only reinforce fears and tendencies to view Islam as synonymous with oppression of minorities.

The call for more education made by those who present themselves as defenders of liberal-secular values constitutes the second leading instrument for the resolution of conflicts. Both obtuse and intolerant populists and Muslims fond of demonstrating their faith excessively and too "ostentatiously" need to be given explicit instructions about the codes of liberal manners. But this pedagogy is problematic because it claims to create and teach in an artificial way the conditions of equality, whereas paradoxically equality is already produced, without being mentioned or codified, through the controversy itself. The latter belongs to the same category of power face-offs as the lovers' quarrel. In both cases, the parties don't seek consensus but seek to have the last word.[18] But the possibility of this household scene supposes the existence of a relation of equality and reciprocity:

When two subjects argue according to a set exchange of remarks and with a view to having the "last word," these two subjects are *already married*: for them the scene is an exercise of a right, the practice of a language of which they are co-owners. . . . This is the meaning of what is euphemistically called dialogue: not to listen to each other, but to submit in common to an egalitarian principle of the distribution of language goods.[19]

The criticisms leveled at Muslims during the Ground Zero mosque controversy do not derive from the logic of a clash of civilizations. They express disappointment about an unmet expectation; they express blame and reproach. But blame makes sense only within a relational framework if not of perfect equality, then at least of reciprocity.[20] One does not blame someone whom one cares nothing about, holds in contempt, does not know, or completely dominates. The participants in the controversies discussed here create, de facto, a relation of equality that falls outside the logic of a clash of civilizations. Paradoxically, it's the liberal-secular pedagogues who, by wishing to speak, codify, and teach the conditions of an equality of consensus, reactivate the culturalist logic. Anti-Muslim discourse is largely confabulation and delirium—the myth of invasion, of conquest, and so on. But the very act of fabulating presupposes "a pre-existing equality between a wish to speak and a wish to hear."[21] As well intentioned as it may be, the turn to pedagogy produces exactly the opposite of the desired effect. The reason, as Rancière points out, is that the community of equals "is not a goal to be reached" through pedagogy and morals "but a supposition to be posited from the outset and endlessly reposited."[22] Making equality explicit serves no purpose if one has not already presupposed equality: "All that strategies or pedagogies of the community of equals can do is cause that community to fall into the arena of active unreason, of explanatory/explained inequality."[23] This probably explains the very low success rate of institutions that aim to work toward intercultural and interreligious dialogue. It may also explain the inconclusive results of the strategy implemented by Muslim organizations in the West that seek to counter the negative representations of themselves with other positive messages. These organizations' very reason for being is the project of explaining a community—reduced to an ensemble of codes—to another community, it too reduced to an ensemble of codes. However, even if the actions and encounters that arise from such a project do for a time alleviate misunderstanding and facilitate understanding, the very essence of the project of explaining is inegalitarian: "Every explanation is a fiction of inequality. I explain a sentence to someone because I assume that he would not understand it if I did not explain it to him. That is to say, I explain to him that if I did not explain he would not understand. I explain to him, in short, that he is less intelligent than I am, and that that is why he deserves to be where he is and I deserve to be where I am."[24] These teaching projects also result in the depoliticizing of social relations. If one accepts that the essence of politics is dissensus, not in the sense of an expression of different interests and opinions but in the sense of the "manifestation of a gap in the sensible itself," then the pedagogy project is, on the contrary, oriented exclusively toward producing consensus. The project presupposes the existence of collective, rational subjects endowed with a certain number of meanings. But "a collectivity can have no *wish* to speak to anyone."[25] Every community is fundamentally lacking consistence. There exists no homogeneous white Protestant community truly threatened by the mosque at Ground Zero, and there exists no victimized or dominated Muslim community. Yet it is precisely this lack of consistency that makes equality possible and renders vain all explanatory projects. The community of equals "occurs, but it has no place."[26]

The question, then, is not to find out how to make it so that discussions of the just and the fair take better account of different conceptions of the good or of the diverse power relations and historical memories present in society, as a number of philosophers of communitarian and postcolonial persuasions would have us do. It is also not about knowing by what cultural institutions or pedagogical treatises one could translate this code into another code. The point is not to give substantive consistency to the liberal-secular ideal but, on the contrary, to give back to it its function as theoretical hypothesis. The goal is to disconnect this ideal from the ensemble of codes and norms of exclusion that it is currently so closely associated with. The "secularization of the secular" proposed by Étienne Balibar implies that one cease reifying the liberal ideals of justice and fairness in the form of Charters of Laïcité, courses on secular morals, codes of good behavior, and republican and nationalist manifestos.[27]

The reason is that the problem is not fundamentally a cognitive one, nor is it epistemological or even axiological. The principal enemy of the American citizen who goes to war against Islam is finally neither the Muslim nor the liberal-secularist; it is the world. In a context that appears to him as more and more uncertain and threatening, the entire world is his enemy. Therefore, it has to be made into a code in order to master it.

"The world," Barthes says, "is . . . *an obligation to share. The world (the worldly) is my rival. I am continually disturbed by Troublemakers [Fâcheux]*."[28] Muslims and liberals are troublemakers, among many others. Faced with such a situation, is it really more words that one needs? The bidding war of words, well intentioned though it may be, serves no purpose because "the scene is neither practical nor dialectical."[29] It unfolds independently of whatever the interlocutors may wish to demonstrate. It's not by stacking words upon words or by opposing positive clichés to negative ones that we will break the cycle of this narcissistic dueling where each party tries to be right. One must first break this discursive chain of scenes and controversies. Conditions must be created for an encounter between individuals, for a spontaneous political conviviality with no pedagogy behind it, that would permit the emergence of the equality of dissensus. The liberation from stereotypes, the creation of an original relation to the other and the real, necessitates the suspension, however surreptitious, of the madness of words: "I divine that the true site of originality and strength is neither the other nor myself, but our relation itself. *It is the originality of the relation which must be conquered*. Most of my injuries come from the stereotype: I am obliged to make myself a lover, like everyone else: to be jealous, neglected, frustrated, like everyone else."[30] Only a human encounter may create some play, a gap in this irrefutable logic of words. It can make appear the possibility of an original relation, unstereotyped, to the world and the other, a relation of copresence and egalitarian dissensus rather than dialogue.

NOTES

INTRODUCTION TO THE AMERICAN EDITION

1. Emily Bazelon, "What Are the Limits of 'Religious Liberty,'" *New York Times*, July 7, 2015, http://www.nytimes.com/2015/07/12/magazine/what-are-the-limits-of-religious-liberty.html?hp&action=click&pgtype=Homepage&module=mini-moth&region=top-stories-below&WT.nav=top-stories-below&_r=1.

2. Pierre-Yves Crochet, "Interdite de collège pour une jupe jugée trop longue: La laïcité va-t-elle trop loin?" *Sud Ouest*, April 30, 2015, http://www.sudouest.fr/2015/04/30/interdite-de-college-pour-une-jupe-jugee-trop-longue-la-laicite-va-t-elle-trop-loin-1908322-4834.php, and "Laïcité à l'école: Une collégienne interdite de cours à cause d'une jupe jugée comme un signe religieux ostentatoire," *Huffington Post*, April 28, 2015, http://www.huffingtonpost.fr/2015/04/28/laicite-ecole-interdiction-cours-jupe-longue-jugee-signe-religieux-ostentatoire_n_7164546.html.

3. These anchors were obviously proven wrong by London police. The mayor of Paris, Anne Hidalgo, threatened to sue Fox News for wrongful information and inadequately describing some Parisian arrondissements as no-go zones. See also Tom McCarthy, "Paris Moves to Sue Fox News for False Reporting on Muslim 'No-Go Zones,'" *Guardian*, February 12, 2015, http://www.theguardian.com/world/2015/feb/12/paris-lawsuit-fox-news-reporting-no-go-zones-non-muslims.

4. Adam Shatz, "Moral Clarity," *LRB Blog, London Review of Books*, January 9, 2015, http://www.lrb.co.uk/blog/2015/01/09/adam-shatz/moral-clarity/.

5. "Nous sommes tous américains" (We Are All Americans) [editorial], *Le Monde*, September 13, 2001.

6. Garry Trudeau, "The Abuse of Satire," *Atlantic*, April 11, 2015, http://www.theatlantic.com/international/archive/2015/04/the-abuse-of-satire/390312/.

7. Anthony Faiola, "French Muslims Feel Deeply Torn by Viral 'I Am Charlie' Slogan," *Washington Post*, January 13, 2015, https://www.washingtonpost.com/world/europe/they -are-not-charlie/2015/01/13/7c9d6998-9aae-11e4-86a3-1b56f64925f6_story.html.

8. Quoted in Amanda Taub, "#JeSuisAhmed: A Crucial Message That Everyone Should Hear," January 9, 2015, VoxReligion, http://www.vox.com/2015/1/9/7521151/charlie-hebdo -jesuisahmed.

9. The six members are Peter Carey, Michael Ondaatje, Francine Prose, Teju Cole, Rachel Kushner, and Taiye Selasi.

10. Jennifer Schuessler, "Six PEN Members Decline Gala After Award for *Charlie Hebdo*," *New York Times*, April 26, 2015, http://www.nytimes.com/2015/04/27/nyregion/six-pen -members-decline-gala-after-award-for-charlie-hebdo.html?_r=0.

11. Glenn Greenwald, "204 PEN Writers (Thus Far) Have Objected to the *Charlie Hebdo* Award—Not Just 6," *The Intercept*, April 30, 2015, https://firstlook.org/theintercept/2015/04/30 /145-pen-writers-thus-far-objected-charlie-hedbo-award-6/.

12. Quoted in Myriam François-Cerrah, "Olivier Roy on *Laïcité* as Ideology, the Myth of 'National Identity' and Racism in the French Republic," *Jadaliyya*, May 16, 2015, http://www .jadaliyya.com/pages/index/21640/olivier-roy-on-laicite-as-ideology-the-myth-of-nat.

13. Abdellali Hajjat and Marwan Mohammed, *Islamophobie: Comment les élites françaises fabriquent le "problème musulman,"* Cahiers libres (Paris: La Découverte, 2013); Houda Asal, "Islamophobie: La fabrique d'un nouveau concept, État des lieux de la recherche," *Sociologie* 5, no. 1 (2014), http://sociologie.revues.org/2185.

14. Mayanthi Fernando, *The Republic Unsettled: Muslim French and the Contradictions of Secularism* (Durham, N.C.: Duke University Press, 2014); John Bowen, *Why the French Don't Like Headscarves: Islam, the State, and Public Space* (Princeton, N.J.: Princeton University Press, 2008).

15. Michael Walzer, "Islamism and the Left," *Dissent*, Winter 2015, https://www.dissent magazine.org/article/islamism-and-the-left. See also Andrew March, "Islamism and the Left: An Exchange," *Dissent*, Winter 2015, https://www.dissentmagazine.org/article /islamism-and-left-exchange.

16. A virulent wave of critiques against "*islamo-gauchisme*" was triggered by the publication of Vincent Geisser's *La nouvelle islamophobie* (Paris: La Découverte, 2003). Polemical articles on this topic have been published in right-wing magazines such as *Causeur* and *Riposte Laïque*. For an academic discussion of the French political science approach to Islamism and post-Islamism, see the landmark debate organized by the journal *Esprit*, August 2001, http://www.esprit.presse.fr/archive/review/detail.php?code=2001_8. For a more recent critique of the Left's discourse on Islamism, see Jean Birnbaum, *Un silence religieux: La gauche face au djihadisme* (Paris: Seuil, 2016).

17. Pascal Bruckner was one of the most vocal critiques of the notion of Islamophobia in France. See his interview "L'islamophobie, ça n'existe pas," *Causeur*, October 29, 2012, http://www.causeur.fr/pascal-bruckner-islamophobie-19758.html#.

18. Adam Shatz, "Drawing Blood," *New Yorker*, October 19, 2015, http://www.newyorker .com/magazine/2015/10/19/drawing-blood.

19. Marine Le Pen, "To Call This Threat by Its Name," *New York Times*, January 18, 2015, http://www.nytimes.com/2015/01/19/opinion/marine-le-pen-france-was-attacked-by-islamic-fundamentalism.html.

20. Michel Houellebecq, "How France's Leaders Failed Its People," *New York Times*, November 19, 2015, http://www.nytimes.com/2015/11/21/opinion/how-frances-leaders-failed-its-people.html.

21. Nilüfer Göle, *Musulmans au quotidien: Une enquête européenne sur les controverses autour de l'islam* (Paris: La Découverte, 2015).

22. François Cusset, *French Theory: Foucault, Derrida, Deleuze et Cie et les mutations de la vie intellectuelle aux États-Unis* (Paris: La Découverte, 2005); Justin Vaïsse, *Neoconservatism: The Biography of a Movement* (Cambridge, Mass.: Harvard University Press, 2011).

23. On the reception of the work of Saba Mahmood in France, see Nadia Marzouki, "La réception française de Saba Mahmood et de l'asadisme," *Tracés*, no. 15 (2015): 33–51, doi:10.4000/traces.6256.

24. "Thomas Jefferson's Iftar," Embassy of the United States of America, http://iipdigital.usembassy.gov/st/english/inbrief/2011/07/20110729153019kram0.3508199.html #axzz3wkjM7XMW.

25. "Remarks by the President at Iftar Dinner," White House, August 10, 21012, https://www.whitehouse.gov/the-press-office/2012/08/10/remarks-president-iftar-dinner.

26. Jocelyne Dakhlia and Bernard Vincent, eds., *Les musulmans dans l'histoire de l'Europe*, vol. 1, *Une intégration invisible* (Paris: Albin Michel, 2011).

27. Denise Spellberg, *Thomas Jefferson's Quran: Islam and the Founders* (New York: Knopf, 2013); Kambiz GhaneaBassiri, *A History of Islam in America: From the New World to the New World Order* (Cambridge: Cambridge University Press, 2010).

28. Yvonne Yazbeck Haddad, *Not Quite American: The Shaping of Arab and Muslim Identity in the United States* (Waco, Tex.: Baylor University Press, 2004); Yvonne Yazbeck Haddad and Jane Idleman Smith, eds., *Muslim Communities in North America* (Albany: State University of New York Press, 1994); Sulayman S. Nyang, *Islam in the United States of America* (Chicago: ABC International Group, 1999).

29. William Lancaster, "Speech in the Ratifying Convention," July 30, 1788, Center for the Study of the American Constitution, http://csac.history.wisc.edu/nc_lancaster.pdf; Denise Spellberg, "Could a Muslim Be President? An Eighteenth-Century Constitutional Debate," *Eighteenth-Century Studies* 39, no. 4 (2006): 485.

30. Asifa Quraishi-Landes, *Sharia and Diversity: Why Some Americans Are Missing the Point*, January 16, 2013, Institute for Social Policy and Understanding, http://www.ispu.org/GetReports/35/2620/Publications.aspx#sthash.GeABoMo5.dpuf.

31. Dina Samir Shehata, "Anti-Sharia Bill Dead, but Sentiment Alive," *Austin Chronicle*, May 22, 2015, http://www.austinchronicle.com/news/2015-05-22/anti-sharia-bill-dead-but-sentiment-alive/.

32. Association of Statisticians of American Religious Bodies, "2010 U.S. Religion Census: Religious Congregations and Membership Study," http://rcms2010.org. An updated survey of the Muslim population in the United States, undertaken by the Pew Research

Center, projects that the number of American Muslims will double by 2050, growing from 1 to 2 percent of the general U.S. population. See Besheer Mohamed, "A New Estimate of the U.S. Muslim Population," January 8, 2016, Pew Research Center, http://www.pewresearch.org/fact-tank/2016/01/06/a-new-estimate-of-the-u-s-muslim-population/.

33. Daniel Mach and Jamil Dakwar, "Anti-Sharia Law: A Solution in Search of a Problem," *Huffington Post*, July 20, 2011, http://www.huffingtonpost.com/2011/05/20/anti-sharia-law-a-solutio_n_864389.html.

34. Mucahit Bilici, *Finding Mecca in America: How Islam Is Becoming an American Religion* (Chicago: University of Chicago Press), 9.

35. Steve Friess, "Proposed Mosque in Detroit Suburb Draws Strong Opposition," September 8, 2015, Al Jazeera America, http://america.aljazeera.com/articles/2015/9/8/proposed-mosque-in-detroit-suburb-draws-sharp-opposition.html; Niraj Warikoo, "Proposed Mosque in Sterling Heights Stirs Opposition," *Detroit Free Press*, September 10, 2015, http://www.freep.com/story/news/local/michigan/macomb/2015/09/09/proposed-mosque-sterling-heights-stirs-opposition/71885024/.

36. Quoted in Aaron Morrison, "Sterling Heights Mosque Proposal Rejected: Michigan Officials Deny Group's Planning Commission Application amid Cheers, Anti-Muslim Epithets," *International Business Times*, September 11, 2015, http://www.ibtimes.com/sterling-heights-mosque-proposal-rejected-michigan-officials-deny-groups-planning-2092858.

37. Niraj Warikoo, "Longtime Leader of Dearborn Mosque Leaves amid Split," *Detroit Free Press*, June 6, 2015, http://www.freep.com/story/news/local/michigan/wayne/2015/06/05/imam-qazwini-resigns-dearborn-mosque/28581129/.

38. For an in-depth study of the internal debates of American Muslim communities and their ambivalent modes of identification to America or to an imagined global *ummah*, see Zareena Grewal, *Islam Is a Foreign Country: American Muslims and the Global Crisis of Authority* (New York: New York University Press, 2013).

39. Graeme Wood, "What ISIS Really Wants," *Atlantic*, March 2015, http://www.theatlantic.com/magazine/archive/2015/03/what-isis-really-wants/384980/. Among explanations based on social and geopolitical structures, there are a few notable exceptions, such as the compelling critique by Brookings expert Will McCants of the call for a reformation of Islam in "Islamic Scripture Is Not the Problem: And Muslim Reformers Is Not the Solution," *Foreign Affairs*, July–August 2015, https://www.foreignaffairs.com/articles/2015-06-16/islamic-scripture-not-problem.

40. Lisa Stampnitzky, *Disciplining Terror: How Experts Invented "Terrorism"* (Cambridge: Cambridge University Press, 2013).

41. Darryl Li, "A Jihadism Anti-Primer," *Middle East Report* 276 (2015), http://www.merip.org/mer/mer276/jihadism-anti-primer.

42. For a similar critique, see Amal Ghazal and Larbi Sadiki, "ISIS: The 'Islamic State' Between Orientalism and the Interiority of MENA's Intellectuals," *Jadaliyya*, January 19, 2016, http://www.jadaliyya.com/pages/index/23616/isis_the-islamic-state-between-orientalism-and-the.

43. Li, "Jihadism Anti-Primer."

44. When, on November 20, 2015, a reporter asked Donald Trump whether he endorsed the idea of constituting a "database" to track Muslims in the country, the Republican candidate answered positively, albeit elusively: "There should be a lot of systems, beyond databases" (quoted in Lauren Carroll, "In Context: Donald Trump's Comments on a Database of American Muslims," November 24, 2015, PolitiFact, http://www.politifact .com/truth-o-meter/article/2015/nov/24/donald-trumps-comments-database -american-muslims/; and in Vaughn Hillyard, "Donald Trump's Plan for a Muslim Database Draws Comparison to Nazi Germany," November 20, 2015, NBC News, http:// www.nbcnews.com/politics/2016-election/trump-says-he-would-certainly-implement -muslim-database-n466716).

45. Ed Pilkington, "Donald Trump: Ban All Muslims Entering US," *Guardian*, December 7, 2015, http://www.theguardian.com/us-news/2015/dec/07/donald-trump-ban-all-muslims -entering-us-san-bernardino-shooting; Max Boot, "The GOP Makes Radical Islam's Case," *Commentary*, October 2, 2015, https://www.commentarymagazine.com/politics-ideas /conservatives-republicans/the-gop-makes-radical-islams-case/; Jacob Heilbrunn, "After 2012, the GOP Set Out to Be More Inclusive: What Happened?" *Politico*, November 21, 2015, http://www.politico.com/magazine/story/2015/11/gop-islam-refugees-213383; Ed Pilkington, Ryan Felton, and Nicky Woolf, " 'Beyond Terrifying': Muslim Americans Shocked by Trump and Carson Quotes," *Guardian*, November 20, 2015, http://www.theguardian.com /us-news/2015/nov/20/muslim-americans-outrage-donald-trump-ben-carson.

46. Amy Davidson, "Trump and the Man in the T-Shirt," *New Yorker*, September 18, 2015, http://www.newyorker.com/news/amy-davidson/trump-and-the-man-in-the-t-shirt; Theodore Schleifer, "Trump Doesn't Challenge Anti-Muslim Questioner at Event," September 18, 2015, CNN, http://edition.cnn.com/2015/09/17/politics/donald-trump -obama-muslim-new-hampshire/.

47. "CAIR Announces Quran Giveaway in Response to Ben Carson's Anti-Muslim Remarks," September 21, 2012, YouTube, https://www.youtube.com/watch?v=sTHVEo1pcAI.

48. E. J. Dionne, *Why the Right Went Wrong: Conservatism from Goldwater to the Tea Party and Beyond* (New York: Simon and Schuster, 2016).

49. Quoted in Alexander Burns, "Once Embraced by Chris Christie, New Jersey's Muslims Feel Betrayed," *New York Times*, December 2, 2015, http://www.nytimes.com/2015/12/03 /nyregion/new-jersey-muslims-feel-sense-of-betrayal-by-christie.html?_r=0.

50. Serina Sandhu, "State of the Union: President Obama Says Anti-Muslim Rhetoric Is 'Just Wrong,' " *Independent*, January 13, 2016, http://www.independent.co.uk/news/world /americas/state-of-the-union-president-obama-says-the-anti-muslim-rhetoric-is-just -wrong-a6808596.html.

51. "Remarks by the President at Islamic Society of Baltimore," White House, February 3, 2016, https://www.whitehouse.gov/the-press-office/2016/02/03/remarks-president-islamic -society-baltimore.

52. Christopher Bail, *Terrified: How Anti-Muslim Fringe Organizations Became Mainstream* (Princeton, N.J.: Princeton University Press, 2015).

53. "CAIR Report: Number of Incidents Targeting U.S. Mosque in 2015 Highest Ever Recorded," December 17, 2015, Council on American-Islamic Relations, http://www.cair .com/press-center/press-releases/13313-mosques-targeted.html; Christopher Mathias, "A Running List of Shameful Islamophobic Acts Since the Paris Attacks," *Huffington Post*, November 20, 2015, http://www.huffingtonpost.com/entry/all-the-islamophobic -acts-in-us-canada-since-paris_us_564cee09e4b031745cef9dda.

54. Mussarut Jabeen and Yusor Abu-Salha, StoryCorps, *Morning Edition*, NPR, February 13, 2015, https://storycorps.org/listen/yusor-abu-salha-and-mussarut-jabeen/; Bill Chappell, " 'We're All One,' Chapel Hill Shooting Victim Said in StoryCorps Talk," February 12, 2015, NPR, http://www.npr.org/sections/thetwo-way/2015/02/12/385714242/were-all-one-chapel -hill-shooting-victim-said-in-storycorps-talk.

55. Nadia Marzouki, Duncan McDonnell, and Olivier Roy, eds., *Saving the People: How Populists Hijack Religion* (Oxford: Oxford University Press, 2016).

56. Adam Nossiter, "French Proposal to Strip Citizenship over Terrorism Sets off Alarms," *New York Times*, January 8, 2016, http://www.nytimes.com/2016/01/09/world/europe /french-proposal-to-strip-citizenship-over-terrorism-sets-off-alarms.html? _r=0.

57. However, a study prepared by a consulting firm based in Toronto, 416 Lab, shows that the *New York Times*'s depiction of Islam in the past twenty-five years has been more negative than the portraying of alcohol, cocaine, or cancer. See Dorgham Abusalim, "Study: 'NYT' Portrays Islam More Negatively Than Alcohol, Cancer, and Cocaine," March 5, 2016, Washington Report on Middle East Affairs, http://mondoweiss.net/2016/03/study-nyt -portrays-islam-more-negatively-than-alcohol-cancer-and-cocaine/. On the condemnation of Islamaphobia, see Elahe Izadi, "Obama, Thomas Jefferson and the Fascinating History of Founding Fathers Defending Muslim Rights," *Washington Post*, February 3, 2015, https://www.washingtonpost.com/news/the-fix/wp/2015/12/11/how-thomas-jefferson -and-other-founding-fathers-defended-muslim-rights/?postshare=711449961904599&tid =ss_tw-bottom; and David W. Dunlap, "Record of Mosque Hints at Muslims' Long History in New York," *New York Times*, December 9, 2015, http://www.nytimes.com /2015/12/10/nyregion/mosque-shows-that-muslims-have-long-been-a-part-of-new -york.html?smid=tw-share.

58. Sonya Faure, Cécile Daumas, and Anastasia Vécrin, " 'Culture de l'excuse': Les sociologues répondent a Valls," *Liberation*, January 12, 2016, http://www.liberation.fr /debats/2016/01/12/culture-de-l-excuse-les-sociologues-repondent-a-valls_1425855.

59. Denise A. Spellberg, "Ben Carson Would Fail U.S. History," *Time*, September 21, 2015, http://time.com/4042435/ben-carson-would-fail-u-s-history/.

60. Denise A. Spellberg, "Ahmed Mohamed and Thomas Jefferson: A Tale of Two Clocks," *The Hill*, October, 16, 2015, http://thehill.com/blogs/congress-blog/religious-rights/257035 -ahmed-mohamed-and-thomas-jefferson-a-tale-of-two-clocks.

61. Wilson Fache, "New York's Forgotten Mosque," December 29, 2015, Middle East Eye, http://www.middleeasteye.net/in-depth/features/new-york-s-forgotten-mosque -1191150126.

62. Dunlap, "Record of Mosque Hints at Muslims' Long History in New York."

63. Benjamin Weiser, "Lawsuit over New York Police Surveillance of Muslims Is Revived," *New York Times*, October 13, 2015, http://www.nytimes.com/2015/10/14/nyregion /appeals-court-reinstates-lawsuit-over-police-surveillance-of-muslims.html?_r=0.

64. Bilici, *Finding Mecca in America*, 192.

65. The template for this kind of "monster" humor would be the cartoons and movies of the Addams Family.

66. Laura Durkay, " 'Homeland' Is the Most Bigoted Show on Television," *Washington Post*, October 2, 2014, https://www.washingtonpost.com/posteverything/wp/2014/10/02 /homeland-is-the-most-bigoted-show-on-television/.

67. Claire Phipps, " 'Homeland Is Racist': Artists Sneak Subversive Graffiti on to TV Show," *Guardian*, October 15, 2015, http://www.theguardian.com/tv-and-radio/2015/oct/15/homeland -is-racist-artists-subversive-graffiti-tv-show.

68. Quoted in Michael Paulson, "American Identity, Muslim Identity," *New York Times*, October 24, 2014, http://www.nytimes.com/2014/10/26/theater/american-identity-muslim -identity-.html?_r=0.

69. Robert N. Bellah "Civil Religion in America," in "Religion in America," special issue, *Dædalus, Journal of the American Academy of Arts and Sciences* 96, no. 1 (1967): 1–2. For a critical discussion of the concept of civil religion, see, among others, "Reconsidering Civil Religion," July 30, 2010, *The Immanent Frame: Secularism, Religion, and the Public Sphere* (blog), Social Science Research Council, http://blogs.ssrc.org/tif/category /exchanges/religion-american-politics/reconsidering-civil-religion/; and Robert Wuthnow, "In America, All Religions Are True," in *American Mythos: Why Our Best Efforts to Be a Better Nation Fall Short* (Princeton, N.J.: Princeton University Press, 2008), 128–63.

70. Kareem Abdul-Jabbar, "Why I Converted to Islam," March 29, 2015, Al Jazeera America, http://america.aljazeera.com/opinions/2015/3/why-i-converted-to-islam.html; Paulson, "American Identity, Muslim Identity."

71. Talal Asad, *Genealogies of Religion: Discipline and Reasons of Power in Christianity and Islam* (Baltimore: Johns Hopkins University Press, 1993); Courtney Bender and Pamela E. Klassen, eds., *After Pluralism: Reimagining Religious Engagement* (New York: Columbia University Press, 2010).

72. Rosemary Hicks, "Religious Pluralism, Secularism and Interfaith Endeavors," in *The Cambridge Companion to American Islam*, ed. Julianne Hammer and Omid Safi (Cambridge: Cambridge University Press, 2013), 158.

73. Bilici, *Finding Mecca in America*, 201.

74. Ibid., 202.

75. Ibid.

76. Conor Friedersdorf, "The New Intolerance of Student Activism," *Atlantic*, November 9, 2015, http://www.theatlantic.com/politics/archive/2015/11/the-new-intolerance-of-student -activism-at-yale/414810/; Isaac Stanley-Becker, "A Confrontation over Race at Yale: Hundreds of Students Demand Answers from the School's First Black Dean," *Washington Post*, November 5, 2015, https://www.washingtonpost.com/news/grade-point /wp/2015/11/05/a-confrontation-over-race-at-yale-hundreds-of-students-demand -answers-from-the-schools-first-black-dean/.

INTRODUCTION

1. Leon Wieseltier, "The Catastrophist," review of *The Second Plane: September 11: Terror and Boredom*, by Martin Amis, *New York Times Book Review*, April 27, 2008, http://www.nytimes.com/2008/04/27/books/review/Wieseltier-t.html?em&_r=0.

2. Frank Newport, "Many Americans Can't Name Obama's Religion," June 22, 2012, Gallup, http://www.gallup.com/poll/155315/many-americans-cant-name-obamas-religion.aspx.

3. On the liberal argument, see Cécile Laborde, *Critical Republicanism: The Hijab Controversy and Political Philosophy* (New York: Oxford University Press, 2008); and Andrew March, *Islam and Liberal Citizenship: The Search for an Overlapping Consensus* (New York: Oxford University Press, 2009). On the republican argument, see Patrick Weil, "Lifting the Veil," *French Politics, Culture & Society* 22, no. 3 (2004): 142. On the postcolonial argument, see Joan Wallach Scott, *The Politics of the Veil* (Princeton, N.J.: Princeton University Press, 2010).

4. Ayaan Hirsi Ali, *Heretic: Why Islam Needs a Reformation Now* (New York: Harper, 2015); Rémi Brague, *On the God of the Christians: And on One or Two Others* (South Bend, Ind.: St. Augustine's Press, 2013).

5. Olivier Roy, *Holy Ignorance: When Religion and Culture Part Ways* (New York: Columbia University Press, 2010); Patrick Haenni, *L'Islam de marché: L'autre révolution conservatrice* (Paris: Seuil, 2005); Nilüfer Göle, *Interpénétrations: L'Islam et l'Europe* (Paris: Galaade, 2005).

1. MUSLIM AMERICANS

1. Pew Forum on Religion and Public Life, *U.S. Religious Landscape Survey: Religious Affiliation: Diverse and Dynamic*, February 2008, http://religions.pewforum.org/pdf/report-religious-landscape-study-full.pdf.

2. For a complete presentation and exhaustive analysis of the history of relations between religions and politics in the United States, see, for example, Denis Lacorne, *De la religion en Amérique: Essai d'histoire politique* (Paris: Gallimard, 2007); Franck Lambert, *The Founding Fathers and the Place of Religion in America* (Princeton, N.J.: Princeton University Press, 2003); and Robert Wuthnow, *America and the Challenges of Religious Diversity* (Princeton, N.J.: Princeton University Press, 2007).

3. Pew Research, Summary of Key Findings, "America's Changing Religious Landscape," May 12, 2015, http://www.pewforum.org/2015/05/12/americas-changing-religious-landscape/.

4. Among Muslim immigrants, 41 percent come from the Middle East or North Africa, 26 percent from Southeast Asia, 11 percent from Sub-Saharan Africa, 7 percent from Europe, 5 percent from Iran, and 9 percent from other countries.

5. There is a higher rate of naturalization among Muslims. The average naturalization rate across all immigrant groups is 47 percent.

6. Abu Dhabi Gallup Center, "Muslim Americans: Faith, Freedom and the Future. Examining U.S. Muslims' Political, Social, and Spiritual Engagement 10 Years After September 11" (presentation deck from the August 2, 2011, Report Launch Event), http://www.gallup.com/poll/148931/Presentation-Muslim-Americans-Faith-Freedom-Future.aspx.

7. Ibid., 17.

8. Studies of this type attribute a normative value to criteria of ideological moderation, participation, and conformity to mainstream practices without genuinely questioning these concepts. They also tend not to state explicitly what criteria are used to describe a given form of religiousness as moderate or dogmatic. Thus the Gallup study classifies Muslims into three categories: the isolated, the tolerant, and the fundamentalist. None of these recent studies inquires into the significance of the category of religion.

9. Robert P. Jones, Daniel Cox, William Galston, and E. J. Dionne Jr., *What It Means to Be an American: Attitudes in an Increasingly Diverse America Ten Years After 9/11* (Washington, D.C.: Brookings Institution and Public Religion Research Institute, 2011), https://www.brookings.edu/research/what-it-means-to-be-an-american-attitudes-in-an-increasingly-diverse-america-ten-years-after-911/.

10. Ibid., 37.

11. Pew Research Center, *Muslim Americans: No Sign of Growth in Alienation or Support for Extremism* (Washington, D.C.: Pew Research Center, 2011), 6.

12. For the historian David W. Bebbington, the four main features of Evangelical Protestantism are the importance of conversion, the focus on the Bible, the centrality of the crucifixion, and active engagement, as discussed in *Evangelicism in Modern Britain: A History from the 1730s to the 1980s* (London: Unwin Hyman, 1989), 2–17.

13. Sébastien Fath, *Dieu bénisse l'Amérique: La religion de la Maison Blanche* (Paris: Seuil), 89. Fath, a specialist on Evangelical Protestantism, defines fundamentalism as "an orthodox reaction to the progressive liberalization of Protestant theology at the end of the nineteenth century. . . . [It] particularly defends the infallibility of the Bible, Millennialism, and separatism" (*Militants de la Bible aux États-Unis: Évangéliques et fondamentalistes du Sud* [Paris: Autrement, 2004], 202). See also Michael D. Lindsay, *Faith in the Halls of Power: How Evangelicals Joined the American Elite* (Oxford: Oxford University Press, 2007).

14. Evangelicals' support for Israel and, consequently, their opposition to a number of Muslim countries also have a theological basis. Fundamentalists subscribe to the millennial doctrine that states that the re-creation of Israel is the precondition for the return of Christ. See Fath, *Dieu bénisse l'Amérique*, 96.

15. Kambiz GhaneaBassiri, *A History of Islam in America: From the New World to the New World Order* (Cambridge: Cambridge University Press, 2010), 20.

16. Cyrus Griffin, "The Unfortunate Moor," *Natchez Southern Galaxy*, December 13, 1827, in *African Muslims in Antebellum America: A Sourcebook*, ed. Allan D. Austin (New York: Garland, 1984), 135, cited in GhaneaBassiri, *History of Islam in America*, 20.

17. *Freedom's Journal of New York City*, June 20, 1828, in *African Muslims in Antebellum America*, ed. Austin, 157, cited in GhaneaBassiri, *History of Islam in America*, 28.

18. In France, nineteenth-century thinkers, military officers, and colonial officials adhering to Auguste Comte's philosophy argued that Islam was theologically superior to other religions because it is, according to them, more rational and less metaphysical than others and therefore closer to the positivist philosophy. They opposed Ernest Renan's racist theories in "Islamism and science." They included people such as Charles Mismer and Christian Cherfils, a French deputy who converted to Islam. On the history of orientalism and admiration for Islam in France, see Maxime Rodinson, *La fascination de l'Islam* (Paris: La Découverte, 2003); and Sadek Sellam, *La France et ses musulmans: Un siècle de politique musulmane, 1895–2005* (Paris: Fayard, 2006).

19. George E. Post, "Arabic-Speaking Negro Mohammedans in Africa," *African Repository*, May 1869, 129–33, cited in GhaneaBassiri, *History of Islam in America*, 52.

20. GhaneaBassiri, *History of Islam in America*, 30.

21. James Freeman Clarke, *Ten Great Religions: An Essay in Comparative Theology* (Boston: Osgood, 1871), 18.

22. Charles Carroll Bonney, "Worlds of Welcome," in *The Dawn of Religious Pluralism: Voices from the World's Parliament of Religions, 1893*, ed. Richard Hughes Seager (La Salle, Ill.: Open Court, 1993), 17. The full text of Bonney's speech is available at https://archive.org/stream/worldscongressadoobonn/worldscongressadoobonn_djvu.txt.

23. Only a select few African American ministers in attendance attempted to criticize the triumphalism of the Parliament of Religions, one example being Bishop Benjamin Arnett of the African Methodist Episcopal Church.

24. Edward Wilmot Blyden, *Christianity, Islam and the Negro Race* (Edinburgh: Edinburgh University Press, 1887), 10.

25. Gilles Kepel, *À l'ouest d'Allah* (Paris: Seuil, 1997).

26. GhaneaBassiri, *History of Islam in America*, 219.

27. Yusuf Nuruddin, "African-American Muslims and the Question of Identity, Between Tradition Islam African Heritage and the American Way," in *Muslims on the Americanization Path?*, ed. Yvonne Yazbeck Haddad and John L. Esposito (New York: Oxford University Press, 2000), 215–62. See also Aminah Beverly McCloud, *African American Islam* (New York: Routledge, 1995); Richard Brent Turner, *Islam in the African-American Experience*, 2nd ed. (Bloomington: Indiana University Press, 2003); Ernest Allen Jr., "Identity and Destiny, the Formative Views of the Moorish Science Temple and the Nation of Islam," in *Muslims on the Americanization Path?*, ed. Haddad and Esposito, 163–214; Sohail Daulatzai, *Black Star, Crescent Moon: The Muslim International and Black Freedom Beyond America* (Minneapolis: University of Minnesota Press, 2015); and Robert Dannin, *Black Pilgrimage to Islam* (New York: Oxford University Press, 2002). See also Sherman A. Jackson, *Islam and the Blackamerican: Looking Toward the Third Resurrection* (Oxford: Oxford University Press, 2005); Martha F. Lee, *The Nation of Islam: An American Millenarian Movement* (Lewiston, N.Y.: Mellen Press, 1988); and C. Eric Lincoln, *The Black Muslims in America* (Boston: Beacon Press, 1961).

28. On Malcolm X and his legacy, see Edward E. Curtis, "Why Malcolm X Never Developed an Islamic Approach to Civil Rights," *Religion* 32 (2002): 227–42; and David Remnick,

"This American Life: The Making and Remaking of Malcolm X," *New Yorker*, April 25, 2011, http://www.newyorker.com/magazine/2011/04/25/this-american-life.

29. Opposed to this thesis, Lawrence Mamiya argues that although Elijah Muhammad, the NOI's founder, first addressed lower-class blacks, he turned his attention very quickly to try to attract middle-class members, in "From Black Muslims to Bilalian: The Evolution of a Movement," *Journal for the Scientific Study of Religion* 21, no. 2 (1982): 138–52. His son, Warith Deen Muhammad, a Republican, was well liked in middle-class African American communities, whereas Louis Farrakhan, who took over direction of the NOI in 1981, aimed to represent the lower classes.

30. GhaneaBassiri, *History of Islam in America*, 141.

31. Ibid., 153.

32. Angel Rabasa, Cheryl Bernard, Lowell H. Schwartz, and Peter Sickle, *Building Moderate Muslim Networks* (Santa Monica, Calif.: Rand Center for Middle East Public Policy, 2007). For a detailed analysis of this approach, see Nadia Marzouki, "De l'endiguement à l'engagement: Le discours des think tanks américains sur l'islam depuis 2001," *Archives de sciences sociales des religions* 155, no. 3 (2001): 21–39.

33. Angel M. Rabasa, Cheryl Bernard, Peter Chalk, C. Christine Fair, Theodore Karasik, Rollie Lal, Ian Lesser, and David Thaler, *The Muslim World After 9/11* (Santa Monica, Calif.: Rand, Project Air Force, 2004), http://www.rand.org/content/dam/rand/pubs/monographs/2004/RAND_MG246.pdf.

34. Jean-Marie Donégani, *La liberté de choisir: Pluralisme religieux et pluralisme politique dans le catholicisme français contemporain* (Paris: Presses de la Fondation nationale des sciences politiques, 1993), 40. Donégani distinguishes between *intransigeantisme* and *intégralisme*.

35. See, for example, Juan Cole, *Engaging the Muslim World* (New York: Palgrave Macmillan, 2009); and Emile Nakhlé, *Necessary Engagement: Reinventing America's Relations with the Muslim World* (Princeton, N.J.: Princeton University Press, 2009).

36. Barack Obama, "A New Beginning" (speech presented at Cairo University, June 4, 2009), https://www.whitehouse.gov/the_press_office/Remarks-by-the-President-at-Cairo-University-6-04-09.

37. Samuel J. Rascoff, "Establishing Official Islam? The Law and Strategy of Counter-Radicalization," *Stanford Law Review* 64, no. 1 (2012): 125–90.

38. Scott Thompson, "House of Wisdom or a House of Cards? Why Teaching Islam in U.S. Foreign Detention Facilities Violates the Establishment Clause," *Nebraska Law Review* 88, no. 2 (2009): 344n.29, cited in Rascoff, "Establishing Official Islam?," 139.

39. Lorenzo Vidino, "Countering Radicalization in America: Lessons from Europe," United States Institute of Peace, Special Report 11. The full text is available at http://www.usip.org/sites/default/files/SR262%20-%20Countering_Radicalization_in_America.pdf.

40. Laurie Goodstein, "U.S. Muslims Take on ISIS' Recruiting Machine," *New York Times*, February 19, 2015, http://mobile.nytimes.com/2015/02/20/us/muslim-leaders-in-us-seek-to-counteract-extremist-recruiters.html?_r=1.

41. The first attempt by Muslim Americans to unite and defend their civil and political rights dates from the early 1950s. The Federation of Islamic Associations of the United States

and Canada was created in 1954 by Abdullah Igram. The organization seeks especially to unite Muslim immigrants of Lebanese origin and does not encourage its members to get involved in civic life. The Muslim Students' Association (MSA) was created in 1963 in Urbana, Illinois. Identifying its mission as in line with the reformist project of thinkers such as Sayid Abul Ala Mawdudi and Sayid Qutb, the MSA's principal aim is to help students arriving from Muslim countries in their daily affairs. Quite quickly, however, the MSA expanded into preaching activities (da'wa) and established several professional organizations, notably the Islamic Medical Association, the Association of Muslim Scientists and Engineers, and the Association of Muslim Social Scientists. See Gutbi Mahdi Ahmed, "Muslim Organizations in the U.S." in *The Muslims of America*, ed. Yvonne Yazbeck Haddad (New York: Oxford University Press, 1993), 11–25.

42. The Muslim Public Affairs Council was founded in 1988 with three missions: defend the civil rights of Muslims, foster dialogue between American Muslims and the rest of society, and encourage the participation of Muslims in political affairs. To further consolidate a Muslim American identity, MPAC works at building alliances with non-Muslim associations and developing cordial relations with the media and members of Congress. The objective of the Council on American-Islamic Relations, founded in 1994, is to defend the image, interests, and rights of Muslims. It ensures that the civil liberties of Muslims are respected, makes efforts to disseminate a positive image of Islam and of Muslims to the American public, and aspires to give more weight, unity, and empowerment to the Muslim community. In its choice of language and mode of operation, CAIR resembles other civil rights organizations, such as the American Civil Liberties Union, more than it resembles a religious organization. Nevertheless, CAIR also claims to want to contribute to improving society and the political life of Americans through the positive lessons of Muslim values.

43. The Ohio Department of Public Safety published "A Guide to Arabic and Islamic Culture," which explains that jihad "does not signify holy war, as many would have it, but rather a fight to achieve personal betterment." This guide also indicates that "if extremists kill in the name of *jihad*, ordinary Muslims consider such actions as deviating completely from the true religion of Islam." The federal government also created new posts, such as the State Department's special representative for Muslim communities, a post occupied by Farah Pandith from 2009 to 2014. See Rascoff, "Establishing Official Islam?," 153–60.

44. Ibid., 162.

45. The complete First Amendment reads: "Congress shall make no law respecting an establishment of religion, or prohibiting the free exercise thereof; or abridging the freedom of speech, or of the press; or the right of the people peaceably to assemble, and to petition the Government for a redress of grievances."

46. Thomas Jefferson, "Letter to the Danbury Baptists," January 1, 1802, Library of Congress, https://www.loc.gov/loc/lcib/9806/danpre.html.

47. *Reynolds v. United States*, 98 U.S. 145 (1878), Legal Information Institute, https://www.law.cornell.edu/supremecourt/text/98/145#writing-type-1-WAITE.

48. Ibid. See also Winnifred Fallers Sullivan, *The Impossibility of Religious Freedom* (Princeton, N.J.: Princeton University Press, 2007).

49.   *Sherbert v. Verner*, 374 U.S. 398 (1963), Legal Information Institute, https://www.law.cornell
      .edu/supremecourt/text/374/398.

50.   *Employment Division, Department of Human Resources of the State of Oregon, et al., Pe-*
      titioners, v. Alfred L. Smith. Employment Division, Department of Human Resources of
      the State of Oregon, et al., Petitioners, v. Galen W. Black, 494 U.S 872 (1990), Legal In-
      formation Institute, https://www.law.cornell.edu/supremecourt/text/494/872. It was in
      reaction to this more restrictive interpretation of religious freedom that the Religious
      Freedom Restoration Act was passed in 1993—a law that reestablishes the criterion of a
      compelling state interest.

51.   *Lynch v. Donnelly*, 465 U.S. 668 (1984), Justia, https://supreme.justia.com/cases/federal/us
      /465/668/case.html. With this expression, the Court was referring to the Lemon criterion
      defined in *Lemon v. Kurtzman* (1971). In this case, which concerned the government's
      financing of the salaries of teachers at who were employed at religious schools but who
      were teaching nonreligious subjects, the Court established the Lemon test to define the
      circumstances under which a law may violate the establishment clause. The Lemon test
      stipulates three conditions to guarantee respect of the establishment clause: "First, the
      statute must have a secular legislative purpose; second, its principal or primary effect
      must be one that neither advances nor inhibits religion; finally, the statute must not foster
      an excessive government entanglement with religion."

52.   *Lynch v. Donnelly*, from the concurring opinion of Justice Sandra Day O'Connor, who
      sided with Justice Warren Burger (author of the opinion of the Court) along with Justices
      Byron White, Lewis F. Powell Jr., and William Rehnquist.

53.   Ibid., from the dissenting opinion of Justices William Brennan, Thurgood Marshall,
      Harry Blackmun, and John Paul Stevens.

54.   Winnifred Fallers Sullivan, "The Religious Expert in American Courts," *Archives de sci-*
      ences sociales des religions 155, no. 3 (2011): 41–60, https://assr.revues.org/23305.

55.   Sullivan, *Impossibility of Religious Freedom*, 8.

56.   Council on American-Islamic Relations, *Same Hate, New Target: Islamophobia and Its*
      Impact in the United States (Washington D.C.: CAIR, 2010), http://www.cair.com/images
      /islamophobia/2010IslamophobiaReport.pdf.

57.   Ibid., 6.

58.   Ibid.

59.   Ibid.

60.   Wajahat Ali, Eli Clifton, Matthew Duss, Lee Fang, Scott Keyes, and Faiz Shakir, *Fear,*
      Inc.: The Roots of the Islamophobia Network in America (Washington, D.C.: Center for
      American Progress, 2011), 9.

61.   Southern Poverty Law Center, "30 New Activists Heading Up the Radical Right," May 26,
      2012, http://www.splcenter.org/get-informed/intelligence-report/browse-all-issues/2012
      /summer/30-to-watch.

62.   Christopher Hitchens, "Facing the Islamist Menace," review of *America Alone: The End*
      of the World as We Know It, by Mark Steyn, *City Journal*, Winter 2007, http://www.city
      -journal.org/html/17_1_urbanities-steyn.html.

63. U.S. Department of Justice, *Report on the Tenth Anniversary of the Religious Land Use and Institutionalized Persons Act*, September 22, 2010.

64. Stephen Sheehi, *Islamophobia: The Ideological Campaign Against Muslims* (Atlanta: Clarity Press, 2011).

65. Deepa Kumar, *Islamophobia and the Politics of Empire* (Chicago: Haymarket Books, 2012).

66. Martha Nussbaum, *New Religious Intolerance: Overcoming the Politics of Fear in an Anxious Age* (Cambridge, Mass.: Harvard University Press, 2012).

67. Ibid., chap. 7.

68. Jennifer Maytorena Taylor, dir. *New Muslim Cool* (Specific Pictures, 2009).

69. The show was shocking precisely for its soporific banality. Thus the Florida Family Association attempted to prove that with such ordinary images of Muslims, the television channel was complicit in a clandestine project to spread Muslim law, or Sharia, across the land by sedating the usual wide-awake vigilance of the average American.

2. THE MOSQUE CONTROVERSIES

1. Akbar Ahmed, *Journey into America: The Challenge of Islam* (Washington, D.C.: Brookings Institution Press, 2010); Akel Ismail Kahera, *Deconstructing the American Mosque: Space, Gender, and Aesthetics* (Austin: University of Texas Press, 2002).

2. The Religious Land Use and Institutionalized Persons Act (http://www.justice.gov/crt /about/spl/documents/rluipa.php) replaces an earlier law from 1993, the Religious Freedom Restoration Act (RFRA), which was overturned by the Supreme Court in 1997 in the case *City of Boerne v. Flores*. The RFRA required the state to show more flexibility when it came to demands made in the name of religious freedom. As such, it was found to violate the non-establishment clause of the First Amendment, and its application in the states was terminated.

3. Quoted in "Statement of the Department of Justice on the Land-Use Provisions of the Religious Land Use and Institutionalized Persons Act (RLUIPA)," September 22, 2010, http://www.justice.gov/crt/rluipa_q_a_9-22-10.pdf.

4. Religious Land Use and Institutionalized Persons Act (2000), https://www.justice.gov /crt/religious-land-use-and-institutionalized-persons-act.

5. Pew Research Center, "Controversies over Mosques and Islamic Centers Across the U.S.," September 27, 2012, http://www.pewforum.org/2012/09/27/controversies-over-mosques -and-islamic-centers-across-the-u-s-2/.

6. For a detailed discussion, see Nadia Marzouki, "Offense morale contre liberté religieuse, la controverse de Ground Zero," *Revue française de science politique* 61, no. 5 (2011): 839–65.

7. The name of Geller's blog alludes to the best-selling book of the conservative, libertarian philosopher-novelist Ayn Rand, *Atlas Shrugged* (New York: Random House, 1957).

8. The English Defense League is a British right-wing movement whose leading mission is fighting against "Islamic radicalism." See Matthew Taylor, "The English Defense League: Inside the Violent World of Britain's New Far Right," *Guardian*, May 28, 2010.

9. Robert Spencer, *The Truth About Muhammad: Founder of the World's Most Intolerant Religion* (Washington, D.C.: Regenery, 2006). The book is banned in many Muslim countries, notably Pakistan.

10. Pamela Geller and Robert Spencer, *The Post-American Presidency: The Obama Administration's War on America* (New York: Simon and Schuster, 2010).

11. Robert Spencer, "Why There Should Be No Mosques at Ground Zero," *Jihad Watch*, May 24, 2010.

12. New York City is divided into five administrative units, or boroughs: Manhattan, the Bronx, Brooklyn, Queens, and Staten Island. Each borough is directed by a borough president whose role is to inform and advise the mayor about the borough's problems and its budget. Each borough also has community boards, whose members are appointed by the borough president to make recommendations to government agencies about problems in their neighborhoods. There are fifty-nine community boards spread over New York City.

13. Mosab Hassan Yousef, *Son of Hamas: A Gripping Account of Terror, Betrayal, Political Intrigue, and Unthinkable Choices* (New York: Tyndale House, 2010).

14. The Landmarks Preservation Commission is charged with applying the law that relates to the preservation of historic buildings and monuments. The New York commission was created in 1965.

15. Andrew Cuomo is quoted in the *New York Post* on July 5, 2010, as saying, "America's very foundation is diversity and tolerance, and this is why we should let this project go forward, even though it's understandable that it makes certain people uncomfortable and is offensive to some."

16. Andrew Cuomo was elected governor of New York in November 2010.

17. Carl Paladino was a registered Democrat from 1974 to 2005 and then became known for his conservative positions, similar to those of former president Ronald Reagan.

18. Paladino called for changing New York's state constitution, which in his view had wrongfully transformed New York into a "European-style welfare state." He notably favored the elimination of the Medicaid program. See Anemona Hartocollis, "Paterson's No. 2 Calls for Medicaid Overhaul," *New York Times*, September 19, 2010, http://www.nytimes.com/2010/09/20/nyregion/20medicaid.html?_r=2&ref=nyregion.

19. The power of eminent domain allows the government to seize property and expropriate a citizen of his private property without his consent in order to build on it something of general public good.

20. Michael Bloomberg, "Mayor Bloomberg Discusses the Landmarks Preservation Commission Vote on 45–47 Park Place," August 3, 2010, http://www1.nyc.gov/office-of-the-mayor/news/337-10/mayor-bloomberg-the-landmarks-preservation-commission-vote-45-47-park-place#/0. Bloomberg concluded, "Political controversies come and go, but our values and our traditions endure—and there is no neighborhood in this City that is off limits to God's love and mercy, as the religious leaders here with us today can attest."

21. Joshua Green, "The Tea Party's Brain," *Atlantic*, November 2010, http://www.theatlantic.com/magazine/archive/2010/11/the-tea-party-8317-s-brain/8280/.

22. Ron Paul, "Demagoguing the Mosque: The Grand Distraction at Ground Zero," LewRockwell.com, August 23, 2010, https://stevenjohnhibbs.wordpress.com/2010/08/24 /demagoguing-the-mosque-the-grand-distraction-at-ground-zero/.

23. Peter Wallsten, "Norquist and Gingrich: Debating a Mosque Near Ground Zero," *Wall Street Journal*, August 18, 2010, http://blogs.wsj.com/washwire/2010/08/18/norquist-and -gingrich-debating-a-mosque-near-ground-zero/.

24. Public hearing organized by the Landmarks Preservation Commission, July 13, 2010, Hunter College. Some videos from the hearing are accessible at YouTube, https://www .youtube.com/watch?v=OsGI296X_Ac; and at "The 'Silent' Majority No More," https:// thesilentmajoritynomore.com/2010/07/14/videoground-zero-mosque-landmarks -preservation-commission-meeting/.

25. Landmarks Preservation Commission, public hearing.

26. Ibid.

27. Mateo Tassig-Rubbo, "Sacred Property: Searching for Value in the Rubble of 9/11," in *After Secular Law*, ed. Winnifred F. Sullivan, Robert A. Yelle, and Mateo Taussig-Rubbo (Stanford, Calif.: Stanford University Press / Stanford Law Books, 2011), 322–41.

28. Glenn A. Fine to Robert S. Mueller III, "Investigation Regarding Removal of a Tiffany Globe from the Fresh Kills Recovery Site" (memorandum), 11, December 17, 2003, U.S. Department of Justice, Office of the Inspector General, https://oig.justice.gov/special /0403a/final.pdf.

29. Taussig-Rubbo, "Sacred Property," 326.

30. David Silverman, "Atheists File Suit to Block WTC Memorial 'Cross,'" July 25, 2011, American Atheists, http://www.atheists.org.

31. "Rep. Grimm to Introduce Bill Making 9/11 Cross a National Monument," September 5, 2011, FedSmith, http://www.fedsmith.com/2011/09/05/rep-grimm-introduce-bill-making-cross/.

32. Landmarks Preservation Commission, public hearing.

33. Anti-Defamation League, "Statement on Islamic Community Center Near Ground Zero" (press release), July 28, 2010, http://www.adl.org/press-center/press-releases/civil-rights /statement-on-islamic.html.

34. Geneviève Zubrzycki, *The Crosses of Auschwitz: Nationalism and Religion in Post-Communist Poland* (Chicago: University of Chicago Press, 2006).

35. *Brown v. New York City Landmarks Preservation Commission*, July 7, 2011, Justia, http:// law.justia.com/cases/new-york/other-courts/2011/2011-51273.html.

36. Created in 1985, the Dove World Outreach Center is a charismatic evangelical church. Functioning almost like a sect, the church has been directed in an authoritarian way by Pastor Terry Jones and his wife, Sylvia, since 2001. Since its founding, the church has been noted for its stands against abortion and homosexuality, and for its Islamophobic declarations.

37. Governor Phil Bredesen signed the bill into law (House Bill 1598) on July 1, 2009. The law adopts the criteria of the state's superior compelling interest concerning the free exercise of religion. When someone claims that his right to religious freedom is substantially burdened by a law, it is up to the state to demonstrate that its superior compelling interest is in jeopardy. This law was a new local reaction to the U.S. Supreme Court decision in

City of Boerne v. Flores (521 U.S. 507 [1997]), which held that a similar law—the Religious Freedom Restauration Act of 1993—was unconstitutional.

38. Quoted in Christian Grantham, "Residents Express Concerns over New Islamic Community Center," *Murfreesboro (Tenn.) Post*, June 18, 2010.

39. Tennessee Open Meetings Act, Tennessee Code § 8-44-101.

40. What follows is largely taken from information and quotations that appeared in this newspaper.

41. "Zelenik Issues Statement on Proposed Islamic Center," *Murfreesboro Post*, June 24, 2010, http://www.murfreesboropost.com/zelenik-issues-statement-on-proposed-islamic-center-cms-23606.

42. Amicus curiae brief for *James Estes, et al., v. Rutherford County Regional Planning Commission, and the Rutherford County Board of Commissioners, et al.*, http://www.justice.gov/crt/spec_topics/religiousdiscrimination/rutherford_amicus_brief.pdf.

43. Christian Grantham, "Plaintiffs Ask if Islam Is a Religion in Mosque Trial," *Murfreesboro Post*, October 20, 2010, http://www.murfreesboropost.com/plaintiffs-ask-if-islam-is-a-religion-in-mosque-trial-cms-24801.

44. Christian Grantham, "U.S. Attorneys Make Presence Known in Murfreesboro Mosque Trial," *Murfreesboro Post*, October 22, 2010, http://www.murfreesboropost.com/u-s-attorneys-make-presence-known-in-murfreesboro-mosque-trial-cms-24817.

45. Quoted in Christian Grantham, "Witnesses Fund Lawsuit Against Local Mosque," *Murfreesboro Post*, October 21, 2010, http://www.murfreesboropost.com/witnesses-fund-lawsuit-against-local-mosque-cms-24812.

46. Ibid.

47. Bob Smietana, "Anti-Muslim Crusaders Make Millions Spreading Fear," *Tennessean* (Nashville), October 24, 2010.

48. Derek Prince was born in India to British parents. He studied philosophy, notably with Wittgenstein, and humanities at Cambridge University. He was sent to Palestine for his military service from 1942 to 1945. Some years after the war, he immigrated to the United States with his Danish wife, Lydia Christensen, and founded the Derek Prince Ministries.

49. Sébastien Fath, *Dieu XXL: La révolution des "megachurches"* (Paris: Autrement, 2008). See also Anne C. Loveland and Otis B. Wheeler, *From Meetinghouse to Megachurch: A Material and Cultural History* (Columbia: University of Missouri Press, 2003).

50. Christian Grantham, "Judge Denies Mosque Injunction," *Murfreesboro Post*, November 17, 2010, http://www.murfreesboropost.com/judge-denies-mosque-injunction-cms-25105.

51. Quoted in Rob Boston, "Religious Freedom: Tenn. Court Affirms That Isn't Just for Christians Any More," August 31, 2011, *Wall of Separation* (blog), Americans United for Separation of Church and State, https://www.au.org/blogs/wall-of-separation/religious-freedom-tenn-court-affirms-that-isn%E2%80%99t-just-for-christians-any.

52. The Tennessee Freedom Coalition is a nonprofit organization with 501c3 status whose stated mission is to educate the public; militate in favor of lower taxes and against Social Security, abortion, and Islamic radicalization; and advocate for a better balance between the population and the federal government. It presents itself as a grassroots movement of determined individuals who want to restore freedom and America's "traditional values."

53. Quoted in Richard Lloyd, "Dutch Anti-Islam Zealot Geert Wilders Finds a Sympathetic Ear at Madison's Cornerstone Church," *Nashville Scene*, May 19, 2011, http://www .nashvillescene.com/nashville/dutch-anti-islam-zealot-geert-wilders-finds-a-sympathetic -ear-at-madisons-cornerstone-church/Content?oid=2450397.

54. Tennessee Code Annotated § 8-44-103, Notice of Public Meetings, https://www .comptroller.tn.gov/openrecords/pdf/open%20meetings%20draft8-44-101.pdf.

55. *Kevin Fisher et al. v. Rutherford Country Regional Planning Commission et al.*, Court of Appeals of Tennessee, June 1, 2012, http://tncourts.gov/sites/default/files/fisherk_opn.pdf.

56. *United States of America vs. Rutherford County*, United States District Court, Middle District of Tennessee, July 10, 2012, http://www.justice.gov/crt/about/hce/documents /rutherford_county_tro.pdf.

57. "The litigation against the mosque's opening finally came to an end on June 2, 2014 when a bid by opponents to appeal the ruling to the Supreme Court of the United States was rebuffed, with the court declining to take the case" ("Islamic Center of Murfreesboro," Wikipedia, http://en.wikipedia.org/wiki/Islamic_Center_of_Murfreesboro).

58. Osama Bahloul, interview with the author, Murfreesboro, October 26, 2011; Lena Sbenaty, interview with the author, October 27, 2011, Murfreesboro.

59. NewGround was founded in 2006 with the aim of creating dialogue between the Muslim Public Affairs Council and the Progressive Jewish Alliance. Its goal is to improve relations between Jews and Muslims through various intercommunity activities, internships, study abroad programs, and conferences.

60. CAC presents itself as a grassroots organization of citizens whose aim is to fight against the infiltration of the Islamic threat in suburban and small town America. CAC's three leading causes are opposing the construction of mosques, the wearing of Islamic religious symbols in schools, and Sharia. Mano Bakh is one of the most active members within this organization.

61. Steven Cuevas, "Controversy over Building New Mosques in the US spills over into the Temecula Valley," August 24, 2010, 89.3 KPCC: Southern California Public Radio, http:// www.scpr.org/news/2010/08/24/18630/temecula-mosque/.

62. CAC has close ties with the Center for Security Policy, the think tank of the neoconservative Frank Gaffney, a leader of the anti-Sharia movement.

63. Quoted in Cuevas, "Controversy over Building New Mosques in the US."

64. Paul W. Kahn, *Political Theology: Four New Chapters on the Concept of Sovereignty* (New York: Columbia University Press, 2011), 7.

65. For Kahn, this opposition is what defines the different political visions in Europe and America:

> European constitutional courts, for example, have no trouble declaring legislation unconstitutional. They do so, however, in the name of individual rights, not in the name of the popular sovereign. The American Supreme Court founds its claim for legitimacy on its capacity to speak in the voice of a transhistorical popular sovereign. The method of legal reasoning for European courts, on the other hand, is "proportionality" review, which is just another name for balancing the various interests—including rights—that are at stake in a situation. (Ibid., 13)

66. Thomas M. Scanlon, *Moral Dimensions: Permissibility, Meaning, Blame* (Cambridge, Mass.: Harvard University Press, 2008).

67. Patricia Paperman, "L'absence d'émotion comme offense," in *La Couleur des pensées: Sentiments, émotions, intentions*, ed. Patricia Paper and Ruwen Ogien (Paris: Éditions de l'EHESS, 1995), 175–97.

68. Even though they may cite, for example, a study conducted by researchers at Duke University that shows regular attendance at a mosque lowers the risk of a person becoming radicalized. See David Schanzer, Charles Kurzman, and Ebrahim Moosa, *Anti-Terror Lessons of Muslim-Americans* (Durham, N.C.: Sanford School of Public Policy, Duke University, January 6, 2010).

69. Judith Butler, *Excitable Speech: A Politics of the Performative* (New York: Routledge, 1997).

3. THE ANTI-SHARIA MOVEMENT

1. Newt Gingrich, "America at Risk: The War with No Name" (speech delivered at the American Enterprise Institute, Washington, D.C., July 21, 2010).

2. Citizens United's mission appears on its website: http://www.citizensunited.org/. Under the rubric "About" and "Who We Are," is the following summary:

> Citizens United is an organization dedicated to restoring our government to citizens' control. Through a combination of education, advocacy, and grass roots organization, Citizens United seeks to reassert the traditional American values of limited government, freedom of enterprise, strong families, and national sovereignty and security. Citizens United's goal is to restore the founding fathers' vision of a free nation, guided by the honesty, common sense, and good will of its citizens. (http://www.citizensunited.org/who-we-are.aspx)

3. The documentary especially deplores the fact that the expression "global war on terror" was replaced by "Overseas Contingency Operation," and that the words "Islamic extremism" and "jihad" were removed from strategic documents about national security. See Scott Wilson and Al Kamen, "Global War on Terror Is Given New Name," *Washington Post*, March 25, 2009.

4. Oak Initiative, "Our Purpose," http://www.theoakinitiative.org/our-purpose. The organization represents American Christians as alienated slaves under the control of a foreign malevolent power.

5. Kyle Mantyla, "Boykin: Islam 'Should Not Be Protected Under the First Amendment,'" December 6, 2010, Right Wing Watch, http://www.rightwingwatch.org/content/boykin-islam-should-not-be-protected-under-first-amendment.

6. Quoted in Kenda Marr, "Santorum: Sharia Is 'Evil,'" *Politico*, March 3, 2011, http://www.politico.com/story/2011/03/rick-santorum-sharia-is-evil-051166.

7. Center for Security Policy, "About Us," http://news.cision.com/center-for-security-policy.

8. The academic committee is composed uniquely of university professors who wish to educate a new generation of students devoted to the philosophy of "peace through

strength" and prepare them for careers in defense and homeland security. The creation of this committee was required, according to the CSP, because of the general incapacity of the current American university system "to contribute to the war effort."

9. Former Muslims United, a small group created in 2009, is very active in antimosque activities, especially educating public opinion about Islamic intolerance and about the duplicity of so-called moderate Muslims. The group is represented by media personalities such as Nonie Darwish, Wafa Sultan, Walid Shoebat, and Ibn Warraq.

10. The study, originally published by the CSP on September 22, 2010, in Washington, is now available in an expanded 370-page version on Amazon, which is linked to by the CSP affiliated website http://shariahthethreat.org/.

11. Andrew McCarthy was in charge of the trial against Omar Abdel Rahman in 1995 and is the author of numerous polemical books opposed to Islam, the American Left, and the Obama administration. See, for example, *The Grand Jihad: How Islam and the Left Sabotage America* (New York: Encounter Books, 2010), and *How Obama Embraces Islam's Sharia Agenda* (New York: Encounter Books, 2010).

12. Center for Security Policy, *Shariah: The Threat to America: An Exercise in Competitive Analysis* (Washington, D.C.: Center for Security Policy, 2010), 120.

13. Ibid., 121.

14. Ibid., 119.

15. Several pieces of information that follow come from Andrea Elliott's well-documented profile "The Man Behind the Anti-Shariah Movement," *New York Times*, July 30, 2011, http://www.nytimes.com/2011/07/31/us/31shariah.html?pagewanted=all&_r=0.

16. Ibid.

17. David Yerushalmi, "On Race: A Tentative Discussion," *McAdam Report*, May 12, 2006, 10, http://littlegreenfootballs.com/weblog/pdf/Yerushalmi-On-Race.pdf.

18. This observation is quoted in Samuel G. Freedman, "Waging a One-Man War on American Muslims," *New York Times*, December 16, 2011, http://www.nytimes.com/2011/12/17/us/on-religion-a-one-man-war-on-american-muslims.html.

19. Elliott, "Man Behind the Anti-Shariah Movement."

20. *S. D. v. M. J. R.*, Superior Court of New Jersey, Appellate Division, July 23, 2010, http://www.judiciary.state.nj.us/mcs/case_law/sd_v_mjr.pdf.

21. Ibid.

22. Asifa Quraishi-Landes, "Rumors of the Sharia Threat Are Greatly Exaggerated: What American Judges Really Do with Islamic Family Law in Their Courtrooms," *New York Law School Law Review* 57, no. 2 (2012–2013): 244–57. See also Nadia Marzouki, "Les débats sur le droit islamique aux États-Unis et au Canada, entre égalité formelle et pluralisme," in *La Charia aujourd'hui*, ed. Baudouin Dupret (Paris: La Découverte, 2012), 280–94.

23. Quoted in Elliott, "Man Behind the Anti-Shariah Movement."

24. State Question 755, House Joint Resolution 1056, HJR 1056, Section C, drafted May 25, 2010, and submitted to a vote on November 2, 2010.

25. Quoted in James C. McKinley Jr., "Oklahoma Surprise: Islam as an Election Issue," *New York Times*, November 14, 2010. Note how Reynolds slides from Judeo-Christian

principles to Christian values, thus omitting any reference to Judaism in the second part of the sentence.

26. United States Constitution, Article VI, clause 2.

27. *Muneer Awad v. Paul Ziriax, Oklahoma State Board of Elections, et al.*, United States District Court, Western District of Oklahoma, November 29, 2010, American Civil Liberties Union, https://www.aclu.org/legal-document/awad-v-ziriax-district-court-decision.

28. Ibid., 1.

29. Ibid., 15.

30. Ibid., 7.

31. This federal appeals court hears cases that cover a district comprising six states: Colorado, Kansas, New Mexico, Oklahoma, Utah, and Wyoming.

32. *Muneer Awad v. Paul Ziraix*, United States Court of Appeals, Tenth Circuit, January 10, 2012, 35, American Civil Liberties Union, https://www.aclu.org/legal-document/awad-v-ziriax-appeals-court-decision.

33. Ibid., 28.

34. Ibid., 29.

35. The template of this "model legislation" is available on the website of the American Public Policy Alliance: http://publicpolicyalliance.org/legislation/american-laws-for-american-courts/.

36. Jill Schachner Chanen, "Anti-Sharia Bills Under Review," *Abajournal*, May 1, 2011.

37. Elizabeth Tenety, "Sharia Law Ban Proposed in Tennessee," On Faith, http://www.faithstreet.com/onfaith/2011/02/24/sharia-law-ban-proposed-in-tennessee/1593.

38. Saeed A. Khan and Alejandro J. Beutel, *Manufacturing Bigotry: A State-by-State Legislative Effort to Push Back Against 2050 by Targeting Muslims and Other Minorities*, January 2015, Institute for Social Policy and Understanding, http://www.ispu.org/pdfs/ISPU_Manufacturing_Bigotry[4].pdf.

39. Frank Gaffney, "Statement on Oklahoma Shariah Ruling," January 11, 2012, Center for Security Policy, http://www.centerforsecuritypolicy.org/2012/01/11/frank-gaffney-on-oklahoma-shariah-ruling-2/.

40. Tim Murphy, "Missouri Jumps on the Anti-Sharia Bandwagon," *Mother Jones*, March 2, 2011, http://www.motherjones.com/mojo/2011/03/missouri-jumps-anti-sharia-bandwagon.

41. In June 2011, the ACLU and MPAC organized "A Solution in Search of a Problem," a day of debate about the anti-Sharia movement,

42. American Civil Liberties Union, *Nothing to Fear: Debunking the Mythical "Sharia Threat" to Our Judicial System* (New York: ACLU, May 2011), https://www.aclu.org/report/nothing-fear-debunking-mythical-sharia-threat-our-judicial-system; American Public Policy Alliance (APPA), *Representative Civil Legal Cases Involving Shariah*, November 8, 2010, http://publicpolicyalliance.org/wp-content/uploads/2010/11/Shariah_Cases_11states_11-08-2010.pdf.

43. Quoted in Elliott, "Man Behind the Anti-Shariah Movement."

44. David Yerushalmi, "Using the Courts to Defend America," YouTube, 9:50/14:09, https://www.youtube.com/watch?v=66fZSE7kmq8.

45. Ibid.

46. Ibid., 12:13/14:09.

47. See, for example, Jews Against Islamophobia Coalition, https://www.facebook.com/Jews-Against-Islamophobia-Coalition-336413369790913/; and Network Against Islamophobia, A Project for Jewish Peace, newsletter, December 2014, https://jewishvoiceforpeace.org/wp-content/uploads/2015/07/Network-Against-Islamophobia-Newsletter.pdf.

48. Quoted in Justin Elliott, "Jews and Muslims United for Sharia?" *Salon*, May 6, 2011, http://www.salon.com/2011/05/06/jews_against_anti_sharia_laws/.

49. Paul Kahn, "A Political Theology for a Civil Religion" (lecture delivered at the European University Institute, Florence, January 2012), 17, http://www.eui.eu/Projects/ReligioWest/Documents/events/LecturesSeries/LectureKahn.pdf.

50. Ibid., 18.

51. Ibid., 20.

52. The Christian Legal Centre is a lobby composed of lawyers whose aim is to advocate in favor of a Christian point of view in British law and politics.

53. Patrick Haenni and Stépane Lathion, *Les minarets de la discorde: Éclairages sur un débat suisse et européen* (Fribourg, Switzerland: Religioscope, 2009).

54. Michael Kimmelmann, "When Fear Turns Graphic," *New York Times*, January 14, 2010.

55. Janet Hook and Tom Hamburger, "New York Mosque Debate Splits GOP," *Los Angeles Times*, August 17, 2010.

56. Ben Armbruster, "Pam Geller Rebuffs Norquist's Call for the Right to 'Knock Down' Islamophobia: 'Grover's Got to Go,'" February 14, 2011, ThinkProgress, http://thinkprogress.org/politics/2011/02/14/144096/geller-norquist-islamophobia/.

57. Adam Serwer, "Chris Christie Smacks Down the Sharia Crowd," *Washington Post*, August 4, 2011, http://www.washingtonpost.com/blogs/plum-line/post/chris-christie-smacks-down-the-sharia-crowd/2011/03/04/gIQARsBBuI_blog.html.

58. Sally Steenland, "Young Muslim American Voices: Setting the Record Straight on Sharia: An Interview with Intisar Rabb," March 8, 2011, Center for American Progress, https://www.americanprogress.org/issues/religion/news/2011/03/08/9263/setting-the-record-straight-on-sharia/.

59. *Muneer Awad v. Paul Ziriax, Oklahoma State Board of Elections, et al.*, United States District Court, Western District of Oklahoma, 11–12 (my emphasis).

60. On this point, see the detailed study by the research team Religare: Alidadi Katayoun, Marie-Claire Foblets, and Jogchum Vrielink, *A Test of Faith? Religious Diversity and Accommodation in the European Workplace* (Burlington, Vt.: Ashgate, 2012).

4. THE FACE OF ANTI-MUSLIM POPULISM

1. Michael Kazin, *The Populist Persuasion: An American History*, rev. ed. (Ithaca, N.Y.: Cornell University Press, 1998).

2. Ibid., 4.

3. Ibid., 13.

4. Ibid., 266.

5.   Ibid., 276.

6.   Quoted in Richard Hofstadter, *The Paranoid Style in American Politics, and Other Essays* (Cambridge, Mass.: Harvard University Press, 1996), 13. Hofstadter's essay originally appeared in the November 1964 issue of *Harper's Magazine* and is available in its online archive: http://harpers.org/archive/1964/11/the-paranoid-style-in-american-politics/. Subsequent page references are to the reedition of the essay in book form, also available online: http://studyplace.ccnmtl.columbia.edu/files/courses/reserve/Hofstadter-1996 -Paranoid-Style-American-Politics-1-to-40.pdf.

7.   Hofstadter, *Paranoid Style in American Politics*, 21. See also David Brion Davis, ed., *The Fear of Conspiracy: Images of Un-American Subversion from the Revolution to the Present* (Ithaca, N.Y.: Cornell University Press, 1971).

8.   Quoted in Kambiz GhaneaBassiri, *A History of Islam in America: From the New World to the New World Order* (New York: Cambridge University Press, 2010), 104. See also Denis Lacorne, *De la religion en Amérique: Essai d'histoire politique* (Paris: Gallimard, 2007), 106 ; and James Freeman Clark, *Ten Great Religions: An Essay in Comparative Theology*, http://www.gutenberg.org/files/14674/14674-h/14674-h.htm.

9.   Norman Cohn, *The Pursuit of the Millennium: Revolutionary Millenarians and Mystical Anarchists of the Middle Ages* (1957; repr., New York: Oxford University Press, 1992), quoted in Hofstadter, *Paranoid Style in American Politics*, 38.

10. Hofstadter, *Paranoid Style in American Politics*, 37.

11. Ibid.

12. Ibid., 4.

13. For a comparison of the discourse of European and American populist movements about religion and Islam, see Nadia Marzouki, Duncan McDonnell, and Olivier Roy, eds., *Saving the People: How Populists Hijack Religion* (Oxford: Oxford University Press, 2016). See also Hanz-Georg Betz, "Culture, Identity and the Question of Islam: The Nativist Agenda of the Radical Right," in *The Far Right in Europe: An Encyclopedia*, ed. Peter Davies and Paul Jackson (Oxford: Greenwood World Press, 2008), 114–15; and Hans-Georg Betz and Susi Meret, "Revisiting Lepanto: The Political Mobilization Against Islam in Contemporary Western Europe," *Patterns of Prejudice* 43, nos. 3–4 (2009): 313–34. For a detailed account of the links among different Far Right anti-Muslim figures and movements, see Institute of Race Relations, "Breivik: The Conspiracy Theory and the Oslo Massacre," *Briefing Paper*, no. 5, September 2011, http://www.irr.org.uk/pdf2/ERA_BriefingPaper5. pdf. On the Eurabia paradigm, see Matt Carr, "You Are Now Entering Eurabia," *Race and Culture* 48, no. 1 (2006): 1–22.

14. Sindre Bangstaad, *Anders Breivik and the Rise of Islamophobia* (London: Zed Books, 2014); Liz Fekete, "The Muslim Conspiracy Theory and the Oslo Massacre," *Race & Class* 53, no. 3 (2012): 30–47.

15. Alan Lake is the pseudonym of the English millionaire Alan Ayling, a central figure in European anti-Muslim movements and a leading financial backer of the English Defense League. See Nigel Copsey, "The English Defense League: Challenging Our Country and our Values of Social Inclusion, Fairness, and Equality," *Faith Matters*, October 2010, http://faith-matters.org/images/stories/fm-reports/english-defense-league-report.pdf.

16. Die Freiheit, founded in 2010 in Berlin, seeks to restrict immigration and fights against the Islamization of Europe. Its founder's Islamophobic positions led him to be expelled from Germany's Christian Democratic Union party.

17. "Dhimmitude" comes from the Arabic word *dhimmi*, which refers to indigenous Jews and Christians governed and protected by Islamic law.

18. Quoted in Institute of Race Relations, "Breivik," 3.

19. Quoted in Lesley Hazleton, "Sleaze," *Accidental Theologist* (blog), May 27, 2011.

20. Quoted in Andreas Lindqvist, "Lars Hedegaard: Muslimer er voldtægtsmænd og løgnere," *Politiken*, December 21, 2010, http://politiken.dk/indland/ECE865702/lars-hedegaard -muslimer-er-voldtaegtsmaend-og-loegnere/.

21. Patrick Haenni and Stéphane Lathion, eds., *Les minarets de la discorde: Éclairages sur un débat suisse et européen* (Fribourg, Switzerland: Religioscope, 2009).

22. Secularism implies an accepted secularization that is welcomed, even decided on, by a group, community, or society. On the place of Islam in European discussions of feminism and religion, see Schirin Amir-Moazami, Christine M. Jacobsen, and Maleiha Malik, "Islam and Gender in Europe: Subjectivities, Politics and Piety," *Feminist Review* 98, no. 1 (2011): 1–8; Schirin Amir-Moazami, "Muslim Challenges to the Secular Consensus: A German Case Study," *Journal of Contemporary European Studies* 13, no. 3 (2005): 267–86; and Jane Freedman, "Women, Islam and Rights in Europe: Beyond a Universalist /Culturalist Dichotomy," *Review of International Studies* 33, no. 1 (2007): 29–44.

23. Olivier Roy, *Secularism Confronts Islam* (New York: Columbia University Press, 2009); Jean Baubérot, *La laïcité falsifiée* (Paris: La Découverte, 2012); Valérie Amiraux, "L'affaire du foulard en France: Retour sur une affaire qui n'en est pas encore une," *Sociologie et sociétés* 41, no. 2 (2009): 273–98; François Lorcerie, ed., *La politisation du voile en France, en Europe et dans le monde arabe* (Paris: L'Harmattan, 2005).

24. Tom Robbins, "NYPD Cops' Training Included an Anti-Muslim Horror Flick," *Village Voice*, January 19, 2012, http://www.villagevoice.com/news/nypd-cops-training-included -an-anti-muslim-horror-flick-6429945. For an analysis of this controversy, see Jeremy F. Walton, "America's Muslim Anxiety: Lessons from *The Third Jihad*," *Revealer*, February 2, 2012.

25. "Following Up: *The Third Jihad*," Zuhdi Jasser, interview with Brian Lehrer, *Brian Lehrer Show*, WNYC, January 27, 2012, http://www.wnyc.org/story/183470-following-third-jihad/.

26. Mitt Romney made these remarks during a Republican Party primary campaign stop in Milwaukee, Wisconsin, April 3, 2012.

27. Rick Santorum, interview on *Meet the Press*, NBC, February 26, 2012.

28. Rick Santorum, interview on *This Week*, ABC, February 26, 2012.

29. Quoted in Faiz Shakir, "Kansas Legislature Passes Discriminatory Anti-Muslim Bill by Calling It a 'Women's Rights Issue,'" May 13, 2012, Think Progress, http://thinkprogress .org/justice/2012/05/13/483278/kansas-legislature-passes-discriminatory-anti-muslim -bill-by-calling-it-a-womens-right-issue/.

30. Barbara Miller Solomon, *Ancestors and Immigrants: A Changing New England's Traditions* (Chicago: University of Chicago Press, 1956), 32–42.

31. Quoted in Michael W. Hughey, "Americanism and Its Discontents: Protestantism, Nativism, and Political Heresy in America," *International Journal of Politics, Culture and Society* 5, no. 4 (1992): 544.

32. Ibid.

33. Kai T. Erikson, *Wayward Puritans: A Study in the Sociology of Deviance* (New York: Prentice Hall, 2004).

34. Ibid., 545.

35. Ibid., 538.

36. Ibid., 545.

37. "Rick Santelli and the 'Rant of the Year,'" YouTube, https://www.youtube.com/watch?v=bEZB4taSEoA.

38. Theda Skocpol and Vanessa Williamson, *The Tea Party and the Remaking of Republican Conservatism* (Oxford: Oxford University Press, 2012). See also Joseph E. Lowndes, *From the New Deal to the New Right: Race and the Southern Origins of Modern Conservatism* (New Haven, Conn.: Yale University Press, 2009); and John M. O'Hara and Michelle Malkin, *A New American Tea Party: The Counterrevolution Against Bailouts, Handouts, Reckless Spending, and More Taxes* (New York: Wiley, 2010).

39. Skocpol and Williamson, *Tea Party*, 56.

40. Ibid., 84.

41. Ibid., 22.

42. According to Skocpol and Williamson, "Overall, the Tea Party does not manifest this classic pattern of federated activity in which local groups elect higher-level leaders. . . . National organizers involved in the Tea Party are not elected or accountable" (Ibid., 98).

43. Jane Mayer, "Covert Operations: The Billionaire Brothers Who Are Waging a War Against Obama," *New Yorker*, August 20, 2010, http://www.newyorker.com/magazine/2010/08/30/covert-operations.

44. Even if the twin themes of reducing taxes and the size of government are central to the Republican Party, they are pursued more or less ruthlessly in different contexts. For certain key figures within the party, such as John Boehner, former Minority Leader (2007–2011) and Speaker (2011–2015) of the House of Representatives, government ought to conserve a certain number of prerogatives and should not be reduced in its functions as drastically as the Koch brothers would wish.

45. Adam Bonica, "Introducing the 112th Congress," *Ideological Cartography*, November 5, 2010. See also E. J. Dionne, *Why the Right Went Wrong: Conservatism from Goldwater to the Tea Party and Beyond* (New York: Simon and Shuster, 2016).

46. Jill Lepore, *The Whites of Their Eyes: The Tea Party's Revolution and the Battle over American History* (Princeton, N.J.: Princeton University Press, 2010), 15.

47. Skocpol and Williamson, *Tea Party*, 50.

48. Lepore, *Whites of Their Eyes*, 137.

49. Glenn Beck, *Glenn Beck's Common Sense: The Case Against Out-of-Control Government, Inspired by Thomas Paine* (New York: Mercury Radio Arts / Threshold Editions, 2009).

50. Lepore, *Whites of Their Eyes*, 147.

51. Skocpol and Williamson, *Tea Party*, 198.
52. Ibid., 10. On FreedomWorks, see http://www.freedomworks.org/about/about-freedomworks; and "FreedomWorks," Wikipedia, https://en.wikipedia.org/wiki/FreedomWorks.
53. Skocpol and Williamson, *Tea Party*, 183.
54. Beck, *Glenn Beck's Common Sense*, 4–5.
55. Scott Clement and John C. Green, "The Tea Party, Religion and Social Issues," Pew Forum on Religion and Public Life, February 23, 2011, http://pewresearch.org/pubs/1903/tea-party-movement-religion-social-issues-conservative-christian.
56. Tom Mullen, "Jesus Christ, Libertarian," December 24, 2010, *Tom Mullen's Blog*, http://thomasmullen.blogspot.fr/2010/12/jesus-christ-libertarian.html.
57. Tom Mullen *A Return to Common Sense: Reawakening Liberty in the Inhabitants of America* (Apollo Beach, Fla.: Mullen, 2013).
58. A poll led by Gallup in October 2015 confirms this trend toward a decline in popular support for the Tea Party. See Jim Norman, "In U.S., Support for Tea Party Drops to New Low," October 26, 2015, Gallup, http://www.gallup.com/poll/186338/support-tea-party-drops-new-low.aspx?version=print.
59. Moustafa Bayoumi, "Did Islamophobia Fuel the Oak Creek Massacre?" *Nation*, August 10, 2012, http://www.thenation.com/article/did-islamophobia-fuel-oak-creek-massacre/.

5. FORCING THE FIRST AMENDMENT

1. Elizabeth Shakman Hurd, "The Global Securitization of Religion," March 23, 2010, *The Immanent Frame: Secularism, Religion, and the Public Sphere* (blog), Social Science Research Council, http://blogs.ssrc.org/tif/2010/03/23/global-securitization/.
2. Fawaz Gerges, *America and Political Islam: Clash of Cultures or Clash of Interests?* (Cambridge: Cambridge University Press, 1999).
3. See, for example, Michael L. Ross, "How Do Natural Resources Influence Civil War: Evidence from Thirteen Cases," *International Organization* 58, no. 1 (2004): 35–67.
4. Douglas Johnston and Cynthia Sampson, eds., *Religion: The Missing Dimension of Statecraft* (Oxford: Oxford University Press, 1995).
5. Chicago Council on Global Affairs, *Engaging Religious Communities Abroad: A New Imperative for U.S. Foreign Policy* (Chicago: Chicago Council on Global Affairs, April 2010), 17n.7, http://www.thechicagocouncil.org/publication/engaging-religious-communities-abroad-new-imperative-us-foreign-policy.
6. Ibid., 19.
7. Ibid., 64.
8. Ibid., 65.
9. Liora Danan and Alice Hunt, *Mixed Blessings: U.S. Engagement with Religion in Conflict-Prone Settings* (Washington, D.C.: Center for Strategic and International Studies, August 2007), 3, http://csis.org/files/media/csis/pubs/070820_religion.pdf.

10. Quoted in ibid., 39.

11. William McCants, "Islamic Scripture Is Not the Problem. and Funding Muslim Reformers Is Not the Solution," *Foreign Affairs*, July–August 2015, https://www.foreignaffairs.com/articles/2015-06-16/islamic-scripture-not-problem.

12. Robert W. Hefner and Krishna Kumar, *Summary Assessment of the Islam and Civil Society Program in Indonesia: Promoting Democracy and Pluralism in the Muslim World*, February 2006, 2, United States Agency for International Development, http://pdf.usaid.gov/pdf_docs/pdacg325.pdf.

13. Ibid., 5.

14. Jesse R. Merriam, "Establishment Clause-trophobia: Building a Framework for Escaping the Confines of Domestic Church-State Jurisprudence," *Columbia Human Rights Law Review*, April 2010, 698–752, especially 710–11, http://works.bepress.com/cgi/viewcontent.cgi?article=1016&context=jesse_merriam.

15. Ibid., 702. See also Colum Lynch, "In Fighting Radical Islam, Tricky Course for U.S. Aid," *Washington Post*, July 30, 2009, http://www.washingtonpost.com/wp-dyn/content/article/2009/07/29/AR2009072903515.html.

16. Office of the Inspector General (OIG), *Audit of USAID's Faith-Based and Community Initiatives*, July 17, 2009, United States Agency for International Development, https://oig.usaid.gov/sites/default/files/audit-reports/9-000-09-009-p.pdf.

17. Ibid., 12.

18. Ibid., 5.

19. Ibid., 7.

20. John H. Mansfield, "The Religion Clauses of the First Amendment and Foreign Relations," *DePaul Law Review* 36, no. 1 (1986): 1–40, http://via.library.depaul.edu/cgi/viewcontent.cgi?article=2129&context=law-review.

21. Ibid., 34–35.

22. *Reid v. Covert* (354 U.S. 1 [1957]) concerned the conviction by a military tribunal of Clarice Covert, who was on trial for having murdered her husband in the United Kingdom. An accord existed at the time between the United States and the United Kingdom that stipulated that American military courts had the sole right to conduct trials for crimes committed by American soldiers stationed in the United Kingdom. Judge John Harlan stated that the Constitution ought to apply abroad unless it was impracticable or anomalous. He went on to oppose Covert's claim to protection under the Fifth Amendment on the grounds that it was impracticable and anomalous. In its decision in *Boumediene v. Bush* (553 U.S. 723 [2008]), the Supreme Court decided that it was proper to apply the principles of habeas corpus to foreign enemy combatants. Judge Anthony Kennedy argued that the habeas corpus provisions guaranteed by the Constitution extended to prisoners held at Guantanamo.

23. Jesse R. Merriam, "A Clarification of the Constitution's Application Abroad: Making the 'Impracticable and Anomalous' Standard More Practicable and Less Anomalous," *William & Mary Bill of Rights Journal*, Fall 2012, 47. http://works.bepress.com/cgi/viewcontent.cgi?article=1024&context=jesse_merriam.

24. OIG, *Audit of USAID's Faith-Based and Community Initiatives*, 6.

25. Participation by Religious Organizations in USAID Programs, Proposed Rules, 76 Federal Register 16713 (March 25, 2011), http://www.gpo.gov/fdsys/pkg/FR-2011-03-25/pdf/FR-2011-03-25.pdf.

26. *Agostini et al. v. Felton et al.*, 521 U.S. 203 (1997). In this ruling, the Supreme Court asserted that the establishment clause is not violated if public-school teachers taught in religious schools, as long as the subjects that they taught were not religious.

27. *Tilton v. Richardson*, 403 U.S. 672 (1971). In this ruling, the Supreme Court authorized the use of public funds to build infrastructure within religious institutions. It was considered that, insofar as the buildings were not themselves religious edifices, it did represent excessive interference by the government into religious matters.

28. Melissa Rogers, Robert Tuttle, Frederick Gedicks, Kent Greenawalt, Ira Lupu, and David Saperstein to Ari Alexander, May 9, 2011. https://www.whitehouse.gov/sites/default/files/omb/assets/oira_0412/0412_09142011-2.pdf.

29. Executive Order 13498, 74 Federal Register 6533 (February 5, 2009), http://www.gpo.gov/fdsys/pkg/FR-2009-02-09/pdf/E9-2893.pdf.

30. Elizabeth Shakman Hurd, *Beyond Religious Freedom: The New Global Politics of Religion* (Princeton N.J.: Princeton University Press, 2015), 79.

31. Ibid., 82.

32. For a complete history of the genesis of the International Religious Freedom Act, see Alan Hertzke, *Freeing God's Children: The Unlikely Alliance for Global Human Rights* (Lanham, Md.: Rowman & Littlefield, 2004).

33. For an analysis of the U.S. policy of promoting and exporting religious freedom before IRFA, see Anna Su, *Exporting Freedom, Religious Liberty and American Power* (Cambridge, Mass.: Harvard University Press, 2016).

34. International Religious Freedom Act of 1998, H.R. 2431, http://www.state.gov/documents/organization/2297.pdf.

35. Quoted in Elizabeth Shakman Hurd, "Believing in Religious Freedom," *The Immanent Frame: Secularism, Religion, and the Public Sphere* (blog), Social Science Research Council, http://blogs.ssrc.org/tif/2012/03/01/believing-in-religious-freedom/. See also Donald S. Lopez Jr., "Belief," in *Critical Terms for Religious Studies*, ed. Mark C. Taylor (Chicago: University of Chicago Press, 1998), 21–35.

36. Hurd, "Believing in Religious Freedom."

37. Ibid.

38. Webb Keane, *Christian Moderns: Freedom and Fetish in the Mission Encounter* (Berkeley: University of California Press, 2007).

39. Webb Keane, "What Is Religious Freedom Supposed to Free," April 3, 2012, *The Immanent Frame: Secularism, Religion, and the Public Sphere* (blog), Social Science Research Council, http://blogs.ssrc.org/tif/2012/04/03/what-is-religious-freedom-supposed-to-free/. On the debate about caricatures of the prophet, and the discussion about the supposedly specific relationship of Muslims to the sacred, see Andrew March, "Speaking About Muhammad, Speaking for Muslims," *Critical Inquiry* 37, no. 4 (2011): 806–21.

40. Quoted in Elizabeth Shakman Hurd, "Muslims Need Not Apply," *Boston Review*, January 24, 2013, http://www.bostonreview.net/world/muslims-need-not-apply. Hurd notes that Shea publicly denied using the words "hiring a Muslim" and refuses the insinuation that she is "a religious bigot." See also Michelle Boorstein, "Agency That Monitors Religious Freedom Abroad Accused of Bias," *Washington Post*, February 17, 2010, http://www.washingtonpost.com/wp-dyn/content/article/2010/02/16/AR2010021605517.html?sid=ST2010021700241.

41. Letter to Senators Inouye, McConnell, and Durbin, "Re: Expressing Concern over the Appointment of Dr. Zuhdi Jasser to the United States Commission on International Religious Freedom (USCIRF)," April 12, 2012, Council of American-Islamic Relations, https://www.cair.com/images/islamophobia/JasserLetter.pdf.

42. Quoted in Joshua Green, "God's Foreign Policy," *Washington Monthly*, November 2001, 28. On the power of evangelicals in the framing of foreign policy directions, see Michael D. Lindsay, *Faith in the Halls of Power: How Evangelicals Joined the American Elite* (New York: Oxford University Press, 2007).

43. The Puebla Institute has since been integrated within the organization Freedom House.

44. Melani McAlister, "Politics of Persecution," *Middle East Research and Information Project*, no. 249 (2008): 24, http://www.merip.org/mer/mer249/politics-persecution. See also Elizabeth Castelli, "Praying for the Persecuted Church: U.S. Christian Activism in the Global Arena," *Journal of Human Rights* 4 (2005): 321–51.

45. On violence against Copts in Egypt, see Mariz Tadros, *Copts at the Crossroads: The Challenge of Building Inclusive Democracy in Egypt* (Cairo: University of Cairo Press, 2013).

46. The text of the covenant is available online. Article 27 reads: "In those States in which ethnic, religious or linguistic minorities exist, persons belonging to such minorities shall not be denied the right, in community with the other members of their group, to enjoy their own culture, to profess and practise their own religion, or to use their own language" (International Covenant on Civil and Political Rights, https://treaties.un.org/doc/Publication/UNTS/Volume%20999/volume-999-I-14668-English.pdf).

47. Heather Sharkey, *American Evangelicals in Egypt: Missionary Encounters in an Age of Empire* (Princeton, N.J.: Princeton University Press, 2008). For discussions about the instrumentalization of liberal-secular norms by Western imperialist projects, see Wendy Brown, *Regulating Aversion: Tolerance in the Age of Identity and Empire* (Princeton, N.J.: Princeton University Press, 2006); Mahmood Mamdani, *Good Muslim, Bad Muslim: America, the Cold War, and the Roots of Terror* (New York: Pantheon, 2004); Samuel Moyn, *The Last Utopia: Human Rights in History* (Cambridge, Mass.: Harvard University Press, 2011); and Anne Norton, *Leo Strauss and the Politics of American Empire* (New Haven, Conn.: Yale University Press, 2004).

48. Saba Mahmood, *Religious Difference in a Secular Age: A Minority Report* (Princeton, N.J.: Princeton University Press, 2015).

49. Saba Mahmood, "Religious Freedom, Minority Rights, and Geopolitics," *The Immanent Frame: Secularism, Religion, and the Public Sphere* (blog), Social Science Research Council, http://blogs.ssrc.org/tif/2012/03/05/religious-freedom-minority-rights-and-geopolitics/, later published as "Religious Freedom, the Minority Question, and

Geopolitics in the Middle East," *Comparative Studies in Society and History* 15, no. 2 (2012): 418–46.

50. Paul Sedra, "Reconstituting the Coptic Community Amidst Revolution," *Middle East Report* 265 (2012): 34–38, and "Class Cleavages and Ethnic Conflict: Coptic Christian Communities in Modern Egyptian Politics," *Islam and Christian-Muslim Relations* 2, no. 10 (1999): 219–35; Mariz Tadros, "Vicissitudes in the Entente Between the Coptic Orthodox Church and the State in Egypt (1952–2007)," *International Journal of Middle East Studies* 41, no. 2 (2009): 269–87.

51. Magdi Khalil is one of the most determined advocates of this idea. Certain Coptic Egyptians have joined with intellectual Muslims to criticize the IRFA as an imperial political tool. One example is Samir Murqus, a researcher at the Coptic Center for Social Studies, who insists on the ideal of nonconfessional citizenship and national unity. See Mahmood, "Religious Freedom, the Minority Question."

52. "Text of Calling on the Egyptian Government to respect human rights and freedoms of religion and expression in Egypt," H. Res. 1303, 110 Cong., 2nd sess., June 24, 2008, GovTrack.us, http://www.govtrack.us/congress/billtext.xpd?bill=hr110-1303.

53. Thomas F. Farr and William L. Saunders Jr., "The Bush Administration and America's International Religious Freedom Policy," *Harvard Journal of Law and Public Policy* 32, no. 3 (2009): 949–70.

54. Ibid., 956.

55. The report is quoted in ibid., 962.

56. Thomas Farr, "The Intellectual Sources of Diplomacy's Religion Deficit," *Oxford Journal of Law and Religion* 1, no. 1 (2012): 283.

57. Department of State, *Report on International Religious Freedom*, 2007, http://www.state.gov/j/drl/rls/irf/2007/.

58. Center for Religious Freedom of the Hudson Institute, *Saudi Arabia's Curriculum of Intolerance*, 2008. http://www.hudson.org/content/researchattachments/attachment/656/saudi_textbooks_final.pdf.

59. Farr and Saunders, "Bush Administration," 964.

60. Thomas Farr, "The Trouble with American Foreign Policy and Islam," *Review of Faith and International Affairs* 9, no. 2 (2011): 68.

61. Winnifred Sullivan, "The World That *Smith* Made," March 7, 2012, *The Immanent Frame: Secularism, Religion, and the Public Sphere* (blog), Social Science Research Council, http://blogs.ssrc.org/tif/2012/03/07/the-world-that-smith-made/.

62. Quoted in Adam Liptak, "Religious Groups Given 'Exception' to Work Bias Law," *New York Times*, January 11, 2012, http://www.nytimes.com/2012/01/12/us/supreme-court-recognizes-religious-exception-to-job-discrimination-laws.html?pagewanted=all.

63. *Hosanna-Tabor Evangelical Lutheran Church and School v. Equal Employment Opportunity Commission et al.*, 565 U.S. ___ (2012), Legal Information Institute, https://www.law.cornell.edu/supremecourt/text/10-553.

64. http://mittromney.com/blogs/mitts-view/2012/02/president-obama-versus-religious-liberty (no longer available); however, see Michael D. Shear, "White House May Look to Compromise on Contraception Decision," *The Caucus* (blog), *New York Times*,

February 7, 2012, http://thecaucus.blogs.nytimes.com/2012/02/07/the-politics-of-obamas-contraception-decision/.

65. Quoted in "Cardinal-Designate Dolan Speaks Out Against HHS Rule, Calls for Action in New Web Video," January 20, 2012, United States Conference of Catholic Bishops, http://www.usccb.org/news/2012/12-013.cfm.

66. Quoted in Michael Stratford, "This Law Is Saying We Are No Longer Free" (interview with Michael Galligan-Stierle), *Chronicle of Higher Education*, February 2, 2012, http://chronicle.com/article/5-Minutes-With-the-Leader-of-a/130657/.

67. "US Catholic Bishops Concerned: Religious Liberty Threatened" (op-ed), *Eurasia Review*, January 29, 2012, http://www.eurasiareview.com/29012012-us-catholic-bishops-concerned-religious-liberty-threatened-oped/.

68. The magazine was founded by Richard John Neuhaus, the author of *The Naked Public Square: Religion and Democracy in America* (Grand Rapids, Mich.: Eerdmans, 1984), as well as *Catholic Matters: Confusion, Controversy, and the Splendor of Truth* (New York: Basic Books, 2006).

69. "In Defense of Religious Freedom: A Statement by Evangelicals and Catholics Together," *First Things* (blog), March 2012, http://www.firstthings.com/article/2012/02/in-defense-of-religious-freedom.

70. Blandine Chelini-Pont, "La diffamation des religions: Un bras de fer international (1999–2009)," *Conscience et liberté* 71 (2010): 42–68.

71. International Covenant on Civil and Political Rights, Article 20, para. 2, https://treaties.un.org/doc/Publication/UNTS/Volume%20999/volume-999-I-14668-English.pdf.

72. Ronan McCrea, *Religion and the Public Order of the European Union* (Oxford: Oxford University Press, 2010), 132, 134.

73. Pasquale Annicchino, "Winning the Battle by Losing the War: The *Lautsi* Case and the Holy Alliance Between American Conservative Evangelicals, the Russian Orthodox Church and the Vatican to Reshape European Identity," *Religion and Human Rights* 6, no. 3 (2011): 213–19, http://papers.ssrn.com/sol3/papers.cfm?abstract_id=2200053.

74. Grégor Puppinck, "*Lautsi v. Italy*: The Leading Case on Majority Religions in European Secular States" (presentation prepared for the annual International Law and Religion Symposium, Provo, Utah, October 3–6, 2010), 2, http://eclj.org/pdf/ECLJ-LAUTSIvI-TALY-secular-states-20110315.pdf.

CONCLUSION

1. The myth of an Islamization of Europe through immigration, high birth rates, and conversion became more widespread in the past decade, but on the basis of a crazy interpretation of actual sociological data, as convincingly shown in Raphaël Liogier, *Le mythe de l'islamisation: Essai sur une obsession collective* (Paris: Seuil, 2012), 121–47.

2. Olivier Roy, *Globalized Islam: The Search for a New Ummah* (New York: Columbia University Press, 2006).

3. Liogier, *Le mythe de l'islamisation*, 153–67.

4. Maurice Barrès was a conservative French novelist, journalist, and politician. Ostensibly a republican, he was nevertheless close to Charles Maurras, the founder of the monarchist party Action Française. Barrès was an ethnic nationalist who popularized the word "nationalism" and worked to have June 24 established as a day of remembrance for St. Joan of Arc—Trans.

5. Frédéric Lowenfeld, "Le peuple substitué: La campagne néo-légitimiste de Nicolas Sarkozy," May 27, 2012, nonfiction.fr, http://www.nonfiction.fr/articleprint-5847-le_peuple_substitue__la_campagne_neo_legitimiste_de_nicolas_sarkozy.htm.

6. Nils Muižnieks, "Anti-Muslim Prejudice Hinders Integration," July 24, 2012, Council of Europe, http://www.coe.int/hu/web/commissioner/-/anti-muslim-prejudice-hinders-integrati-1.

7. Quoted in Nancy Cordes, "Michele Bachman Refuses to Back Down on Claims About Huma Abedin," July 19, 2012, CBS News, http://www.cbsnews.com/8301-505267_162-57475483/michele-bachmann-refuses-to-back-down-on-claims-about-huma-adedin/.

8. Edward Rollins, "Bachmann's Former Campaign Chief: Shame on You, Michele," July 18, 2012, Fox News, http://www.foxnews.com/opinion/2012/07/18/bachmann-former-campaign-chief-shame-on-michele/.

9. Among the winning anti-Muslim candidates were Trent Franks (R-Ariz.), Louis Gohmert (R-Tex.), Lynn Westmoreland (R-Ga.), Diane Black (R-Tenn.), and Steve King (R-Iowa).

10. The anti-Muslim complaints extend the seventeenth-century genre of the jeremiad, a rhetorical form used by Puritan pastors to lecture the faithful about their sins and put them on their guard against the risk of breaking the covenant. See Edmund Morgan, *Visible Saints: The History of a Puritan Idea* (Ithaca, N.Y.: Cornell University Press, 1963); and Perry Miller, *The New England Mind: From Colony to Province* (Cambridge, Mass.: Harvard University Press, 1953), 27–40.

11. Faisel Devji, *The Terrorist in Search of Humanity: Militant Islam and Global Politics* (New York: Columbia University Press, 2009).

12. Michael Sandel, *Public Philosophy: Essays on Morality in Politics* (Cambridge, Mass.: Harvard University Press, 2006); Charles Taylor, *A Secular Age* (Cambridge, Mass.: Harvard University Press, 2007).

13. Michel de Certeau, "Une pratique sociale de la différence: Croire," in *Faire croire: Modalités de la diffusion et de la réception des messages religieux du XIIe au XVe siècle* (Rome: École Française de Rome, 1981).

14. Jacques Rancière, *Aux bords du politique* (Paris: Gallimard, 1998), 184: "cet Un du sentiment en Un du concept."

15. Ibid., 186.

16. Ibid., 188.

17. "Freedom of Religion or Belief," European Union, External Action, http://eeas.europa.eu/human_rights/frb/index_en.htm.

18. Roland Barthes, *Fragments d'un discours amoureux* (Paris: Seuil, 1977), translated as *A Lover's Discourse: Fragments*, trans. Richard Howard (New York: Hill and Wang, 1978). According to Barthes, "Every party to a scene dreams of having the last word. To speak last, to 'conclude,' is to assign a destiny to everything that's been said. . . . With the last

word, I'm going to disorganize, 'liquidate' my adversary. . . . The scene unfolds with this triumph in mind" (247 [trans. C. Jon Delogu, adapted from Howard]).

19. Barthes, Lover's Discourse, trans. Howard, 243.

20. Thomas Scanlon, Moral Dimensions: Permissibility, Meaning, Blame (Cambridge, Mass.: Harvard University Press, 2010).

21. Jacques Rancière, On the Shores of Politics, trans. Liz Heron (London: Verso, 1995), 82.

22. Ibid., 84.

23. Ibid.

24. Ibid., 83.

25. Ibid.

26. Ibid., 82.

27. Étienne Balibar, Saeculum, Culture, religion, idéologie (Paris: Galilée, 2012).

28. Barthes, Fragments d'un discours amoureux, 246. Howard translates Fâcheux as "intruders."

29. Ibid., 207.

30. Ibid., 35–36 (my emphasis).

SELECTED BIBLIOGRAPHY

Ahmed, Akbar S. *Journey into America: The Challenge of Islam*. Washington, D.C.: Brookings Institution Press, 2010.

Ahmed, Gutbi Mahdi. "Muslim Organizations in the U.S." In *The Muslims of America*, edited by Yvonne Yazbeck Haddad, 11–25. New York: Oxford University Press, 1993.

Akkerman, Tjitskeet, and Anniken Hagelund. "Women and Children First! Anti-Immigration Parties and Gender in Norway and the Netherlands." *Patterns of Prejudice* 41, no. 2 (2007): 197–214.

Albertazzi, Daniele, and Duncan McDonnell. "The Lega Nord Back in Government." *West European Politics* 33, no. 6 (2010): 1318–40.

Allen, Ernest, Jr. "Identity and Destiny: The Formative Views of the Moorish Science Temple and the Nation of Islam." In *Muslims on the Americanization Path*, edited by Yvonne Yazbeck Haddad and John L. Esposito, 163–214. New York: Oxford University Press, 2000.

Amiraux, Valérie. "L'affaire du foulard en France: Retour sur une affaire qui n'en est pas encore une." *Sociologie et sociétés* 41, no. 2 (2009): 273–98.

Amir-Moazami, Schirin. "Muslim Challenges to the Secular Consensus: A German Case Study." *Journal of Contemporary European Studies* 13, no. 3 (2005): 267–86.

Amir-Moazami, Schirin, Christine M. Jacobsen, and Maleiha Malik. "Islam and Gender in Europe: Subjectivities, Politics and Piety." *Feminist Review* 98, no. 1 (2011): 1–8.

Asad, Talal. *Genealogies of Religion: Discipline and Reasons of Power in Christianity and Islam*. Baltimore: Johns Hopkins University Press, 1993.

Asal, Houda. "Islamophobie: La fabrique d'un nouveau concept, État des lieux de la recherche." *Sociologie* 5, no. 1 (2014).

Bail, Christopher. *Terrified: How Anti-Muslim Fringe Organizations Became Mainstream*. Princeton, N.J.: Princeton University Press, 2015.

Balibar, Étienne. *Saeculum: Culture, religion, idéologie*. Paris: Galilée, 2012.

Bangstaad, Sindre. *Anders Breivik and the Rise of Islamophobia*. London: Zed Books, 2014.

Baubérot, Jean. *La laïcité falsifiée*. Paris: La Découverte, 2012.

Beck, Glenn. *Glenn Beck's Common Sense: The Case Against Out-of-Control Government, Inspired by Thomas Paine*. New York: Mercury Radio Arts / Threshold Editions, 2009.

Bellah, Robert. "Civil Religion in America." *Dædalus, Journal of the American Academy of Arts and Sciences* 96, no. 1 (1967): 1–2.

Bender, Courtney, and Pamela E. Klassen, eds. *After Pluralism: Reimagining Religious Engagement*. New York: Columbia University Press, 2010.

Betz, Hanz-Georg. "Culture, Identity and the Question of Islam: The Nativist Agenda of the Radical Right." In *The Far Right in Europe: An Encyclopedia*, edited by Peter Davies and Paul Jackson, 114–15. Oxford: Greenwood World Press, 2008.

Betz, Hans-Georg, and Susi Meret. "Revisiting Lepanto: The Political Mobilization Against Islam in Contemporary Western Europe." *Patterns of Prejudice* 43, nos. 3–4 (2009): 313–34.

Bilici, Mucahit. *Finding Mecca in America: How Islam Is Becoming an American Religion*. Chicago: University of Chicago Press, 2012.

Birnbaum, Jean. *Un silence religieux: La gauche face au djihadisme*. Paris: Seuil, 2016.

Blyden, Edward Wilmot. *Christianity, Islam and the Negro Race*. Edinburgh: Edinburgh University Press, 1887.

Bonney, Charles Carroll. "Worlds of Welcome." In *The Dawn of Religious Pluralism: Voices from the Parliament of Religions, 1893*, edited by Richard H. Seager, 17–22. La Salle, Ill.: Open Court, 1993.

Bowen, John. *Why the French Don't Like Headscarves: Islam, the State, and Public Space*. Princeton, N.J.: Princeton University Press, 2008.

Brown, Wendy. *Regulating Aversion: Tolerance in the Age of Identity and Empire*. Princeton, N.J.: Princeton University Press, 2006.

Bulliet, Richard. *The Case for Islamo-Christian Civilization*. New York: Columbia University Press, 2004.

Butler, Judith. *Excitable Speech: A Politics of the Performative*. New York: Routledge, 1997.

Castelli, Elizabeth. "Praying for the Persecuted Church: U.S. Christian Activism in the Global Arena." *Journal of Human Rights* 4 (2005): 321–51.

Clarke, James Freeman. *Ten Great Religions: An Essay in Comparative Theology*. Boston: Osgood, 1871.

Cohn, Norman. *The Pursuit of the Millennium: Revolutionary Millenarians and Mystical Anarchists of the Middle Ages*. New York: Oxford University Press, 1992.

Cole, Juan. *Engaging the Muslim World*. New York: Palgrave Macmillan, 2009.

Dakhlia, Jocelyne, and Bernard Vincent, eds. *Les Musulmans dans l'histoire de l'Europe*. Vol. 1, *Une intégration invisible*. Paris: Albin Michel, 2011.

Danan, Liora, and Alice Hunt. *Mixed Blessings: U.S. Engagement with Religion in Conflict-Prone Settings*. Washington, D.C.: Center for Strategic and International Studies, August 2007.

Dannin, Robert. *Black Pilgrimage to Islam*. New York: Oxford University Press, 2002.

Daulatzai, Sohail. *Black Star, Crescent Moon: The Muslim International and Black Freedom Beyond America*. Minneapolis: University of Minnesota Press, 2015.

Davis, David Brion, ed. *The Fear of Conspiracy: Images of Un-American Subversion from the Revolution to the Present*. Ithaca, N.Y.: Cornell University Press, 1971.

de Certeau, Michel. "Une pratique sociale de la différence: Croire." In *Faire croire: Modalités de la diffusion et de la réception des messages religieux du XIIe au XVe siècle*. Rome: École Française de Rome, 1981.

Devji, Faisel. *The Terrorist in Search of Humanity: Militant Islam and Global Politics*. New York: Columbia University Press, 2009.

Dionne, E. J. *Why the Right Went Wrong: Conservatism from Goldwater to the Tea Party and Beyond*. New York: Simon and Schuster, 2016.

Erikson, Kai T. *Wayward Puritans: A Study in the Sociology of Deviance*. New York: Prentice Hall, 2004.

Fekete, Liz, "The Muslim Conspiracy Theory and the Oslo Massacre." *Race & Class* 53, no. 3 (2012): 30–47.

Fernando, Mayanthi. *The Republic Unsettled: Muslim French and the Contradictions of Secularism*. Durham, N.C.: Duke University Press, 2014.

Freedman, Jane. "Women, Islam and Rights in Europe: Beyond a Universalist/Culturalist Dichotomy." *Review of International Studies* 33, no. 1 (2007): 29–44.

Geisser, Vincent. *La nouvelle islamophobie*. Paris: La Découverte, 2003.

Gerges, Fawaz A. *America and Political Islam: Clash of Cultures or Clash of Interests?* Cambridge: Cambridge University Press, 1999.

GhaneaBassiri, Kambiz. *A History of Islam in America: From the New World to the New World Order*. New York: Cambridge University Press, 2010.

Göle, Nilüfer. *Interpénétrations: L'Islam et l'Europe*. Paris: Galaade, 2005.

——. *Musulmans au quotidien: Une enquête européenne sur les controverses autour de l'Islam*. Paris: La Découverte, 2015.

Green, Joshua. "God's Foreign Policy: Why the Biggest Threat to Bush's War Strategy Isn't Coming from Muslims, but from Christians." *Washington Monthly*, November 2001, 26–33.

Grewal, Zareena. *Islam Is a Foreign Country: American Muslims and the Global Crisis of Authority*. New York: New York University Press, 2013.

Haddad, Yvonne Yazbeck, ed. *The Muslims of America*. New York: Oxford University Press, 1993.

——. *Not Quite American: The Shaping of Arab and Muslim Identity in the United States*. Waco, Tex.: Baylor University Press, 2004.

Haddad, Yvonne, and Jane I. Smith, eds. *Muslim Minorities in the West: Visible and Invisible*. Walnut Creek, Calif.: AltaMira Press, 2002.

Haenni, Patrick. *L'Islam de marché: L'autre révolution conservatrice*. Paris: Seuil, 2005.

Haenni, Patrick, and Stépane Lathion. *Les minarets de la discorde: Éclairages sur un débat suisse et européen*. Fribourg, Switzerlanc: Religioscope, 2009.

Hajjat, Abdellali, and Marwan Mohammed. *Islamophobie: Comment les élites françaises fabriquent le "problème musulman."* Cahiers libres. Paris: La Découverte, 2013.

Hertzke, Alan. *Freeing God's Children: The Unlikely Alliance for Global Human Rights*. Lanham, Md.: Rowman & Littlefield, 2004.

Hicks, Rosemary. "Religious Pluralism, Secularism, and Interfaith Endeavors." In *The Cambridge Companion to American Islam*, edited by Julianne Hammer and Omid Safi, 156–69. Cambridge: Cambridge University Press, 2013.

Hofstadter, Richard. *The Paranoid Style in American Politics, and Other Essays.* Cambridge, Mass.: Harvard University Press, 1996.

Hughey, Michael W. "Americanism and Its Discontents: Protestantism, Nativism, and Political Heresy in America." *International Journal of Politics, Culture and Society* 5, no. 4 (1992): 533–53.

Hurd, Elizabeth Shakman, *Beyond Religious Freedom: The New Global Politics of Religion.* Princeton, N.J.: Princeton University Press, 2015.

——. *The Politics of Secularism in International Relations.* Princeton, N.J.: Princeton University Press, 2008.

Jackson, Sherman. *Islam and the Blackamerican: Looking Toward the Third Resurrection.* Oxford: Oxford University Press, 2005.

Johnston, Douglas, and Cynthia Sampson, eds. *Religion: The Missing Dimension of Statecraft.* New York: Oxford University Press, 1995.

Jones, Robert P., Daniel Cox, William Galston, and E. J. Dionne Jr. *What It Means to Be an American: Attitudes in an Increasingly Diverse America Ten Years After 9/11.* Washington, D.C.: Brookings Institution and Public Religion Research Institute, 2011.

Kahera, Akel Ismail. *Deconstructing the American Mosque: Space, Gender, and Aesthetics.* Austin: University of Texas Press, 2002.

Kahn, Paul. *Political Theology: Four New Chapters on the Concept of Sovereignty.* New York: Columbia University Press, 2012.

Katayoun, Alidadi, Marie-Claire Foblets, and Jogchum Vrielink. *A Test of Faith? Religious Diversity and Accommodation in the European Workplace.* Burlington, Vt.: Ashgate, 2012.

Kazin, Michael. *The Populist Persuasion: An American History.* Rev. ed. Ithaca, N.Y.: Cornell University Press, 1998.

Keane, Webb. *Christian Moderns: Freedom and Fetish in the Mission Encounter.* Berkeley: University of California Press, 2007.

Kumar, Deepa. *Islamophobia and the Politics of Empire.* Chicago: Haymarket Books, 2012.

Laborde, Cécile. *Critical Republicanism: The Hijab Controversy and Political Philosophy.* New York: Oxford University Press, 2008.

Lacorne, Denis. *De la religion en Amérique: Essai d'histoire politique.* Paris: Gallimard, 2007.

Lambert, Franck. *The Founding Fathers and the Place of Religion in America.* Princeton, N.J.: Princeton University Press, 2003.

Laurence, Jonathan. *The Emancipation of Europe's Muslims: The State's Role in Minority Integration.* Princeton, N.J.: Princeton University Press, 2012.

Lee, Martha F. *The Nation of Islam: An American Millenarian Movement.* Lewiston, N.Y.: Mellen Press, 1988.

Lepore, Jill. *The Whites of Their Eyes: The Tea Party's Revolution and the Battle over American History.* Princeton, N.J.: Princeton University Press, 2010.

Lincoln, C. Eric. *The Black Muslims in America.* Boston: Beacon Press, 1961.

Lindsay, Michael D. *Faith in the Halls of Power: How Evangelicals Joined the American Elite.* New York: Oxford University Press, 2007.

Liogier, Raphaël. *Le mythe de l'islamisation: Essai sur une obsession collective.* Paris: Seuil, 2012.

Lopez, Donald S., Jr. "Belief." In *Critical Terms for Religious Studies*, edited by Mark C. Taylor, 21–35. Chicago: University of Chicago Press, 1998.

Lorcerie, François, ed. *La politisation du voile en France, en Europe et dans le monde arabe*. Paris: L'Harmattan, 2005.

Loveland, Anne C., and Otis B. Wheeler. *From Meetinghouse to Megachurch: A Material and Cultural History*. Columbia: University of Missouri Press, 2003.

Lowndes, Joseph E. *From the New Deal to the New Right: Race and the Southern Origins of Modern Conservatism*. New Haven, Conn.: Yale University Press, 2009.

Mahmood, Saba. *Religious Difference in a Secular Age: A Minority Report*. Princeton, N.J.: Princeton University Press, 2015.

——. "Religious Freedom, the Minority Question, and Geopolitics in the Middle East." *Comparative Studies in Society and History* 15, no. 2 (2012): 418–46.

Mamdani, Mahmood. *Good Muslim, Bad Muslim: America, the Cold War, and the Roots of Terror*. New York: Pantheon, 2004.

Mamiya, Lawrence. "From Black Muslims to Bilalian: The Evolution of a Movement." *Journal for the Scientific Study of Religion* 21, no. 2 (1982): 138–52.

Mansfield, John H. "The Religion Clauses of the First Amendment and Foreign Relations." *DePaul Law Review* 36, no. 1 (1986): 1–40.

March, Andrew. *Islam and Liberal Citizenship: The Search for an Overlapping Consensus*. New York: Oxford University Press, 2009.

——. "Speaking About Muhammad, Speaking for Muslims." *Critical Inquiry* 37, no. 4 (2011): 806–21.

Marzouki, Nadia. "De l'endiguement à l'engagement: Le discours des think tanks américains sur l'islam depuis 2001." *Archives de sciences sociales des religions* 155, no. 3 (2001): 21–39.

——. "La réception française de Saba Mahmood et de l'asadisme." *Tracés*, no. 15 (2015): 33–51.

——. "Les débats sur le droit islamique aux États-Unis et au Canada, entre égalité formelle et pluralisme." In *La Charia aujourd'hui*, edited by Baudouin Dupret, 280–94. Paris: La Découverte, 2012.

——. "Offense morale contre liberté religieuse, la controverse de Ground Zero." *Revue française de science politique* 61, no. 5 (2011): 839–65.

Marzouki, Nadia, Duncan McDonnell, and Olivier Roy, eds. *Saving the People: How Populists Hijack Religion*. Oxford: Oxford University Press, 2016.

McAlister, Melani. "Politics of Persecution." *Middle East Report*, no. 249 (2008): 18–27.

McCloud, Aminah Beverly. *African-American Islam*. New York: Routledge, 1995.

McCrea, Ronan. *Religion and the Public Order of the European Union*. Oxford: Oxford University Press, 2010.

Merriam, Jesse. "Establishment Clause-trophobia: Building a Framework for Escaping the Confines of Domestic Church-State Jurisprudence." *Columbia Human Rights Law Review* 41, no. 699 (2010): 699–764.

Metcalf, Barbara, ed. *Making Muslim Space in North America and Europe*. Berkeley: University of California Press, 1996.

Miller, Perry. *The New England Mind: From Colony to Province*. Cambridge, Mass.: Harvard University Press, 1953.

Morgan, Edmund. *Visible Saints: The History of a Puritan Idea*. Ithaca, N.Y.: Cornell University Press, 1963.

Moyn, Samuel. *The Last Utopia: Human Rights in History*. Cambridge, Mass.: Harvard University Press, 2011.

Nakhlé, Emile. *Necessary Engagement: Reinventing America's Relations with the Muslim World*. Princeton, N.J.: Princeton University Press, 2009.

Norton, Anne. *Leo Strauss and the Politics of American Empire*. New Haven, Conn.: Yale University Press, 2004.

Nuruddin, Yusuf. "African-American Muslims and the Question of Identity: Between Tradition Islam African Heritage and the American Way." In *Muslims on the Americanization Path?*, edited by Yvonne Yazbeck Haddad and John L. Esposito, 215–62. New York: Oxford University Press, 2000.

Nussbaum, Martha. *New Religious Intolerance: Overcoming the Politics of Fear in an Anxious Age*. Cambridge, Mass.: Harvard University Press, 2012.

Nyang, Sulayman S. *Islam in the United States of America*. Chicago: ABC International Group, 1999.

O'Hara, John M., and Michelle Malkin. *A New American Tea Party: The Counterrevolution Against Bailouts, Handouts, Reckless Spending, and More Taxes*. New York: Wiley, 2010.

Paperman, Patricia. "L'absence d'émotion comme offense." In *La Couleur des pensées: Sentiments, émotions, intentions*, edited by Patricia Paper and Ruwen Ogien, 175–97. Paris: Éditions de l'EHESS, 1995.

Quraishi-Landes, Asifa. "Rumors of the Sharia Threat Are Greatly Exaggerated: What American Judges Really Do with Islamic Family Law in Their Courtrooms." *New York Law School Law Review* 57, no. 2 (2012–2013): 244–57.

Rabasa, Angel M., Cheryl Bernard, Peter Chalk, C. Christine Fair, Theodore Karasik, Rollie Lal, Ian Lesser, and David Thaler. *The Muslim World After 9/11*. Santa Monica, Calif.: Rand, Project Air Force, 2004.

Rabasa, Angel, Cheryl Bernard, Lowell H. Schwartz, and Peter Sickle. *Building Moderate Muslim Networks*. Santa Monica, Calif.: Rand Center for Middle East Public Policy, 2007.

Rancière, Jacques. *Aux bords du politique*. Paris: Gallimard, 1998.

Rascoff, Samuel J. "Establishing Official Islam? The Law and Strategy of Counter-Radicalization." *Stanford Law Review* 64, no. 1 (2012): 125–90.

Remnick, David. "This American Life: The Making and Remaking of Malcolm X." *New Yorker*, April 25, 2011.

Rodinson, Maxime. *La fascination de l'Islam*. Paris: La Découverte, 2003.

Roy, Olivier. *Globalized Islam: The Search for a New Ummah*. New York: Columbia University Press, 2006.

——. *Holy Ignorance: When Religion and Culture Part Ways*. New York: Columbia University Press, 2010.

——. *Secularism Confronts Islam*. New York: Columbia University Press, 2009.

Sandel, Michael. *Public Philosophy: Essays on Morality in Politics*. Cambridge, Mass.: Harvard University Press, 2006.

Scanlon, Thomas M. *Moral Dimensions: Permissibility, Meaning, Blame*. Cambridge, Mass.: Harvard University Press, 2008.

Schanzer, David H., Charles Kurzman, and EbrahimMoosa. *Anti-Terror: Lessons of Muslim-Americans*. Durham, N.C.: Sanford School of Public Policy, Duke University, January 6, 2010.

Scott, Joan Wallace. *The Politics of the Veil.* Princeton, N.J.: Princeton University Press, 2010.

Sedra, Paul. "Class Cleavages and Ethnic Conflict: Coptic Christian Communities in Modern Egyptian Politics." *Islam and Christian-Muslim Relations* 2, no. 10 (1999): 219–35.

——. "Reconstituting the Coptic Community Amidst Revolution." *Middle East Report* 265 (2012): 34–38.

Sellam, Sadek. *La France et ses musulmans: Un siècle de politique musulmane, 1895–2005.* Paris: Fayard, 2006.

Sharkey, Heather. *American Evangelicals in Egypt: Missionary Encounters in an Age of Empire.* Princeton, N.J.: Princeton University Press, 2008.

Sheehi, Stephen. *Islamophobia: The Ideological Campaign Against Muslims.* Atlanta: Clarity Press, 2011.

Skocpol, Theda, and Vanessa Williamson. *The Tea Party and the Remaking of Republican Conservatism.* Oxford: Oxford University Press, 2012

Solomon, Barbara Miller. *Ancestors and Immigrants: A Changing New England's Traditions.* Chicago: University of Chicago Press, 1956.

Spellberg, Denise A. "Could a Muslim Be President? An Eighteenth-Century Constitutional Debate." *Eighteenth-Century Studies* 39, no. 4 (2006): 485–506.

——. *Thomas Jefferson's Qur'an: Islam and the Founders.* New York: Knopf, 2013.

Stampnitzky, Lisa. *Disciplining Terror: How Experts Invented "Terrorism."* Cambridge: Cambridge University Press, 2013.

Su, Anna. *Exporting Freedom: Religious Liberty and American Power.* Cambridge, Mass.: Harvard University Press, 2016.

Sullivan, Winnifred Fallers. *The Impossibility of Religious Freedom.* Princeton, N.J.: Princeton University Press, 2007.

Sullivan, Winnifred Fallers, Robert A. Yelle, and Mateo Taussig-Rubbo, eds. *After Secular Law.* Stanford, Calif.: Stanford University Press / Stanford Law Books, 2011.

Tadros, Mariz. *Copts at the Crossroads: The Challenge of Building Inclusive Democracy in Egypt.* Cairo: University of Cairo Press, 2013.

——. "Vicissitudes in the Entente Between the Coptic Orthodox Church and the State in Egypt (1952–2007)." *International Journal of Middle East Studies* 41, no. 2 (2009): 269–87.

Tassig-Rubbo, Mateo. "Sacred Property: Searching for Value in the Rubble of 9/11." In *After Secular Law,* edited by Winnifred F. Sullivan, Robert A. Yelle, and Mateo Taussig-Rubbo, 322–41. Stanford, Calif.: Stanford University Press / Stanford Law Books, 2011.

Taylor, Charles. *A Secular Age.* Cambridge, Mass.: Harvard University Press, 2007.

Turner, Richard Brent. *Islam in the African-American Experience.* Bloomington: Indiana University Press, 2003.

Vaïsse, Justin. *Neoconservatism: The Biography of a Movement.* Cambridge, Mass.: Harvard University Press, 2011.

Wuthnow, Robert. *America and the Challenge of Religious Diversity.* Princeton, N.J.: Princeton University Press, 2007.

——. "In America, All Religions Are True." In *American Mythos: Why Our Best Efforts to Be a Better Nation Fall Short,* 128–63. Princeton, N.J.: Princeton University Press, 2008.

Zubrzycki, Geneviève. *The Crosses of Auschwitz: Nationalism and Religion in Post-Communist Poland.* Chicago: University of Chicago Press, 2006.

INDEX